Library of
Davidson College

Romantic German Literature

Romantic German Literature

Glyn Tegai Hughes

Edward Arnold

© Glyn Tegai Hughes 1979

First published 1979 by
Edward Arnold (Publishers) Ltd
41 Bedford Square, London WC1B 3DQ

ISBN 0 7131 6192 2

All rights reserved. No part of this publication may be reproduced, stored in a retrieval system or transmitted in any form or by any means, electronic, photocopying, recording or otherwise, without the prior permission of Edward Arnold (Publishers) Ltd.

British Library Cataloguing in Publication Data
Hughes, Glyn Tegai
   Romantic German literature.
   1. German literature—18th century—History and criticism   2. German literature—19th century—History and criticism
   I. Title
   830′.9′006   PT311

ISBN 0 7131 6192 2

Printed in Great Britain by
Butler & Tanner Ltd
Frome and London

Preface

I have concentrated on the major figures of Romanticism and on the works that can still speak to us. There are two consequences. Writers highly regarded in their day, but who now seem important only in the history of taste, get very short shrift; Uhland is a case in point. And themes have to take second place to works; except in summary fashion I have not sought to draw together, say, the Romantic view of language or the relatively dismal history of Romantic drama.

It may be that there is rather too much about the philosophical background, and the history of ideas certainly has its dangers; yet it is difficult to think of another literary period caught in such intellectual ferment.

Problems of demarcation and definition are insoluble. Is Kleist a Romantic? To answer positively either way would be foolhardy; all I can say is that I have excluded him and that perhaps the longish note on his stories will indicate why.

I have tried to give my own interpretations but, at the same time, to keep the reader acquainted with the latest state of scholarship and criticism. A great flood of work on German Romanticism has appeared in the last ten or fifteen years, much of it of very high quality. The notes and bibliography call attention in particular to these more recent works.

On the whole I have translated passages I wished to quote and have given the original, in the text or notes, only when some stylistic or associative reason seemed to demand it. References are, however, always given, so that the German may be found without real difficulty. Titles are translated in the index. Frequently used abbreviations are listed immediately before the notes or, when referring to editions of authors, in the relevant section of the bibliography.

Gregynog, University of Wales   Glyn Tegai Hughes

Contents

Preface	v
1. Background and Backbone	1
2. New Ways of Feeling: Wackenroder, Tieck and 'The Night Watches'	21
3. Profusion and Order: The Brothers Schlegel	41
4. Poetry in Metaphysics: Novalis	61
5. The Legacy of Myth: The Grimms, Brentano and Arnim	79
6. Natural and Supernatural: Eichendorff, with Görres	98
7. The Risks of the Imagination: Hoffmann, with Chamisso, Fouqué and Werner	112
8. Coda: The Swabians	127
Abbreviations	131
Bibliographical Guide	133
Index	177

I

Background and Backbone

Definitions and Preconditions

'Romantic' as a typological word, a whiff of grapeshot in an argument about human attitudes, may be effective in some very general way, but it is a good deal more like an ineradicable nuisance. Here we consider it in a specific historical setting, not as a catch-all to cover *Romeo and Juliet* and a Dior perfume; and used thus it does have meaning as well as resonance.

Yet we must not be too confident in these matters; our betters have long had difficulties even within the historical context. The words 'romantic', 'romantique', 'romantisch' have a rich history, about which much has been written, and which is only partially relevant to the literary phenomenon described in this book. By the end of the eighteenth century the epithet had, both in English and German, acquired an air, not infrequently pejorative, of medieval or outlandish picturesqueness, occasionally touched by sublimity but more often by sentiment or sentimentality. At its best it suggested a relationship to the imagination and to the emotions that presupposed a pleasurable or otherwise meritorious response. Yet ambivalence remained, for the derivation from 'romance' added the possible connotation of 'fictitious' or 'extravagantly improbable'. In German, too, it was until the end of the century possible to use 'romantisch' simply as the adjective from 'Roman', the novel.

We then have to face the awkwardness that writers we distinguish as 'Romantic' themselves used the term in a way little developed from that of the eighteenth century, as was the case with the English Romantic poets or, say, the early Tieck; or, as in Friedrich Schlegel, they elaborated it in a way important for but not coextensive with the usage of later literary historians. What they did not do until quite late, and what many did not do at all, was to use the term as a group designation.

In Germany, as had happened somewhat earlier in England with the word 'Methodist', the first use as a cognomen was by enemies. For a while the German writers later thought of as the 'early Romantics' ('die Frühromantiker' or 'die ältere Romantik') or as the Jena Romantic group (the Schlegels, Novalis, Tieck, Fichte) were called 'the new school' ('die neue Schule'). But the terms 'die Romantik' and 'Romantiker' were beginning to come into use after 1800 and, in the baiting of the later or Heidelberg circle ('die jüngere Romantik': Brentano, Arnim, Görres) by Johann Heinrich Voß and his fellow classicist-rationalists, the new descriptions were applied to both the old and new groups, the high-point of this enemy use being in Jens Baggesen's *Klingklingelalmanach* (1808), where satirical verses list most of those we would now call Romantics. By 1819 Friedrich Bouterwek, in the eleventh volume of his pioneering history of literature, was able to use the term descriptively for the modern movement, though in earlier volumes he had felt it necessary to distinguish more rigorously between 'altromantisch' and 'neuromantisch'.[1]

When Mme de Staël had used the term 'romantique' in *De l'Allemagne* (1813) she had still given it the extended meaning of literature in the medieval tradition. This followed the argument in August Wilhelm Schlegel's Berlin and Vienna lectures where chivalry, Christianity and a new sense of transience and infinity were seen as informing 'romantic' poetry, as opposed to ancient or classical art.[2]

It was the medievalizing and what he regarded as the obscuranticism of the Romantic attitude that provoked Heine's censure in *Die romantische Schule* (1835, though dated 1836), itself a conscious counterblast to *De l'Allemagne*. He thinks little of most of these figures of the preceding thirty or forty years when compared with Lessing, Herder, Schiller or, above all, Goethe; but he is by then comfortably able to attach the label 'Romantic' to them, although he excludes Hoffmann.[3] Eichendorff, in his 'Zur Geschichte der neuern romantischen Poesie in Deutschland'

[1] *Geschichte der Poesie und Beredsamkeit seit dem Ende des dreizehnten Jahrhunderts*, vol. XI, Göttingen, 1819, xxii, 533 pp.; though he still (p. xx) finds it necessary to throw in the qualification 'so-called': 'die Schule der sogenannten Romantiker'.

[2] Philipp Mayer (1798–1827), just before he became tutor to the Archduke Friedrich, concluded his *Theorie und Literatur der deutschen Dichtungsarten*, 3 vols, Vienna, 1824, with a piece on 'Romantische Poesie' (III, 327–32). Though he has already shown himself very sympathetic to Novalis, Tieck and the Schlegels, the essay refers only to Tieck, and that in a sentence. 'Romantic' poetry is still viewed typologically and we are directed to Christianity, Shakespeare, Ariosto, Oriental literature, Goethe, Herder, Jean Paul.

[3] It is the conservatism and Catholicism of Friedrich Schlegel's later years that may be said to feed Heine's polemic and to cast its shadow back over the earlier achievement, with much of which Heine was in sympathy. See Peter Uwe Hohendahl, 'Geschichte und Modernität: Heines Kritik an der Romantik', *JDSG*, xvii (1973), 318–61; also in his *Literaturkritik und Öffentlichkeit*, Munich, Piper, 1974, pp. 50–101.

(1846), is still, however, concerned to distinguish between the new Romantic school and that original romanticism which has always been an expression of religious feeling, particularly of Christianity.

In general, though, it is fair to say that by the 1830s 'Romanticism' was a chronological concept available to literary historians and in general use by them.[4]

Critical Approaches

The first major critical appraisal of the movement was by Rudolf Haym in 1870. The rigorous scholarship and austere judgements of a philosopher and theologian were applied to the early Romantics' attempts at synthesis, and there emerged a monumental intellectual history of the turn of the century. And it was this tradition of the history of ideas that dominated the interpretation of German Romanticism for generations after Haym, from Ricarda Huch's sympathetic attempt to recreate the whole climate of the early and late periods in her two volumes (1899 and 1902) to H. A. Korff's grandiose *Geist der Goethezeit* (*Frühromantik*, 1940; *Hochromantik*, 1953), a vast quarry of concepts. There were, of course, attempts to strike out in other directions: Josef Nadler (1912–18) argued that Romanticism was the triumph of the German East over the West; Fritz Strich (1922), following Wölfflin's basic formal categories in art history, interpreted Classicism as the quest for perfection and completeness, and Romanticism as yearning for infinitude. The Nazi period made much, as might be expected, of the popular, folk elements in Romanticism but showed a good deal of reserve towards other aspects, though Walther Linden (1933) drew attention to the importance of the 'organic' and conservative tendencies of the later Romantics.

Contemporary East German criticism reveals, on the whole, a want of enthusiasm for Romanticism, not only for the conservatism of the Restoration period, but also because of what it regards as the inadequate social response of the earlier figures to the decline of feudalism after the French Revolution. West German Marxists, however, have been a good deal more prepared to discover, or manufacture, Jacobin, radical or

[4] An interesting subdivision is that elaborated by Theodor Echtermeyer and Arnold Ruge in their polemical manifesto, 'Der Protestantismus und die Romantik', in the *Hallische Jahrbücher*, no. 245 (1839)–no. 64 (1840) reprinted with a foreword and commentary by Norbert Oellers, Hildesheim, Gerstenberg, 1972, viii, 146 pp. They distinguish between the forerunners of Romanticism (Jacobi, Hamann, the Storm and Stress writers, Claudius, Heinse), the real Romantics (the Schlegels, Tieck, Wackenroder, Steffens, Creuzer, Adam Müller, Brentano, Arnim), the innumerable imitators after 1810, divided into political and harmless groups (Uhland, Kerner, Kleist, Chamisso, Eichendorff, Hoffmann, with Görres in both camps), and a romantic orientation towards France after 1830 in the Young Germany movement.

anti-capitalist elements in and around many Romantic writers or, for instance, to sophisticate Arnim's anti-semitism out of existence. They achieve useful insights into the role of market forces, the nature of the reading public and other sociological trends, though there remains an unease that the works themselves are being forced into a societal schema.

The great explosion of critical work on the Romantics in the last ten or fifteen years has reopened all options. Romanticism is seen to be many-faceted: its earlier period is still intimately connected with European Enlightenment, its later is turned in on the Germanic; it owes much to German Idealism, but it also reaches back to Spinoza and Böhme; it is both fragmentary and encyclopaedic in its intentions; it is at times deeply committed to the emotions, but can also be austerely theoretical; it centres on the self, but makes valiant attempts to integrate society with its past. Modern criticism is alert to the Romantics' innovative grappling with the creative function of language, to their attempts at relating formal patterns to literary intention, to their constant symbolizing purporting to conjure up in art some higher reality, to their pursuit of myth as well as their concern for the realities of contemporary history.

Origins

A fruitful source of confusion for those not familiar with the commonplaces of German literary history is the sharpness of the distinction drawn between Romanticism and Weimar Classicism. Certainly there is a good deal of overlapping between, say, the aesthetic theories of Schiller and some of those of Friedrich Schlegel, and it is often illuminating to see how both movements grew out of the same intellectual tilth. Nevertheless it is true to say that Goethe distinguished himself firmly from the Romantics and that the emphases of Classicism are, in the baldest terms, towards the values of Greek antiquity, the discovery of the generally valid in the particular, the achievement of harmony and balance through a moral sense responsive to the call of our common humanity, an organically based stylization seizing life in the perfection of types, proportion rather than decoration.

The emphases of Romanticism are different and we shall therefore scarcely be able to avoid picking out of the common background those factors that moved its first representatives away from Classicism.

Stirrings that are tentatively and controversially called 'preromantic' (a twentieth-century systematizing term) exist in many European literatures during the eighteenth century. They have some analogy with the early, loose use of the term 'romantic' itself and may, in general, be thought of as anti-rationalist. The revolt against the rigidities of rationalism occurs at its fiercest in Germany in the Storm and Stress (Sturm und Drang) writers; but the experience remains, as it were, available to Romanticism. Other strands deriving from England, from the emancipation of the bourgeoisie, or from German Pietism's insistence on the inner life and the emotional experience of God, between them made acceptable not only sentiment but a sentimentality in moral and religious attitudes, a cult of tearful friendship and melancholy love, an intertwining of human affections and the natural processes of landscape, an unleashing of the imaginative powers, all that we now know as 'sensibility' ('Empfindsamkeit').[5]

To these one should add other features reinforcing either new complexities within Enlightenment or a retreat from it: Rousseau's exaltation of natural man and of the passions; the rediscovery of folk-poetry in Herder and Bürger, with English and Scottish influences in the background; Herder's understanding of historical relativism and the new approach to the distant in time and space, notably the Middle Ages; the discovery of the South Seas and the resultant anthropological speculations; the opening of religion to the imagination that took place in the shadow of deism; the recognition of the creative and symbolic character of language, especially by Hamann.[6]

In the byways of thought, too, Neoplatonic and mystical ideas had persisted throughout the century. Böhme's amalgam of the heritage of medieval mysticism and the scientific speculations of the Renaissance

---

[5] Preromanticism: see *Le Préromantisme: hypothèque ou hypothèse*, ed. Paul Viallaneix, Paris, Klincksieck, 1975, 631 pp. These proceedings of a colloquium arranged at Clermont-Ferrand in 1972 contain several discussions of the validity of the term, though from a somewhat blinkered French point of view.

Sensibility: for the argument that the Enlightenment contains its own versions of sensibility see the postscript to *Empfindsamkeit: Theoretische und kritische Texte*, ed. Wolfgang Doktor and Gerhard Sauder, Stuttgart, Reclam, 1976, 216 pp. (=UB, 9835).

[6] Rousseau: one should note that the Romantics, particularly the Schlegels and Novalis, were generally hostile to him. See Rudolf Buck, *Rousseau und die deutsche Romantik*, Berlin, 1939, 147 pp. (Tübingen diss., 1937); for Rousseau's more widespread influence see Raymond Trousson, 'Jean-Jacques Rousseau dans la presse périodique allemande de 1750 à 1800', *Dix-huitième siècle*, i (1969), 289–310, and ii (1970), 227–64.

Georg Forster: the importance of Forster, voyager with Cook, Rosicrucian, Jacobin and disillusioned revolutionary, translator of oriental literature, enthusiastic admirer of medieval architecture, has not yet been fully assessed. See the works in 4 vols, Leipzig, Insel, 1972; Kurt Kersten, *Der Weltumsegler Johann Georg Adam Forster 1754–1794*, Bern, Francke, 1957, 400 pp.; Ludwig Uhlig, *Georg Forster. Einheit und Mannigfaltigkeit in seiner geistigen Welt*, Tübingen, Niemeyer, 1965, viii, 343 pp.; Thomas P. Saine, *Georg Forster*, New York, Twayne, 1972, 182 pp., and in *Deutsche Dichter des 18. Jhs*, ed. B. v. Weise, Berlin, Schmidt, 1977, pp. 861–80; Gerhard Steiner, *Georg Forster*, Stuttgart, Metzler, 1977, vi, 136 pp. (=SM, 156); Christa Krüger, *Georg Forsters und Friedrich Schlegels Beurteilung der Französichen Revolution*, Göppingen, Kümmerle, 1974, 243 pp.; and W. D. Robson-Scott, *Literary Background of the Gothic Revival*, 1965, especially pp. 99–105.

was the persistent mycelium from which growths regularly emerged. His later appeal to Tieck and Novalis, Fichte and Schelling, was compounded of interest in his doctrine of the mysterious Will, the forming power in the Godhead, nature and man, with the associated adaptation of the trinitarian principle that prefigured the romantic and Hegelian dialectic. Then there were his symbols, often using the natural elements (light, fire, mercury, sulphur), which were important for Tieck— and indeed for William Blake, and his 'doctrine of signatures'. This claimed that God's creative word or revelation was to be read in the 'books' that are mankind and nature, and the doctrine, uniting as it does the primitive magic of naming with the Graeco-Christian tradition of the creative logos, carries over into the Romantic concept of the hieroglyph and, incidentally, into Stephen's walk on the beach in Joyce's *Ulysses*.

Böhme's speculations were kept alive in Germany by Rosicrucians and Pietists but, above all, through the mediation of the French philosopher Louis Claude de Saint-Martin (1743–1803), who opened the door to mystical and cabbalistic literature for Franz von Baader and G. H. von Schubert.[7] This area in which alchemism, cabbalism, magic numerology, and similar fringe activities of the mind, cohabited with mystical exaltation, a more or less philosophically grounded theosophy and new directions in the natural sciences will require a rather more detailed analysis in a later section.

It is important, however, to appreciate the way in which ideas of all kinds were darting more randomly into the minds of men (and even more of women), with the rapid growth of commercial lending libraries and of reading circles and societies towards the end of the century. Pulp novels may have been the staple fare of some of the borrowers and the range of readers was still, of course, relatively small; but certainly many of the reading societies supplemented the old and well-considered volumes in private libraries with the latest novelties from England and France, with periodicals or almanacs, voyages, contemporary biographies, and even the latest philosophical, theological or pedagogic works. Printing was now also for butterfly minds.[8]

---

[7] In addition to Ernst Benz (1968) and Hans Graßl (1968) see Antoine Faivre, *Kirchberger et l'Illuminisme du dix-huitième siècle*, The Hague, Nijhoff, 1966, xxx, 284 pp., and his *Eckartshausen et la théosophie chrétienne*, Paris, Klincksieck, 1969, 788 pp.; and Mieczyslawa Sekrecka, *Louis Claude de Saint-Martin, le Philosophe inconnu*, Wroclaw, 1968, 224 pp. (=Acta universitatis wratislaviensis, 65). Karl R. H. Frick, *Die Erleuchteten. Gnostisch-theosophische und alchemistisch-rosenkreuzerische Geheimgesellschaften bis zum Ende des 18. Jahrhunderts*, Graz, Akademische Druck- und Verlagsgesellschaft, 1973, xi, 635 pp., presents an overwhelming mass of detail.

[8] Much has been written on this topic recently. Perhaps the most useful works are Albert Ward, *Book Production, Fiction and the German Reading Public 1740–1800*, Oxford, Clarendon

Society and State

The three hundred or so territorial units into which Germany was still divided in 1789 were, in great measure, socially and economically backward. Whole streets had fallen into decay in, for instance, Cologne, while serfdom still existed in much of the North and East. Apart from Prussia's austerely responsible administration the picture everywhere is of misgovernment and stagnation. It is within this framework that the rise of the middle class occurs, bringing with it unsatisfied aspirations, impatience at the restrictions of absolutism, and a dream of a better society.

Some reflection of this may be seen, without pressing the analogy too closely, in the changed dream of the Golden Age by the final quarter of the eighteenth century. The Arcadian idylls, the looking back to natural man, start yielding to a vision of a utopian future; Christian chiliasm, the vision of the thousand-year kingdom, had anyway been kept alive in Swabian Pietism. In Bavaria, Adam Weishaupt's secret society (the Illuminati) assumed the task of overthrowing the Church and transforming society, all, as it happened, on the best Enlightenment principles. Then, suddenly, Utopia was at hand.[9]

'The French Revolution, Fichte's *Theory of Knowledge* and Goethe's *Wilhelm Meister* are the greatest trends of the age' (Friedrich Schlegel, *KA* II, 198). The much quoted *Athenäum* fragment 216 is significant in that it links and limits the Revolution. The initial burst of enthusiasm was particularly marked among the intelligentsia; the common people were little more than curious. Yet the general air of expectancy, the sense that all was now possible, was unmistakable. 'Nothing was dreamt of but the regeneration of the human race,' said Southey, looking back from his Tory middle age. Few who were young in 1789 ever freed themselves from the experience, whatever their later revulsion from the consequences.

Disillusion came for some with the Terror, for others with the realization that the new France was not prepared to stop her revolution at her borders. Tieck, writing to Wackenroder in September 1792, still wished that he were a Frenchman, saw the genius of Greece hovering over Gaul,

---

Press, 1974, ix, 214 pp., and Rolf Engelsing, *Der Bürger als Leser. Lesergeschichte in Deutschland 1500–1800*, Stuttgart, Metzler, 1974, 375 pp., though the detail is almost wholly limited to Bremen.

[9] See Mähl, ... *Novalis* (1965) and H.-J. Heiner, 'Das "goldene Zeitalter" in der deutschen Romantik', *ZDP*, xci (1972), 206–34, with a different analysis, emphasizing the supposed frustration of the Romantic writer at not being able to translate into reality the expectations aroused by the French Revolution. Heiner's argument is that the writer's status in Germany did not permit him to influence public affairs and that he, as it were, turned in upon himself and his friends. This is of doubtful validity even for Hoffmann, whom he discusses; it is not true at all of Arnim, whom he does not.

attested that France filled his thoughts night and day, and that he longed to be there. Yet we must not allow ourselves to be too impressed; he did not go (though Georg Forster, and later Görres, did), it is a very long letter, and France occupies one paragraph. And eventually the Jacobins were more than he could swallow.

Curiously enough, the impetus given by the Revolution to dreams of a better future did not die away with disenchantment at its progress. Several reasons may be advanced. Prussia, having taken only a very inglorious part in the Revolutionary Wars against France from 1792 on, signed a separate peace in 1795 and remained neutral for ten years; a precarious calm reigned in central and northern Germany, including Weimar and Jena. All around them they saw reforms, under direct French rule in the Rhineland, in feverish imitative haste in Bavaria, Baden and Württemberg. The Holy Roman Empire was collapsing and ceased to exist even as a symbol in 1806. Change was all.

Then, again in 1806, Napoleon turned to Prussia and Frederick the Great's creation began to fall apart. Yet the occupation by French forces, the profound humiliation of all the German states, led not to despair but to a resurgence of the national will. The nation was summoned to a consciousness of its fundamental unity by the oratory of Fichte's 'Addresses to the German Nation', delivered in Berlin in the winter of 1807-8 and published (*Reden an die deutsche Nation*) in 1808, lectures in which the former cosmopolitan and radical now developed the myth that the Germans, with a unique national imagination nurtured by the purity of their language, were the only wholly genuine people in the modern world. The 'Addresses' certainly have an unattractive flavour of the totalitarian state, and talk of an 'Urvolk' makes later echoes ring in our ears; but, taken with the similar exaltation of linguistic and racial purity and of militarism in Ernst Moritz Arndt and the mystical folkdom which Friedrich Ludwig Jahn translated into paramilitary gymnastic societies, the regenerative power of patriotism is clearly making itself felt. Above all it appears in the non-revolutionary reform movements in Prussia between 1807 and 1813, where Stein and Hardenberg attempt nothing less than a total reorganization of the state.

Philosophy, Science and Psychology

The influence of philosophical speculation on literature may easily be exaggerated; Proust is more than paraphrased Bergson. Most writers have an uncertain grasp of the technical apparatus of philosophers; for every enquiring Novalis there are a dozen bored Tiecks. Literature is not, in general, written by failed philosophers, and a coarsening of distinctions commonly attends the conversion of analytical thought into art.

Yet it is clear that the great half-century from the publication of Kant's *Kritik der reinen Vernunft* in 1781 to the death of Hegel in 1831 must be reckoned an exception, above all in the earlier part. There were still some writers relatively unaffected by any direct philosophical influence, but an unusual number made a determined effort to understand the Kantian revolution and its subsequent modifications. Mme de Staël claimed that, once the *Kritik* had become known, it 'created such a sensation in Germany that almost everything achieved since then, in literature as well as philosophy, derives from the impetus given by that work' (*De l'Allemagne*, IV, 112). Why should this have been so? What explains the interest in philosophical systems?

In part, no doubt, the explanation lies in contiguity, more especially in Jena; Fichte, Schelling and the Schlegels, quarrels notwithstanding, were intimately connected. Goethe and Schiller were near at hand. In part, too, the new importance attached to aesthetics will have helped. But these considerations will hardly explain all.

The essential feature is that Kant and his successors were consciously creating revolution, the cultural Maoism of the day. Kant himself spoke of his work as the second Copernican revolution; Fichte compared his philosophy with the French Revolution, releasing men from the bondage of the 'thing-in-itself'; Schelling deemed his natural philosophy certain to instigate 'a general and highly desirable revolution'; Dorothea Veit, in a letter to Schleiermacher of 28 October 1799, called him and Schelling 'you revolutionary people'; and their opponents regarded them in the same light.[10]

Certainly they were decidedly self-confident, each convinced that his own philosophical method was the one genuine agent of revolution. At this remove we see the dependence of Fichte and Schelling on Kant even more clearly than their divergence from him. For them, however, there was not one revolution but three.

What was it that they and their contemporaries found so new in these ways of thinking? Essentially it was a re-examination of the creative interchange between self and world. It is typical of the Kantian revolution that, when Kant sketched the four tasks of his philosophy in a letter to Karl Friedrich Stäudlin of 4 May 1793, he should have related all four to the self not to the world of objects. The questions he sets himself are: what can I know? (metaphysics); what should I do? (ethics, morality); what may I hope? (religion); what is man? (anthropology).

---

[10] Kant, in his preface to the first edition of the *Kritik der reinen Vernunft*. The other references are from Fambach IV: Fichte, letter of April (?) 1795, p. 219; Schelling in a polemical pamphlet of April 1800, p. 357; Dorothea Veit, p. 349; opponents, pp. 407-8 (Nicolai in 1801), 523 and 526.

The ordering of the phenomenal world is not a product of objects themselves but of the activity of our understanding, operating on sense-data according to the two forms of human sensibility, time and space, and the categories, such as substance and cause, which are constructive forms of thought. The human mind therefore itself determines the laws that it finds in the phenomenal world. Things-in-themselves do exist as a kind of noumenal substratum, but we cannot know them. Metaphysical speculation is therefore an illusion.

Kant on human knowing had as profound an effect on the Romantic writers as Kant on the moral law had on Classicism. He provided a whole new philosophical language and method; he detached appearance from reality; he liberated speculation from reason (though himself retaining careful rationality of discourse); he confirmed both the creativity and the ethical responsibility of the self. Even the opponents of the Critical philosophy—whether traditional empiricists or rationalists or those, like Hamann, Herder and Jacobi, who upheld the claims of feeling and faith—had to take account of it.

Fichte. Fichte advanced even further the primacy of the self, or rather of the ego, the primeval principle. His breathtaking leap of logic is to make the object wholly dependent on the subject, to subjugate things to man. The external world does not exist in its own right (there are no things-in-themselves); it, the non-ego, is merely posited or asserted by the ego as its own limiting and therefore delimiting opposite. This is the dialectical process by which the world exists.

The creative process implied in all this is of the greatest significance for Romanticism's view of the artist's imaginative power. The ego is pure activity; imagination, the pre-reflective activity, creates the world of objects as it constantly reaches out beyond itself towards infinity. In this creative tension lies the genesis of Romantic irony, as of Friedrich Schlegel's genre theory and Novalis's 'magic idealism'. From here, too, springs Fichte's interpretation of the moral law. His main concern, indeed, is an ethical one. 'My system', he writes to Karl Leonhard Reinhold on 8 January 1800, 'is from its beginning to its end just an analysis of freedom.' This freedom is an activity of the imagination and the will, an exercise in self-expression.

Fichte's views varied significantly during his lifetime, and reactions to them were often affected by attitudes towards Fichte's own personality: independent, energetic, violent. But his system was generally recognized as being the high point of idealism, of nature's dependence on mind. The dualism between nature and mind is resolved by forcible subjugation of the former. A wholly subjective universe is thus made available, and for many contemporaries the distinction between the subjectivity of the absolute ego and the individual self was conveniently blurred. Thus the relationship between freedom and morality, the releasing of the imagination, and the activism that Fichte compared with the French Revolution were living issues contributing to Romantic theory and emotion. It should not, however, be forgotten that the heightening of consciousness achieved for some by the new status of the self was felt by others as exposure to the chill winds of uncertainty.

Schelling. The sorcerer of Romantic philosophy is undoubtedly Schelling, and he had all too many apprentices. Nineteenth-century neo-Hegelian historians of philosophy did less than justice to the imaginative power of his thought and certainly overstressed the inconstancy of his views, though it is fair to distinguish, as he himself did, between the first advance from Fichte to the 'Philosophy of Nature' (Naturphilosophie), then the formulation of the 'System of Identity' (Identitätssystem), and finally the long, bitter years of neglect and struggle for an understanding of the nature of God.[11] Schelling proceeds by magnificent conjectural leaps, which he then has to integrate into a system. Most historians of philosophy have found this a distasteful method, though its fascination is now more readily acknowledged; the consequence, at all events, was that it was generally the intuitions that seized the imagination of his contemporaries and that are of most concern to us.

Fichte had no real feeling for the natural world; the non-ego was a bloodless concept. Schelling was much more the heir of the later eighteenth century's scientific discoveries and of its increasing awareness of natural beauty.

'The system of nature is at the same time the system of our mind' (*Werke*, 1927, I, 689); this is Schelling's advance from Fichte. Nature is not the creation of the ego but its analogue. Both are held together in the unity of consciousness; the same mind is at work in nature and in us. Nature is, it is true, unconscious mind, slumbering intelligence; but the world-soul within it is always striving towards consciousness. Nature is in a perpetual state of activity, of becoming, assuming multifarious forms on its meanderings towards this goal of consciousness. The forms themselves are created, out of original identity, by the principle of polarity exemplified in the phenomenon of terrestrial magnetism, or the negative and positive in electricity, or the relationship of acids and alkalis in chemistry, or, in life, in the interplay between the three powers

---

[11] It used to be argued that the so-called *Systemprogramm* of 1796 contains the germ of most of Schelling's later ideas, but there is now a total lack of agreement about its authorship: Schelling, Hölderlin or Hegel. See *Das älteste Systemprogramm. Studien zur Frühgeschichte des deutschen Idealismus*, ed. Rüdiger Bubner, Bonn, Bouvier, 1973, 265 pp. (=Hegel-Studien, supp. vol. 9).

of stimulation, sensitivity and reproduction.[12] This dynamic view of nature is, and is meant to be, in direct opposition to the Enlightenment's mechanistic view of nature and it has, of course, obvious affinities with Fichte's activist interpretation of being. We can hear echoes of Spinoza and of Giordano Bruno's Renaissance vision of nature as a single organism, without following Schelling further into his System of Identity where the Absolute is the all-embracing, undifferentiated unity, the point where all differences are reconciled or, as Hegel unkindly put it, the night in which all cows are black.

Schelling made three essential contributions to the Romantic movement. In his vision of the poet he gave a new and central meaning to the creative act, and opened for art the resources of the collective unconscious, though he naturally did not use the term.[13] Then he showed that the growth of the natural sciences did not necessarily compel a mechanistic and anti-personal view of the world. Finally, he provided an antidote to the extreme subjectivism of Fichte by forming and giving powerful expression to the desire for unity, the wish to repair the rift in the world.

Science. It should not be thought that the systems of Fichte and Schelling were the only raw material of Romantic speculation. They were closely interwoven with ideas from the whole range of the natural sciences, into which the Romantic writers, gluttons for the encyclopaedic in their search for totality, enthusiastically immersed themselves. Novalis, Arnim and Chamisso were, for that matter, professional scientists of some competence.

Contemporary thought was greatly influenced by the notion of organic unity, a divine creative life permeating the whole universe, Nature as a total organism, God's becoming; man as the microcosm, separated from unity but fitfully capable of grasping it again by art as intuition; the dynamic process initiated and sustained by the principle of polarity; levels and stages in nature, and growth from matter to man: these were

---

[12] Here Schelling was profoundly influenced by the physiologist Carl Friedrich Kielmeyer (1765–1844) and his doctrine of organisms as the product of a common developmental force.

[13] The chief statement of the overriding importance of art in Schelling's thought up to about 1800 is to be found towards the end of the *System des transzendentalen Idealismus* (1800; *Werke*, 1927, II, 627–8). Only in art can philosophy objectify itself, can the unconscious in action be represented outwardly, can the absolute be shown in the finite. For a relationship between Schelling and Freud, and a review of the connexion between Naturphilosophie and medicine, see Odo Marquard, 'Über einige Beziehungen zwischen Ästhetik und Therapeutik in der Philosophie des neunzehnten Jahrhunderts, in *Materialen zu Schelling*, 1975, pp. 341–77.

some of the concerns at large in the late eighteenth and early nineteenth centuries.

They derived from specific scientific advances: the first, faltering steps in evolutionary biology; the discoveries in the chemistry of gases that seemed to confirm both the principle of polarity, in the composition of water, and the notion of an indwelling vital force, oxygen; the beginnings of an understanding of the central nervous system;[14] the observation of electrical effects, particularly Galvani's experiments with frogs' legs in the 1780s, where he thought that the twitching he had observed was the result of 'animal electricity' (an exciting concept)—thought Volta later showed the cause to be in the different metals tied to the legs.

Galvanism had appeared to confirm the theories of 'animal magnetism' propounded and apparently put into practice by Franz Anton Mesmer (1734–1815), and disseminated in more than two hundred books and pamphlets within a decade. Mesmer, who was probably part genuine investigator and part charlatan, believed that the universe was permeated with an invisible fluid (*fluidum universale*) holding everything together. Animal magnetism was only a special case of the organism's receptivity to this universal fluid.

The opportunities for confusion between science and magic in all this are evident enough. Magnetism, galvanism, mesmerism, universal effluvia, hypnotic states, sympathetic relationship of objects: all these obscured the boundaries between the natural sciences, theosophy, occultism and the philosophy of nature. From about 1770 well on into the nineteenth century, there is a vast literature on these fringe sciences, culminating, one might reasonably say, in Joseph Ennemoser's *Geschichte der Magie* (1844).

Naturphilosophie. The philosophy of nature that developed in the wake of Schelling, and to a lesser extent of Hegel, was a kind of transcendental science, an interpretation of natural phenomena in terms of a speculatively derived system; and it undoubtedly encouraged many outlandish theories. The general designation 'Naturphilosophie' is used in a particular sense to characterize this essentially non-scientific attitude,

---

[14] The Scottish doctor, John Brown (1735–88), developed the notion of the sensibility of the nervous system into a doctrine in which life, an unbroken chain of stimuli, is healthy only when these are in balance. This Brunonian system was followed by a large number of doctors and, in practical terms, involved the restoration of a proper balance by the lavish use of laudanum or alcohol, medicaments to which Brown himself was no stranger. Friedrich Schlegel, Tieck and Novalis were all at one time deeply interested in his theories and Schelling was involved in a painful controversy about Brunonian medical procedures on the death of his step-daughter, Auguste Böhmer, in 1800. See Leibbrand (1956) and John Neubauer, 'Dr John Brown (1735–88) and early German Romanticism', *Journal of the History of Ideas*, xxviii (1967), 367–82.

which disdained empirical observation and proceeded by bold analogy and poetic comparisons. Intoxicated with the absolute, with organicism and polarity, the Naturphilosophen relied heavily on imagination.[15]

Typical figures are Troxler, Treviranus, Johann Jakob Wagner and Eschenmayer (extensively annotated by Novalis), in all of whom intuition smartly outran enquiry. Others succeeded in being experimental scientists of some achievement, as their left hand proceeded in ignorance of their right. Among these may be counted the pathologist Kieser, the physiologist Burdach, the botanist Nees von Esenbeck and, pre-eminently, Lorenz Oken who first postulated the cell theory and evolution from primeval slime. As the systematizer of Naturphilosophie, however, Oken attempts an elaborate explanation of the universe from a priori postulates or, less politely, by guesswork. There are brilliant guesses in plenty but they are embedded in a great deal of nonsense, frequently shading off into numerology and other fringe subjects.

A little more must be said about two of Schelling's most enthusiastic admirers, whose connexions with the Romantic writers were very close. Johann Wilhelm Ritter (1776–1810), the discoverer of ultra-violet rays and a physicist of remarkable insights, was on intimate terms with Novalis and Friedrich Schlegel and was immoderately admired by other Romantics, particularly Brentano. He was self-taught, lived in poverty and proceeded almost wholly without system, so that the most remarkable experimental results alternate with speculative absurdities or dark rhetorical intuitions. The restoration of man's lost harmony with nature, the unification of physics and poetry, the search for a general principle of cohesion (largely found in galvanism), the recognition of parallels and hieroglyphic correspondences: these were the stuff of his thought. His exalted and visionary style, at its best and incoherent worst, may be seen in the *Fragmente aus dem Nachlaß eines jungen Physikers* (1810), which may indeed contain some fragments by Novalis, to whom the collection was intended to be a memorial.

The Scandinavian Henrik Steffens (1773–1845) was a central figure in Romantic circles for many years, and his autobiography, *Was ich erlebte*, in ten volumes (1840–4) is one of the most valuable records of the period. Steffens's first important work was his *Beiträge zur inneren Naturgeschichte der Erde* (1801) and in it one gets an apparent attempt to proceed from scientific observation, initially of geological character, to more theoretical speculations. The empirical foundations are, how-

---

[15] The analogy of the Naturphilosoph's way with science and the Romantic writer's sense of his art is pointed in one of Friedrich Schlegel's fragments of 1812: 'Die neue Poesie oder sogenannte neue Schule entspricht sehr bestimmt der Naturphilosophie. Es war eine Revolution in dem ästhetischen Gebiet. Die romantische Poesie als eine kombinatorische und universelle gehört hierhin' (*Schriften und Fragmente*, ed. Ernst Behler, 1956, p. 136).

ever, relatively flimsy and the attempts at synthesis overbold and frequently fantastic. Steffens was fundamentally more interested in the imaginative analogies to be drawn from experiments rather than in the sober results. This leads him, to take one instance from a lecture (related by Friedrich Wöhler in a letter to Liebig), to describe the diamond as a piece of flint that had come to its senses ('ein zu sich selbst gekommener Kiesel'), which invited the travesty by a contemporary geologist that quartz must therefore be a diamond that had gone mad.

In his later years, for example in his *Anthropologie* (1822), Steffens saw man primarily as the microcosm, the abridgement of God and of all natural processes, and the claims of religion and patriotism came to influence him greatly. In this later period he also wrote a good deal of fiction, retelling legends and constructing very workmanlike Märchen, Novellen and historical novels.

Psychology. Naturphilosophie is intimately combined with psychology; discoveries, or deductions, in the natural sciences are applicable to man because of the identity between him and the natural world. Two men in particular, Schubert and Carus, exemplify this connexion.

The physician Gotthilf Heinrich Schubert (1780–1860), a warm and enthusiastic personality who wrote books as readily as some men write letters, came into prominence with a series of lectures, *Ansichten von der Nachtseite der Naturwissenschaft* (1808),[16] which greatly influenced the later Romantic writers. Although his other works, especially *Symbolik des Traumes* (1814) and *Geschichte der Seele* (1830), amplify his views, it is reasonable to take the 'Night-Side' lectures as representing them pretty adequately. He begins, typically enough, by inferring from the evidence of ancient myth the existence of a primordial golden age, when man was in total harmony with nature, a period of his unquestioning acceptance of and subordination to the eternal rhythm of the natural law. But man lost his sense of total dependence on nature, which became an object, a phenomenon for scientific investigation; and not until now, the period of Naturphilosophie, has he rediscovered how to approach her. He is to come to her with a recognition of the underlying harmony of all things, of the world-soul continually at work in its process of creation and organization, unconsciously presaged by myth. This hylozoism, which allows Schubert to draw audacious parallels between, say, planetary orbits and the organs of the human body, is accompanied by a doctrine of the scale of being or developmental ladder. Everything tends to a higher state, strives for the most complete perfection, and at certain

---

[16] It is instructive to compare the 'Night-Side' with Alexander von Humbolt's *Ansichten der Natur*, also 1808, equally poetic in character but objective in its descriptions and non-speculative in method.

moments the germ of the higher existence intrudes into the husk of the present form; in the plant it does this at the moment of full bloom. This is where Schubert, influenced by Ritter, Brown and Mesmer, converts abstract speculation into psychology and physiology. For, in man, the higher future life, the spiritual world which borders on this one, reveals itself in death and its cortege of anticipatory or accompanying states. These psychic anomalies, when the forces of life are in repose, when the boundaries between matter and spirit are blurred, are presentiments (often of death), clairvoyance, *déja-vu* experiences, dreams and reveries, animal magnetism, sympathy (we might now say telepathy), somnambulism, prophetic inspiration, ecstasy, fever and the like. It was in providing a framework for these borderline phenomena, in elevating them beyond rationality and consciousness, that Schubert was important for Romantic writers.

The realm of the subconscious is more lucidly and systematically explored by Carl Gustav Carus (1789–1869), the sub-Goethean figure of later Romanticism. Carus was a doctor who made notable advances in gynaecology, a naturalist, a notable traveller, a psychologist, a physiognomist, an elegant and sculptured writer, and both a theorist of art and a painter of substantial achievement.[17] His work is more disciplined than that of most of the nature philosophers, but the philosophical bases are very similar; the world-soul as the organizing principle (Carus generally calls it 'die Idee') and the doctrines of polarity and of ascent to the human mind, which is 'the fine flowering of the cosmos' (*Natur und Idee*, 1861, p. 2).

Human consciousness is the highest goal of life, but it is sustained by the rhythms and intuitions of the unconscious state, just as plants and lower organisms respond much more readily than men to intangibles such as a coming change in the weather. In *Psyche* (1846, p. 69) he compares the full conscious state to the gleaming spire of a Gothic cathedral, attracting the eye by the richness of its ornamentation and the way it strives towards heaven, but unable to stand without the foundations resting deep and invisible in the earth beneath. Carus distinguishes between a region of the absolute unconscious, where the organic processes of growth and reproduction are at work, and the region of the relative unconscious which contains, as it were, the abandoned experiences of our individual past, the lumber-room of memory from which items can be made available again to the conscious mind. But, as we sink back during sleep or hypnotic and clairvoyant states into the absolute unconscious,

[17] For his painting see Marianne Prause, *Carl Gustav Carus. Leben und Werk*, Berlin, Deutscher Verlag für Kunstwissenschaft, 1968, 187 pp. The influence of Naturphilosophie on landscape painting is revealed in the relationship of Steffens and Carus with Caspar David Friedrich; see Börsch-Supan and Jähnig (1973 and 1974).

the stream of cosmic life, we are linked to the common background of the human race. Jung acknowledged Carus to be, with Eduard von Hartmann, the rediscoverer of the unconscious and there are certainly clear presages of the Jungian system. Similarly the relative unconscious, from which association of ideas may lead us to consciousness, has its undertones of Freud.

Carus embodies much of the anthropology of Romanticism, but when he discusses psychosomatic disorders, or examines prophetic dreams, or traces the invisible antennae of the soul reaching into the world, he is in general rationalizing Naturphilosophie and making it accessible to the post-Hegelian mind. Certainly he seems much the most modern of the Romantic thinkers.

Religion

Steffens, Schubert and Carus all were, or became, intensely concerned with the place of God in the scheme of nature, and we have seen that Schelling increasingly tortured his philosophical system in an attempt to solve the problem. But the romanticization of religion and the decisive shift of Romantic interest towards Christianity is principally the work of two men, the Bavarian Catholic Franz von Baader and the Protestant Schleiermacher.

Baader. Baader (1765–1841) trained first as a doctor and then as a mining engineer at Freiberg before spending four years in England. His writings are extensive but unsystematic and it is difficult to point to any one work, except perhaps *Fermenta cognitionis* (1822–5), as being specially representative of him. There is, however, no doubt of his powerful influence on Romantic writers over a long period, not least by personal contact; it was of him that Friedrich Schlegel wrote to Sulpiz Boisserée in 1811 that, if he could only write as he could speak, there would be less talk of Schelling and Fichte.

In him the schoolmen and mystics of the Middle Ages return once more to German thought. Baader was concerned to re-establish God at the centre of nature, the human mind and society. As early as 1786 he was referring to a world-soul, but not a pantheist one; all is in God, but all is not God.

Our thought is a continuation of God's, a 'knowing-with'; in its highest form it is intuitive understanding, thinking with the heart, a far cry from rationalism and, for some, a release for the imagination, not without overtones of clairvoyance, hypnosis and the like. Baader reached back to the whole complex of Christian symbolism and the medieval and baroque mysticism of Meister Eckhart or Böhme. At the same time he was anticipating the analogies of Naturphilosophie, so that, for instance, love, which is the unifying element in creation, can also be called attraction, cohesion, gravity; or he can attempt to explain the immaterial corporeality of God by reference to para-psychological phenomena, particularly magnetism. There is therefore in his work, in the mid 1780s, a curious and heady combination of philosophical argument, theosophy, mysticism, alchemy, the cabbala, science and pseudo-science and the correspondences and hieroglyphs that were to characterize Naturphilosophie. For the early Romantics it was Baader who made esoteric symbolism, paranormal psychology and mystical eschatology intellectually respectable. He removed things from their customary categories.

He was personally a tolerant man, with considerable sympathy for the workers, little taste for the more reactionary features of the Restoration period, and an understanding of the ills of society that has been compared with that of Engels. Nevertheless his theocentric social and political philosophy is very similar to that of the far more controversial Adam Müller, perhaps the leading political theorist of Romanticism.[18]

Baader's theocentric social and political philosophy is medieval, patriarchal and idealized. Romanticism is here not individualistic; man is seen as part of a cosmic community. The organism of the state has its own structural laws corresponding to the order of the universe. Order presupposes ordering and therefore authority and hierarchy. The governor and the governed have duties towards one another; these are regulated by their common duty towards God and by love, the guiding principle of society. The growth of self-interested capitalism threatens the balance of society; industrialization mechanizes man. The French Revolution spells the dictatorship of the masses, of an aggregation of Godless individuals rather than an organic society; it is the gleam of the dawns of hell. This phrase is taken from a pamphlet written by him in 1815 on the need for a new and closer relationship between religion and politics as a consequence of the Revolution. The combination is characteristic of much Romantic thinking.

Schleiermacher. In July 1797 Friedrich Schlegel went to Berlin carrying the plan of a periodical to which August Wilhelm, Novalis and others were to be contributors. There he met a young preacher, Friedrich

[18] The changing attitudes to Adam Müller mirror the dominant intellectual climate in Germany, from a distrust of his conversion to Catholicism in 1805, through distaste for his collaboration with Metternich, interest in his view of the organic state during the Nazi period, the contemptuous rejection of him as a police-spy reactionary by some present-day critics. His literary criticism and his aesthetic doctrine, based largely on the reconciliation of opposites in poetry as a way of achieving wholeness and universality, are conveniently summarized in Wellek, *The Romantic Age*, 1955, pp. 291–7.

Daniel Ernst Schleiermacher (1768–1834), a regular visitor to the salon of Henriette Herz; Schlegel was much taken with him and saw in him an important moral leavening for the periodical. Schleiermacher, it is clear, was both excited and disturbed by his conversations with Friedrich Schlegel and his new friends, and in late 1798 and the early months of 1799 he wrote his defence of religion, with not only the old rationalists but also the new Romantics in mind. The work was published anonymously in Berlin in 1799 as *Über die Religion. Reden an die Gebildeten unter ihren Verächtern*; it introduced the greatest change in man's view of religion since the Reformation.

Religion is shown to be an independent area of human thought, not as for Kant an appendage to morality, or as for the Enlightenment a form of philosophy. Its basis is feeling, an intuition of the universe, a consciousness of an all-embracing unity, a sense of complete dependence on the absolute. The absolute unity with whom we feel at one, and on whom we depend, is God. In him the real and ideal, being and thought, are one; he is above all contradictions. Man, however, thinks only in terms of contradictions not of perfect knowledge. God is therefore a necessary proposition but not a definable or provable one. A rational theology is not possible.

The impact of the *Reden* depended to some considerable extent on the style; Schleiermacher is one of the few preachers whose rhetoric transfers effectively into print. It is all quite unlike the theological writing of the rest of the eighteenth century; take, for instance, the description of the fleeting instant when intuition and feeling are one: 'I lie in the bosom of the infinite world, and in that moment I am its soul, for I feel all its powers and its infinite life as my very own' (*Über die Religion*, 1799, p. 74). The language is that of *Werther* or Wackenroder.

They were also felt to be profoundly liberating, an accommodation of religion to modern man's requirements. Miracles, revelation, scriptural inspiration, dogma: all these can be explained, not to say explained away. The specifically Christian content is minimal, although recent estimations of Schleiermacher stress the important role of the mediator (Christ) in his thought in the *Reden*; and there is certainly in succeeding editions, and in his later works generally, a distinct movement nearer historic Christianity. The main stress though is unmistakably on unity and infinity; 'religion is a sense of the Infinite and a taste for it' (p. 53). Spinoza's influence is profound, though Schleiermacher regards accusations of pantheism as having no useful meaning.

Both in the *Reden*, and more especially in the *Monologen* (1800), he celebrates the importance of the individual, not the general Fichtean ego but the empirical, existential self. Each human being is an abbreviated, concentrated, but not fully developed version of the universe. At the same time we are all different; we are separate and special versions of the absolute.

The claim has often been made that this view of individuality represents Romantic influence on Schleiermacher at its most acute; but, in fact, extreme individualism is in practice held in check by his Moravian upbringing. The brotherhood that was central to their church life is reflected in his argument that we have to respect the special characteristics of others, and that the individual only fulfils himself in community, where he fits in to the sum of all human experiences.[19] Communities, whether families, schools, churches or states, also have their own individual characteristics and must be allowed their own organic growth—and here we approach Adam Müller's organic theory of the state again. Schleiermacher himself took an active part in the anti-Napoleonic struggle and was, towards the end of his life, a fairly advanced liberal reformer; but what he did for Romanticism's social philosophy was to combine the emphasis on individualism with a deep respect for the collective interplays of people and thus to show the necessity for what we should now call a sociology of religion. His more general achievement was to create a new ideal of religion that could be associated with the cultural movements of the age. This ideal was emotional, imaginative, intuitive rather than rational, dogmatic, normative; it was to be lived rather than argued. Schleiermacher's theological position remains a topic for argument; what contributed substantially to his influence was that he showed in himself how a life of some stature and nobility could be lived by his precepts. He attracted attention because he was a remarkable stylist; he retained it because he was a man of character.

Schleiermacher and Baader were men of intellectual distinction and high imaginative gifts. After the buffetings that Christianity had suffered under rationalism, and the bloodless counter-arguments of orthodoxy, these two made religion seem relevant again, able to comprehend developments in science and the humanities but also open to the excitements of the imagination.

---

[19] The particular interest in Schleiermacher as the originator of modern hermeneutics (the science of interpretation, particularly of the Scriptures) shown by such theologians as Rudolf Bultmann and Wolfhart Pannenberg is associated with these arguments. Briefly, Schleirmacher conceives of hermeneutical theory in very general terms, not limited to Bible texts. Understanding, he says, can only properly begin once the interpreter has identified himself with the author, speaker, reader. This understanding is achieved by intuition based on seeing individuality in the light of generic consciousness or common humanity.

2

New Ways of Feeling:
Wackenroder, Tieck and 'The Night Watches'

If we were now to continue to trace intellectual trends, we should undoubtedly proceed straight to the Schlegels and Novalis. It is, however, not mere chronology but rather a sense of atmosphere that impels most writers on German Romanticism to begin with Wackenroder and Tieck and the consolidation of new ways of feeling.

Wackenroder

Wilhelm Heinrich Wackenroder was born in Berlin, the citadel of the dying Enlightenment, in 1773. His father, an earnest Prussian official of considerable standing, intended him for the law, and regardless of the son's extreme reluctance this was indeed his eventual fate. At school Wackenroder became friendly with the much more extrovert Tieck, on whom he grew very dependent, and both were together at the Universities of Erlangen in the Summer Term of 1793 and Göttingen in the autumn and winter of 1793 to 1794. During their stay at Erlangen they made several excursions through Franconia; Tieck was the more overwhelmed by the landscape, Wackenroder by the towns and the whole cultural atmosphere of the antique South German Catholic world. In 1794, his studies at Göttingen completed, Wackenroder became a junior at the court of appeal in Berlin, after wistful consideration of flight to Italy with Tieck. He escaped from his servitude in 1796, when he and Tieck visited Dresden to see the galleries there. By February 1798 he was dead.

The conflict of parental will and filial inclination is a well-worn subject and exposes one to the danger of sentimentalizing Wackenroder, or of producing an excessively biographical account of his work. The opposite danger is that of some East German critics, who read into his dislike of the law a fundamental critique of Prussian feudalism.[1] What seems more realistic is to say that he found his own everyday world remarkably uncongenial and revelled in all forms of escape from it, or means of redeeming it. Chief among these was art. From his own experience he produced an aesthetic compelling in its sincerity and fundamental originality, even if we can trace some component parts to Herder, the early Goethe, Winckelmann or Karl Philipp Moritz. It was an aesthetic free from the philosophical theorizing of Romanticism; Wackenroder was innocent of any influence from Fichte or Friederich Schlegel.

It was on the visit to Dresden in 1796 that he showed his writing to Tieck, and on the way back they called on the musician Johann Friedrich Reichardt, who both published Wackenroder's Dürer essay in his periodical *Deutschland* and also suggested the word 'Herzensergießungen' for the title of the collection of Wackenroder's essays brought out later that year, anonymously but with a preface by Tieck and some contributions by him.[2] After Wackenroder's death his other writings were incorporated by Tieck in *Phantasien über die Kunst für Freunde der Kunst* (1799), which contained a good deal more of his own work, then in 1814 he collected Wackenroder's contributions to these volumes under the title *Phantasien über die Kunst von einem kunstliebenden Klosterbruder*.

The *Herzensergießungen eines kunstliebenden Klosterbruders* have as their only connecting thread the figure of the art-loving friar himself, and he is a useful figure in that his mask stylizes, distances and sanctifies. He is, in fact, an almost contemporary figure but his naivete seems to place him in a much earlier period. It is through him that the unpretentious chronicle style of the biographies of painters is acceptable, and these sum-

[1] The section on Wackenroder in *Romantik*, Berlin, 1967, is characteristic, as is that in Johannes Mittenzwei, *Das Musikalische in der Literatur*, Halle (Saale), Verlag Sprache und Literatur, 1962, pp. 107-12, entitled 'Wackenroders Flucht in den musikalischen Elfenbeinturm'.

[2] It is not now thought that Reichardt suggested the figure of the friar, or that the latter was in any way connected with the Klosterbruder in Lessing's *Nathan*. See Richard Alewyn, 'Wackenroders Anteil an den *Herzensergießungen* und den *Phantasien*', *GR*, xix (1944), 48–58. For a discussion of Tieck's part see Gillies's edition and Werner Kohlschmidt, 'Bemerkungen zu Wackenroders und Tiecks Anteil an den *Phantasien über die Kunst*', in *Philologia deutsch. Festschrift Walter Henzen*, ed. Kohlschmidt and Paul Zinsli, Bern, Francke, 1965, pp. 89–99. There is still some uncertainty about the authorship of the various pieces in the *Phantasien*, but Kohlschmidt's arguments for ascribing the two Berglinger letters and the 'Märchen von einem nackten Heiligen' to Tieck, though repeated in his history of literature (1974), have not convinced.

For Reichardt's close connexion with many figures of the Romantic movement see Erich Neuß, *Das Giebichensteiner Dichterparadies. Johann Friedrich Reichardt und die 'Herberge der Romantik'*, Halle, [1932], 205 pp. (=Hallische Nachrichten-Bücherei, 9). For Reichardt generally see Walter Salmen's *Johann Friedrich Reichardt: Komponist, Schriftsteller ...*, Freiburg & Zürich, Atlantis, 1963, 363 pp.

mary versions of Vasari, Bellori and Sandrart hold the essence of Wackenroder's new attitude towards art and the artist. The *Herzensergießungen* also contain theoretical essays, again put in the friar's mouth, and generally appearing to equate art and religion.

Wackenroder speaks primarily of painting and is groping for its symbolic values when he defines it as fusing 'the spiritual and supersensual ... into visible forms' (*WB* I, 67). His symbolism is both religious in purpose and tied to Christian subject-matter; the Virgin Mary, for instance, is imported into one of Raphael's dreams instead of the figure of Galatea. A work of art is the reflection of divine creative power, as indeed it had been for Shaftesbury and the Storm and Stress, but artistic creation is here thought of more especially as religious art and its contemplation as a kind of prayer. The true artist is a selfless and devoted man; the creative and receptive soul both approach the work in rapt quietude and devotion. The description of the psychological processes of creation and appreciation had an impact on his contemporaries that is now difficult for us to grasp, for the pietistic vocabulary and the religiosity of the approach blur the critical edges and mislead us into thinking that there is nothing more here than naive enthusiasm for a golden age of God-inspired art. What Wackenroder does is to project into the past, and into the picture, his own idealizations. The artistic hagiography serves to create an atmosphere in which the emotional charge of religion is also available for the work of art.

The interest in the artist's life is of a piece with the concentration on the subject of a painting rather than on its composition. His knowledge of techniques, particularly in their historical development, was very sketchy and in 'Zwei Gemäldeschilderungen' (Two Descriptions of Paintings), the section of the *Herzensergießungen* in which he announces the impossibility of describing a painting and then tries to reproduce its essence in poetry, what he does is to allow the human subjects of the paintings to speak. Thus he recognizes that a painting is an organic whole, but at the same time neglects form in favour of subject-matter. The Madonna of Pommersfelden, then thought to be by Raphael but now ascribed to the school of Joos van Cleve, is described in detail for his parents in 1793 and it aroused intense enthusiasm in him; but no account is taken of any formal values. It is true that reaction against over-strict rules of composition was very relevant at the time and that it was perhaps more important to stress the religious and mediating role of art; but one suspects that Wackenroder's own deficient sense of form was responsible for his emphasis, rather than any conscious choice. Breathless enthusiasm remains untempered by structural subtleties.

One fundamental merit of his work was that it opened up new areas of the past for the aesthetic experience of the early nineteenth century.

There has recently been a good deal of argument as to whether his sensibility in any way comprehended medieval art, though his knowledge of medieval literature is undisputed.[3] Certainly his most extravagant praise is reserved for the Italian Renaissance, and above all for Raphael. It is also true that Dürer, for whom he had an almost equal enthusiasm, is not a medieval artist. Yet there are strong medieval traits in him and the atmosphere of simple piety and quiet craftsmanship with which Wackenroder (and later Tieck in *Sternbald*) surrounds his Renaissance figures is one clearly appropriate to the Middle Ages. (That they were also boisterous and often brutal times is naturally left out of account in early Romantic sentimentalized projection, and scarcely emerges before Arnim.) Wackenroder himself thought that he was writing about the Middle Ages; he asks, for instance, 'Why do you not condemn the Indian for speaking the Indian language and not ours? Do you then wish to condemn the Middle Ages for not building temples like those of Greece?' (*WB* I, 48). And the delight in the 'medieval' aspects of Nuremberg and the other Franconian towns shows an entirely new sensibility; the picturesque tortuosities of streets and buildings had repelled the Enlightenment, now they charmed. One should therefore avoid being over-nice in one's consideration of Wackenroder's medievalism (even the term 'Mittelalter' was only newly settled in the language of his day), and recognize that the important feature of his turning to the past was a non-historical desire to return to an idealized state of society, located in fact in the High Renaissance but in atmosphere in the Middle Ages, where the artist lived as a believer within a closed community. The pattern of this was one he thought he had himself recognized in Catholic South Germany and this regional appeal was also one that he fed into Romanticism.

Both Wackenroder and Tieck had a direct influence on painting, though obviously on subject-matter rather than on technique. This can be seen in Runge, both in the religious quality of his art and in the symbolic 'language' of the painting and its relationship to the natural world—though in this connexion Böhme is an even more important influence. It is, however, in the Nazarenes that Wackenroder's glorification of Renaissance piety as a source of great art comes to full fruition.[4] In

[3] See particularly W. D. Robson-Scott, *Literary Background of the Gothic Revival*, 1965, and Hans Eichner's introduction to volume four of the Friedrich Schlegel critical edition. For the growth of interest in Raphael see Marielene Putscher, *Raphaels Sixtinische Madonna. Das Werk und seine Wirkung*, Tübingen, Hopfer, 1955, vii, 347 pp., and in Dürer, *Dürer und die Nachwelt*, ed. Heinz Lüdecke and Susanne Heiland, Berlin, Rütten & Loening, 1955, 451 pp., and Jean Philippon, 'Dürer et les romantiques allemands', in *La Gloire de Dürer*, ed. Jean Richer, Paris, Klincksieck, 1974, pp. 153–71.
[4] See Keith Andrews, *The Nazarenes*, Oxford University Press, 1964, 168 pp., Rudolf Bachleitner, *Die Nazarener*, Munich, Wilhelm Heyne, 1976, 203 pp., and Fritz Herbert

July 1809 Friedrich Overbeck, Franz Pforr and four other young Viennese artists formed a group called the Lukasbruderschaft, united in their reverence for sixteenth-century German art and for Raphael and his contemporaries. Early in 1810 Overbeck and Pforr moved to Rome where they soon occupied the empty monastery of San Isidoro being joined later by Cornelius, Schnorr von Carolsfeld, the brothers Veit and others. Some of their work was produced communally and this, together with the disciplined life, the choice of Christian subject-matter, the serious and monumental nature of their paintings, the readiness with which they expatiated on their intentions, makes them the typical executants of one aspect of Romantic art.

Although Wackenroder's artistic ideal was to some extent fulfilled by the Nazarenes, it is significant that its realization is called into question even within the *Herzensergießungen* and the *Phantasien*, in those sections relating to Joseph Berglinger, friend of the friar's youth, composer and Kapellmeister. Wackenroder moves away from painting to music, an even more direct channel of communication with the divine; indeed in 'Ein wunderbares morgenländisches Märchen von einem nackten Heiligen' (A Wondrous Oriental Tale of a Naked Saint) in the *Phantasien* we find music directly releasing the saint's soul from its desperate concern with the turning wheel of time and bearing it straight to heaven.[5] Wackenroder himself had a good musical background, and his generation in Berlin was the first to experience the newly developed instrumental and symphonic music. It is, for instance, possible that he heard a piano recital by the young Beethoven in the summer of 1796. The Joseph Berglinger Novelle and the associated writings by the fictional Berglinger in the *Phantasien* are set in this present age. Joseph's story, as related by the friar, is that of a sensitive child whose main pleasure is music but whose father wishes him to study medicine. Joseph runs away to the capital, where he eventually becomes Kapellmeister. The immediacy of his original musical experience has, however, been affected by his discovery of the dependence of music on rules and order, and his disgust at the indifference of the public is matched only by a disillusionment with the world in which some critics see nihilistic traits. He returns home to see his father on his death-bed, finds his sisters in great poverty and degradation and, in a series of emotional spasms, composes an overpowering

Lehr, *Die Blütezeit romantischer Bildkunst: Franz Pforr, der Meister des Lukasbundes*, Marburg, Verlag des kunstgeschichtlichen Seminars, 1924, xvi, 366 pp.

[5] The wheel of time is convincingly shown by Hertrich, *Joseph Berglinger*, 1969, pp. 169–81, to be the clock of the Enlightenment's mechanistic view of the universe, a view which still retained some of its power for Wackenroder and Tieck, but which was in process of losing its optimism and rationality. Hertrich also examines, and demolishes, various interpretations in which the wheel represents industrialized society, a nihilistic fear of time, or the conventionality from which only art can rescue man.

'Easter Oratorio'. Shortly after he dies of a 'nervous fever'. The autobiographical elements must not be pressed too far, but they can no more be overlooked than can the Wertherian tension between self and world.

What Berglinger deplores is the loss of direct emotional response to music, a consequence of the general retreat of sensibility in the generation that was middle-aged at the turn of the century. In a community that has lost its responsiveness to music, and thus its intuitions of infinity, the artist, the representative of the absolute, cannot function. It is not, as some have claimed, that Berglinger is an inadequate artist, but a sense that the fundamental tension between art and reality becomes unbearable when that reality is as prosaic as that in which Berglinger-Wackenroder believed himself to live. The problematic nature of the artist's existence is also heightened by the ambiguity of his relationship to the unconscious; a prey to 'unknown powers': (*WB* I, 139), his music 'presses on recklessly into wilder labyrinths', calls up 'all the fearful terrors of the world', 'dreadful armies', 'nightmare figures'. In 'dreadful licence', like the magic goddesses of fate, music conjures up the 'mysteries of the soul.' 'Dreadful, oracular, ambiguous darkness' is for man a mark of the divinity of music (*WB* I, 193-4). This is a far cry from the innocent openness of some of the lives of the painters. The modern world has been pressing in on Wackenroder from the beginning; at first he escaped into the past, now he faces it in mingled despair and anticipation. The trappings of the artist's predicament will last throughout the Romantic movement; Hoffmann's Kreisler is a direct descendant of Berglinger. In Wackenroder the urgent note is one of hopeful panic.

Tieck

Tieck is the most impressionable of writers, carrying over into his work his considerable talent for mimicry. He develops hints and exploits novelty, whether derived from personal relationships or from his often undiscriminating reading. Wackenroder's reorientation of the artist is carried a stage further, and some would say vulgarized, in *Sternbald*; folktales combine with the Gothic novel in some of the plays and Märchen; Gozzi and Sterne join the Fichtean ego to colour the plays of fictive illusion. What is remarkable is how this eclecticism produced a body of work recognizable then and now as different in kind from its predecessors and yet not incomprehensibly strange, the first fruits of Romanticism in widely acceptable form. Tieck's great achievement was to have been intensely receptive and adaptable at a crucial point in cultural history. His constant willingness to experiment, his brooding sensitivity, his serious if uninspired search for significance, made him the representative writer of the new movement. One qualification is, however, necessary:

Tieck lived to be nearly eighty and published for over sixty years. He began at the end of the Enlightenment and lived on to the days of Keller and Fontane; and one sees in him, therefore, not only the growth of Romanticism but its gradual modulation into Biedermeier. Revolutionary fervour seldom lasts for sixty years.

Ludwig Tieck was born in 1773 as the first child of a master rope-maker of some cultural pretensions; his sister Sophie was herself a prolific writer and his brother Friedrich became a sculptor of distinction. From an early age, Ludwig read and wrote feverishly. His literary career began with an Oriental tale of patricide, sensuality and gruesome fantasies and it was followed by a tragedy heavy with Oresteian motifs and the appurtenances of spookery. Then came hack-work in Nicolai's 'literary factory', which which he obtained some emotional release in the tale *Peter Lebrecht* (1795) by mocking both the moralistic story and the Gothic novel, interpolating Sternean comments and apologies to the reader. Yet the ironic attitude cannot wholly cancel out these influences on him, and Gothic strands will continue in his work for some time, with an uncertainty of tone evident in the half parody and half writing for effect of the play *Ritter Blaubart* (1796).

A similar uncertainty pervades the novel in letters *William Lovell*, first conceived in 1792 but written mainly between 1794 and 1796. Tieck himself later called it 'the mausoleum of many cherished passions and errors',[6] and it both reflects the moods of despair to which he was prone during his student days and his subsequent rationalization of them. It is, in form, an eighteenth-century novel in the tradition of Richardson, the literary reminiscences abound: Jacobi's *Woldemar*, Rétif de la Bretonne's *Le paysan perverti*, Heinse's *Ardinghello*, Goethe's *Werther*. Repetitive and sensational in plot and over-supplied with stereotyped characters, the novel is nevertheless interesting in its attempt to relate autobiographical experience to contemporary uncertainties. It does this in the figure of Lovell, a young man whose youthful enthusiasm and self-indulgence lead to total commitment to pleasure and then to crime, degradation and eventual destruction. That he is a voluptuary is, however, no more than a concession to eighteenth-century taste; we remember Lovelace. What is significant is the instability of the self. Lovell hovers constantly between excitation and despair, reflected in two recurring concepts, 'chaos' and 'boredom'. Conscious of the emptiness within himself, he enlarges his despair to include the whole world. In partial understanding of Fichte he claims that everything he imagines himself to perceive outside himself can really exist only within himself: 'beings

---

[6] Letter to Solger, 31 March 1815, in Matenko, *Tieck and Solger*, 1933, p. 167. It should be noted that Tieck made changes in the text of the novel for the editions of 1813 and 1828.

are because we think them' (*Lovell*, letter 23). Thus there are no anchors in objectivity, and the natural world is not yet redemptive, as it later becomes in Eichendorff. These are new modes of consciousness, nihilistic commentaries on a world denatured. But in letter form they are distanced, as they were in Tieck's experience. Lovell is a specimen, not an authorial voice.

Bonaventura's 'Nachtwachen'

This anonymous work—half novel, half diary—published in 1804 in the little Saxon town of Penig, seems at first sight to approach *Lovell* quite closely in its nihilistic attitude. But the authorial stance is very different, much more heavily indebted to Jean Paul; and the confusion of tone reflects the later hour.

There has been much speculation about authorship: Schelling, Caroline, Jean Paul himself, Brentano, E. T. A. Hoffmann, Viennese journalist Johann Karl Christian Fischer, a minor *littérateur* Friedrich Gottlob Wetzel (the favourite for over half a century) and now, thanks to the researches of Jost Schillemeit, the likeliest candidate of all, the minor novelist, dramatist and theatre-director, August Klingemann (1777–1831).[7]

The *Nachtwachen* are an undoubted *tour de force* and seem to prefigure much of the existential despair of modern man. The formal division into sixteen 'night watches' soon shades off into the fragmentary, the chaotic, the contradictory; but an ironic authorial control appears, as it were, in the cracks. Hints, allusions, interweaving motifs abound. References to poets and philosophers, parodies, quotations, imitations stretch from Antiquity to the Romantics; the form itself partly parodies the Romantic novel, Romantic criticism, and the Romantic fragment. Much of the quotation is designed to level, to reduce everything and everyone to chaos and despair. The vanity of human life, the corruption of society, the threat to individual identity, the absence of divinity and meaning, all these themes are chilling and spoke powerfully to Expressionism and to the generation immediately after the Second World War. The audacious unmasking (the word 'mask' continually recurs) of human motives, the

---

[7] The 1974 volume of *Aurora* has two new candidates in opposition to Schillemeit's thesis. Ernst Erich Metzner, pp. 96–100, suggests Jens Baggesen and is to publish his arguments in more detail; Wolfgang Proß, pp. 64–74, proposes the Jacobin doctor Johann Benjamin Erhard, who had written a satire on Jean Paul, but this thesis is quietly refuted by Melitta Scherzer, *Aurora*, xxxvii (1977), 115–33. In *LiLi*, iv (1974), 13–29, Dieter Wickmann, 'Zum Bonaventura-Problem. Eine mathematisch-statistische Überprüfung der Klingemann-Hypothese', also comes out against. Rosemarie Hunter-Longheed, *Mitteilungen der E. T. A. Hoffmann-Gesellschaft*, xxiii (1977), 22–43, returns to the possibility of Hoffmann, with some new evidence.

vision of men as marionettes dangling above a void, the rejection of religion, society, philosophy, the sense of a general fraudulence of things, all these undoubtedly conjure up the bleak horror of existence. The narrator Kreuzgang, a name characteristically punning and symbolic, is a confused failure at everything—even at being a lunatic—but makes a relative success of being a night-watchman, as night strips the accidentals away and shows him the harsh truth behind things, the emptiness of all.

What is, however, finally less than satisfying about the *Nachtwachen* is the sense of contrivance, the subordination of despair to device. Ingenuity nearly transforms the clichés, the parodies, the ironic self-criticism, the baroque eccentricities and the mannerist arabesques into profound moral nihilism; but not quite. A piccolo does not blow the last trump.

Tieck

To return to Tieck; in 1797 he met Friedrich Schlegel at Dorothea Veit's and was introduced by him to Schleiermacher. He married, not altogether happily, in 1798 and then spent part of 1799 and 1800 in Jena, where he got to know Fichte and Schelling and, more fruitfully, Novalis, who for six months after their meeting on 17 July 1799 was 'quite infatuated by the Tiecks'.[8] The Schlegels were at this period running Tieck as a rival to Goethe, but they remained aware that he did not share their aesthetic preoccupations and he was not asked to contribute to the *Athenäum*. Looking back in a letter to Solger of 1 September 1815 (Matenko, p. 182), Tieck rather prided himself on not having succumbed to the feverish appeal of 'revolution, philanthropism, Pestalozzi, Kantianism, Fichteanism or Naturphilosophie as the final and exclusive truth'. Yet he certainly felt the attraction of anything new and strange and was substantially affected by the ideas of Steffens, whose acquaintance he made in 1799; and, however crude his understanding of Jacob Böhme, the accident of picking up a copy of *Aurora* in a secondhand bookshop in 1797 or 1798 made him an important mediator of his thought. We may mention here that Tieck had a library of some distinction, and alongside his creative work he also translated *Don Quixote* (1799–1801) and edited old German texts, four volumes of Shakespeare

---

[8] Dorothea to Schleiermacher, 11 November 1799; see Novalis, *KS* IV, 644.
The great gathering of Romantics, the so-called 'Romantikertreffen', in August Wilhelm Schlegel's house in mid-November 1799 brought together August Wilhelm (then aged 32) and Caroline (36), Friedrich (27) and Dorothea Veit (36), Tieck (26) and Amalia (20), Schelling (24), Novalis (27) and his brother Karl (23), and Ritter (23). Schleiermacher (31) was in Berlin; Fichte (37) had just had to leave Jena because of the quarrel about his alleged atheism.

apocrypha and of works by his contemporaries, and the writings of Novalis, Maler Müller, Kleist and Lenz.

Much of this scholarly activity fell within the period between the drama *Kaiser Octavianus* (1803) and the long stay in Dresden, 1819 to 1842, where his creative energy burst out anew. In Dresden he was for some years dramatic adviser to the court theatre, and was a ready counsellor of young writers, both in person and by his reviews. His regular evening readings were features of the city's life (it was said that the best theatre in Germany was in his parlour) and, all in all, Tieck prospered as an urbane man of letters. Soon after his move to Berlin in 1842, at the instigation of the Prussian King Friederich Wilhelm IV, he had a stroke from which he only partially recovered and he died at Potsdam on 28 April 1853.

At first sight it appears that most of what is specifically Romantic in Tieck is concentrated between the years 1797 and 1803, but this is to disregard the persistence of his sense of imbalance between the world and self. What is more to the point about Tieck is that total commitment almost always leads to scepticism; all his significant works are self-questioning. Uncertainty of intention is allied to an ultimate mistrust of apocalyptic. Hot for certainties he finds only compromises.

Often he declines to search and we have the mass of occasional verse and ephemeral stories. Sometimes a literary historical interest attaches even to these; and sometimes Tieck's momentary enthusiasms or brooding uncertainties raise him above himself in works that still speak to us.

Franz Sternbalds Wanderungen combines historical impact with a continuingly attractive limpidity of vision. It is perhaps difficult to look back to its appearance in 1798 without remembering later Romantic novels exploiting similar motifs; yet, for contemporaries, it marked the birth of a new kind of novel: the first really Romantic novel since Cervantes, according to Friedrich Schlegel. Goethe was unimpressed: the packaging was agreeable, but there was nothing inside.[9] And Caroline Schlegel fell asleep as it was being read. Subsequent reactions have been equally mixed: it is an uncertain amalgam of *Wilhelm Meister* and Heinse's *Ardinghello*; it is vague rhapsodizing about art; it is a new examination of the creative process; the possibilities of the contrast between its progressive aesthetic and its naive story are not exploited; the décor is anaemic; the evocation of mood is enchanting; the novel meanders formlessly along; the interpolated stories reflect a careful formal structuring. What can account for the confusion of judgement? The novel is unfinished,

[9] Friedrich Schlegel to August Wilhelm, March 1799; Goethe's letter to Schiller, 5 September 1798: 'Den vortrefflichen Sternbald lege ich bei, es ist unglaublich, wie leer das artige Gefäß ist.' (Not Schiller to Goethe, as Kluckhohn says in *DL*, VI, ii, followed by many others.)

and the two existing parts do not, at first sight, appear to be adequately related. The old German world of the first part is that of the *Herzensergießungen*; Franz Sternbald sets out on his journey through the Germany and Holland of 1521 in order to perfect his vocation as an artist. But what happens to him in the second part is that he escapes from the sixteenth century into the Romantic period. As he wanders into Italy the landscape, vague and mood-laden at best, becomes magical, hypnotic, emotively charged. His sensuous awareness heightens his instability; volatile in his erotic relationships, he swings between doubt and self-confidence in his artistic commitment. Uncertain of his own identity, in a timeless land, half-enchanted by the mysteries of event and character, Sternbald is abandoned to the storm of the imagination. Everything retreats towards infinity: the stream rushing past, the path penetrating further into the forest, the trees stretching heavenwards, the distant hills melting into the sky, the sound of the horn or the mill drawing Franz from the open window into the night, the moon playing the remote home of our dreams, our love, our happiness. Franz snatches the pleasures of life as they come, but over all there broods the mystery of the unattainable, symbolized in Marie, his lost love. It is this groundswell of apprehension and emptiness that gives meaning to what some have thought of as pale longings and sentimental mood-pictures. Sternbald is Tieck's Berglinger, the artist who has experienced the analytical disturbance of the modern world. The third, unwritten, part was to have depicted the synthesis of past, present and eternal; the artist, we may take it, was to have been shown as a divine reconciler, restoring meaning to fragmented experience. The old German pattern was to accommodate the Italian Renaissance and the contemporary revolution. Marie, so unexpectedly—and unsatisfactorily—discovered at the end of Book Two, would be torn away but finally restored to him and the novel would end with Sebastian in Nuremberg. The recently discovered fragment of the continuation contains significant references to the invasion of time by eternity and to the child's instinctive feeling for the magical connexion with the universe.[10] Tieck, not surprisingly, found himself unable to write this synthesis of journeying into the past, opening the senses to the present and providing intimations of immortality from recollections of early childhood. What the novel does, however, is to suggest, even in its unresolved state, an equilibrium ultimately attainable

---

[10] First published by Richard Alewyn in *JFDH*, 1962, pp. 58–68, and reprinted in the Reclam edition of *Sternbald*. Tieck had been under a good deal of pressure to complete the novel and had, as he explains in the postscript to the *Sternbald* volume in the *Schriften* (1843), many times taken up the pen; but the mood had never been right.

For the quotations about childhood see the Reclam edition, p. 496.

through the natural world, whose mystery and perils do not exhaust its significance. It is also revelation, a hieroglyph of the divine, an inkling of wholeness. Schelling's world-soul moves in it, but the concept is not a wholly abstract one; Tieck creates valid pictures, even if the subjective interlacing of emotion and the external world is sometimes facile and formulaic. When Franz's painting is hung in his home church, he looks through the door into the churchyard, and the trees and bushes seem to be praying and lifting their branches like folded hands. 'For the first time, Sternbald perceived that all his powers and feelings were in harmony; he was caught up and protected by the spirit that rules the world and keeps it in its course' (Reclam, p. 72; *WTh* I, 743).

Florestan represents the extreme of subjectivism and rootlessness, the open-ended approach to the world, and his influence certainly dominates sections of the novel. Thus an air of improvidence and dilettantism pervades much of the central core of the work, giving perhaps too much stress to vague aspirations and diaphanous uncertainties. Yet the overriding impression left by the novel is of a commitment to the natural world that, in spite of criticism levelled at Tieck as a lightweight, is of a different order of intensity from the normal eighteenth-century enthusiasm. There may indeed, as contemporary critics suggested, be too many morning or evening scenes; but they created a new mode of vision. Runge, for one, was intoxicated by the novel. Here, to take one instance, the forest is established as the great symbol of all-embracing nature, both in its menace and in its shelter. *Sternbald* is the first novel in which the landscape is the chief character. It is less a 'Künstlerroman' than a 'Naturroman'.

Tieck's other major achievement of this period is the Märchen *Der blonde Eckbert*, written in 1796. It is best seen plain, as first published in *Peter Leberechts Märchen* (vol. I, 1797), not set in the framework of *Phantasus* (1812). Here Tieck gathered some of his published work and added some new material, such as *Die Elfen*, and Boccaccio-like showed a group of friends reading and discussing the contributions. The thin remarks on the Märchen and other literary topics do little more than remind us of the gap between the almost accidental tension of *Der blonde Eckbert* and the conscious—and tamer—allegories of later works. *Der Runenberg*, probably written in 1801 and published late in 1802, though not without incidental descriptions of some power, is an example of the debilitating effect of conscious use of motifs from Novalis and Steffens. The forces of the natural world are too readily identified, too smoothly symbolized, too exemplary. The battle lines of magic and reality are too neatly drawn up. In *Die Elfen* the definition of the two worlds has become even sharper, and we are left with a charming but insubstantial fantasy. As for *Der getreue Eckart* (1799), the spruced-up folktale is so paralysingly silly and the two-part construction so awkward that one wonders how anyone could ever have taken pleasure even in its accidentals.

What makes *Der blonde Eckbert* stand so high above the other Märchen? Why is the problematical experience of the natural world at such a level of intensity here? How did the sense of animated nature burst out so suddenly in Tieck? he had not, in 1796, read Böhme, he had not yet met Novalis or Steffens, and he could have read almost nothing of Schelling's. It is not difficult to list possible sources: the supernatural interests of his youth; the recognition of Shakespeare's ability to hold two worlds, of normality and of magic, in balance; Manichean folk memories; the increasingly active engagement with nature in the eighteenth century as a whole; perhaps even, as Marianne Thalmann suggests, the conflict within himself between townsman and country-lover, the Berliner seduced but appalled by the forests. It might also be worth examining the growth of the view of nature as the dynamic expression of a world force (as, for instance, in Georg Forster), the organic experience of the world.

Somehow all these, and more, fused in *Eckbert* to a new synthesis that would be imitated, but seldom achieved, by succeeding Romantic writers and by Tieck himself. What is presented here is the equivocal nature of reality, and the instability of viewpoint, reflected in the narrative technique, causes the whole Märchen to proceed on a knife edge. There are symbols, certainly: the dog and the bird are aspects of reality and illusion, of nature and wish-fulfilment. But the symbols, too, are insubstantial and elusive; all is relative, all uncertain, dreamlike, perhaps even dreamt. Eckbert's own psychological state seems to make him confuse reality and illusion; his persecution mania blurs all the edges of experience. Does his mind perhaps collapse because of the confusion of boundaries, the uncertain identity of objects, the doubtful validity of experience? Is the supernatural a product of the insecure mind, or a projection of the collective unconscious? Or is it an independent, hostile force: the divine without forgiveness? Or is it rather that the mysterious power of the universe catches man up whatever he consciously wills, confounding his plans, destroying his world, and plunging him into the anarchy of nature? Face to face with the inexorable and hostile confusion of things, the notions of responsibility and guilt become meaningless and the application of a moral to the story falls away. The incest motif is no more than a gratuitous folk heightening of the horror.

Der blonde Eckbert calls normality in question. The senses present us with unreliable data; memory and temporal awareness play tricks (what unimaginable disturbance of the 'natural' order underlies Walther's knowledge of the little dog's name?); all interpretations are elusive. The general atmosphere of the work reinforces the hallucinatory effect. The style is uncomplicated and the limitations of the Märchen form are accepted, though themes and levels of narrative awareness are interwoven. Descriptions are inconclusive and dreamlike.[11] Bertha herself employs in childlike simplicity the yet unthumbed counters of Romanticism: 'unendlich', 'wunderbar', 'seltsam', 'recht inniglich'. The new word-creation 'Waldeinsamkeit' (the solitude of the forest) connects the idyllic and the anchoretic with the sense of loneliness of man confronted with the supreme forces of nature. Every now and again Tieck catches his breath at the abyss of life, and *Eckbert* is the finest expression of this.

It would be easy to go on from here to justify Tieck's use of irony as a protective device against such unnerving consciousness; but this would be to make Tieck more reflective and less intuitive than he is. The Romantic Irony of the plays is, and seems, more literary than metaphysical. The old view of *Der gestiefelte Kater* (1797) as being the dramatic expression of Friedrich Schlegel's theory of irony is now treated with great reserve.[12] August Wilhelm was long ago quite clear about it, and about *Prinz Zerbino oder die Reise nach dem guten Geschmack* (written mainly in 1798); both are allegorical literary criticism of purely contemporary relevance (letter to Auguste de Staël of 19 February 1822, in Körner, *Krisenjahre* II, 393).

In *Der gestiefelte Kater* Tieck takes Perrault's Puss in Boots fairytale and makes of it a statement about aesthetic illusion, a satire on contemporary literary, moral and political attitudes and an elegantly amusing amalgam of comedy and farce. The subject is the attempt by a group of players to present the play 'Puss in Boots.' There is a fictive audience, which comments and interrupts; the players, the fictive playwright, the prompter, the scene shifters all take part in the arguments. The play within a play is continually being affected by the confrontation, and finally the fictive poet stands before the fictive audience with only the bare walls of the theatre behind him. He had tried to make them become as little children again: 'What you ought to have done was to lay aside all your education for a couple of hours.' But they clung too firmly to their enlightenment: 'Our education has cost us enough sweat and toil' (*WTh* II, 267–8).

The satire on rationalism and sentimentality, against classicistic good taste and the lumpishly prosaic nature of contemporary criticism, is in the first place directed against the audience, against the real contem-

---

[11] Brian A. Rowley has, however, convincingly refuted the old argument that Tieck used synaesthetic imagery to create an effect of vagueness: 'The Light of Music and the Music of Light. Synaesthetic Imagery in the Works of Ludwig Tieck', *PEGS*, xxvi (1957), 52–80.

[12] See particularly Raymond M. Immerwahr, *The Esthetic Intent of Tieck's Fantastic Comedy*, 1953, and Heimrich, *Fiktion und Fiktionsironie*, 1968, pp. 60–5.

porary audience through the fictive one; but it also includes a good deal of ephemeral criticism of figures from the underworld of the Enlightenment. Iffland and Kotzebue may still mean something to us, but the modern reader or spectator will not make much of references to Stephanie, or Böttiger or C. G. Cramer.[13]

What interests us more now, and this is true of *Die verkehrte Welt* (written in 1798 and published in 1799) and of *Zerbino*, is the significance of the breaking of the dramatic illusion; though in *Zerbino* this occurs mainly towards the end of the play and is overlaid with other effects in a general and laboured attempt at uniting a variety of experiences, a Romantic 'universal' experiment. There is no want of precedents for the breaking of illusion: Beaumont and Fletcher, Ben Jonson, Gozzi, Holberg (indicated by Tieck himself as a source) or, from a different genre, *Tristram Shandy*. What, if anything, did Tieck add? He does not, we should note, implicate the real audience directly in the breaking of illusion, but the plays do point towards this, and Adam Müller, in his articles in *Phöbus* in 1808, takes *Der gestiefelte Kater* as the starting point for some very twentieth-century sounding speculations (*Schriften*, 1967, I, 245). Müller looks forward to a time when real life in the stalls and ideal life on the stage are so unified, so informed by the same ironic spirit, that the actors merely initiate a dialogue between audience and stage. Representatives of the audience will improvise interruptions that are then taken up by the actors. The curtain will go up not just so that the public can see the actors, but so that the actors can see the public. This dialogue which allows so many different individuals to participate is the function of Romantic comedy, the 'democratic' form as opposed to the 'monarchical', monologue nature of tragedy.

Ingenious attempts have recently been made to define the specifically Romantic type of illusion-breaking by reference to the function of the 'Rollen-Ich', the self as role, the King or Landlord conscious of himself as the manifestation of hundreds of kings or landlords. These considerations usefully point up the allegorical nature of such roles and, one may also add, seem unintentionally to highlight the over-literary quality of much Romantic drama and indeed the impersonal inhumanity of much of their characterization. Nevertheless the step to an interpretation of the 'Rollen-Ich' as an expression of the problematical nature of the Romantic ego is too weighty for Tieck's comedies to bear, as Heimrich acknowledges.[14]

Tieck certainly uses the interplay of dramatic illusion and disillusion

---

[13] The best guide to the whole field of Tieck's literary parodies is still Hans [Friedrich] Günther, *Romantische Kritik und Satire bei Ludwig Tieck*, Leipzig, 1907, 213 pp.

[14] See Heimrich, note 12 above, and Peter Szondi, 'Friedrich Schlegel und die romantische Ironie. Mit einem Anhang über Ludwig Tieck', *Euph*, xlviii (1954), 397–411.

to point the inadequacy of a rationalist, common-sense approach to theatre, to a play. He plays with the play, he allows the alogical free rein, he balances poetry between fantasy and buffoonery. Perhaps indeed there is something here about the nature of reality, about the 'theatre of the world'—a later and rather half-hearted suggestion by Tieck in the *Phantasus* version of *Der gestiefelte Kater* (1812). But the chief impression is one of enthusiastic clowning; Friedrich Schlegel's description, in 'Vom ästhetischen Wert der griechischen Komödie' (1794, *KA* I) of the breaking of dramatic illusion as 'well-considered mischief, exuberant vitality' is here apt enough. One only wishes, particularly in the two later plays, that it were more spontaneously amusing.

It is very odd that nearly all Tieck's dramas should be unplayable. *Der gestiefelte Kater* has had the occasional successful performance, particularly of late with the renewed interest in anti-illusionist theatre. It is, in other words, precisely because it plays with the concept of unplayability, because its theatrical world is called in question, that the *Kater* can still appeal. Yet Tieck was as much a man of the theatre as any writer of his time: in earlier years the passionate theatre-goer and actor *manqué*, the enthusiastic mediator of Shakespeare and Calderón, the facile experimenter with dramatic forms; in later years the dramatic critic and adviser in Dresden and Berlin, the expert on the Elizabethan stage, the innovator simplifying costume and décor. The three long dramas based on Volksbuch traditions, *Leben und Tod der heiligen Genoveva* (1799), *Kaiser Octavianus* (1802–2) and *Fortunat* (1815–16), are nevertheless all book-dramas, one might almost say all theoretical exercises.

Genoveva was an attempt to recreate the mood of the childlike piety of the Crusade period. It is a sprawling, sentimental piece with much virtuosity in the metrical patterns and with some lyrical scenes of considerable beauty. Marianne Thalmann makes great claims for it, and for *Octavianus*, as epoch-making masterpieces, and it is true that *Genoveva* pleased Goethe and powerfully moved many contemporaries. For later readers, however, the artificiality of Tieck's re-creation, the sterile longing, the *longueurs* of the psychological analyses, the over-explicit parade of belief, the almost total lack of dramatic tension, all these seem to disqualify it from serious consideration.[15]

Tieck himself, in the preface to the 1828 edition of his works, defined his purpose in writing *Kaiser Octavianus* as being to set down his view of Romantic poetry allegorically, lyrically and dramatically. The story line is no more than an excuse for a bewildering succession of scenes,

---

[15] One of *Genoveva*'s incidental interests is the witch Winfreda's view of magic as a glorified form of Naturphilosophie (*WTh* II, 484). She has the gift of 'looking into the innermost depths of nature' and sees 'how thought and will assume corporeal form, how fantasy penetrates to the very core of things'. 'All things are just the garb of the world of the spirit.'

reflective, comic, narrative, fantastic, realistic, sentimental, ironic, idealized, parodistic. Similarly there is a profuse formal variety: prose, imitations of the Nibelungen line, Hans Sachs Knittelvers, blank verse sometimes with internal rhyme, and a whole range of Spanish trochaic stanza forms, generally after the pattern of Calderón. What especially appealed to him in the Spanish forms was the lavish use of assonance, that tentative approach to rhyme that binds yet leaves incomplete, the prosodic expression of yearning in which Tieck finds a 'strange magic' as it 'hovers rich in its intimations of the future' (*Schriften*, 1828, I, xxxix). The work is certainly full of mood-pictures, drenched with imagery, often synaesthetic, and its recent admirers may well be right in claiming that it should not be judged by conventional standards of dramatic tension. Yet the overwhelming impression it leaves, is, unhappily, one of a not very significant jumble.

Fortunat has not usually been highly thought of, though it is in many ways more readable than the other dramas. Its two parts are more narrative than dramatic, suggesting a marriage between the fairytale and the picaresque novel. The hero's good luck and, in the second part, the fickleness of fortune for his sons are portrayed in an alternation of fantasy and realism; Tieck indeed regarded some of the scenes as being the most daring he had attempted. But, in truth, there are few fireworks, metrical or other, and with *Fortunat* we are shading off into the quieter period of Tieck's Novellen.

In 1829, in a note to volume eleven of his works, Tieck justified his use of the term Novelle for the tales he was then writing. The Novelle is particularly suited to deal with contrast, with the duality of life; perhaps at times it may resolve the contradictions of human existence. It is, he implies, a vehicle for discussion in a restricted frame. The Novelle's special characteristic, however, is that it has a marked turning-point, a twist that makes the story strange and perhaps unique. The natural, commonplace event suddenly appears in a new light. The everyday is irradiated by the marvellous.

The theory of the 'Wendepunkt', the turning-point, has persisted in the discussions of the nature of the Novelle and has usually been understood somewhat mechanically. The accompanying concept of 'das Wunderbare', the marvellous, has been held to refer to a relationship between Märchen and Novelle, but it has now been argued with much force that there is here a reflection of Solger's influence on Tieck.[16] The marvellous represents the absorption of the absolute by the finite. The

[16] See Manfred Schunicht, 'Der "Falke" am "Wendepunkt". Zu den Novellentheorien Tiecks und Heyses', *GRM*, xli (1960), 44–65, building on Helmut Endrulat's 1957 Münster dissertation 'Ludwig Tiecks Altersnovellistik und das Problem der ästhetischen Subjektivität'.

moment at which the absolute loses itself in temporal reality is the 'turning-point'.

This relationship of the 'turning-point' theory to a late Romantic philosophical system must reduce its general applicability to discussion of the Novelle form, but it is of great interest for Tieck's own works. It would be foolish to expect consistency from Tieck and, in any case, he was moderately sceptical about the application of his theory to his own writing.[17] Nor does the argument as to whether some of his later works were Novellen or Romane seem anything other than sterile. Yet the general implication of the move towards narrative as the medium through which the relationship between the ideal and the real can best be examined is clear enough, and the tension remains an important element even in the works that appear least Romantic. He has no taste for an art that concerns itself merely with amassing details or with minute description. He is no Stifter or Droste, and the comparison of his historical fiction with that of Walter Scott is equally misleading.

The Tieck of these later years retains an ironical view, even if overlaid at times with the fashionably sentimental. His best-known Novelle, *Des Lebens Überfluß* (begun in 1837 and published in the almanac *Urania* for 1839), is characteristic both of the irony and the sentiment. The story of the young couple having to burn the staircase up to their room for the winter firewood is an agreeable anecdote owing something to Jean Paul. It fits the theory of the Novelle very well, with its turning-point, its not too obtrusive symbols (the fire and the wood—the former echoed in the young man's pseudonym Brand; the Caxton Chaucer), its intrusion of the extraordinary into the everyday. Like most of Tieck's Novellen it is carried along by conversation, with diary extracts and reminiscences here providing flashbacks; and, fairly artificially, the wheels always come full circle. As everyday life is reduced to, or below, the barest essentials, the direct criticism of contemporary society so often seen elsewhere in Tieck's later Novellen yields here to oblique indications of the fear of revolution, the breakdown of social order—for better or for worse, the undue sway of materialism.[18] The Novelle is a hymn to married love and to the power of imagination, an attempt to portray an Eden that is urban and contemporary but at the same time abstract, shut off from reality, which is not even visible through the windows. The reduction to the purified essence of existence is, however, achieved by wild improb-

---

[17] See, for instance, Köpke, *Ludwig Tieck*, 1855, II, 234, also in *Dichter über ihre Dichtungen. Ludwig Tieck*, 1971, III, 244–5.

[18] W. J. Lillyman, the most perceptive of current Tieck scholars, argues that *Des Lebens Überfluß* is a portrayal of a crisis in Heinrich's conservatism. He changes his attitude in the course of the tale as he comes into conflict with what he had previously regarded as being the God-given order. See his article in *GQ*, xlvi (1973), 393–409.

ability and by such stupefyingly inattentive ingenuousness on the part of the wife, that Tieck's attempted irony is drowned in mawkishness. That these traits were characteristic of almanac fiction of the time explains but scarcely excuses. Critics in general, it is fair to say, have found a grace and ease in the style, and a humour and whimsicality (used as a term of commendation) in the situation and characterization.

The later Novellen make fewer claims than some are now disposed to suggest for them,[19] though one should guard against assuming that their great contemporary popularity also implies triviality. What one may more justly assume is that Tieck's mildly conservative political and ethical views chimed with those of the almanac readers. He questions his own conservatism at times, it is true, but tentatively and gently. He looks for stability, in love and marriage, in the relationship of the social classes, in the position of the arts and the artist. What most troubles him now is excess, fanaticism. Both his historical novels have this as their subject.

Der Aufruhr in den Cevennen, begun in 1820, published in part in 1826 and never completed, is carefully based on the Calvinist Camisards' uprising in the South of France in 1703. Yet it is not really the historical background that interests Tieck, so much as the human situation in his own main plot. He does indeed present religious problems—of toleration, or enthusiasm, or confessional relationships—that were significant for his own day, though he does it in what some contemporaries thought an inadequately committed fashion. What excites him more, however, is the nature of the disturbed human psyche, in its hysteria, its prophecies and visions, its hallucinations and cruelties. The resources of Romantic horror are still employed to assault the emotions, but the tentative solutions lie in reason and broad humanity, fragile though these may be.[20]

The novel *Vittoria Acccorombona* was written between 1836 and 1840, but Tieck acknowledged that the subject had been suggested by his reading of John Webster's, *The White Devil* in 1792. Though it is set with some exactitude in Renaissance Italy it is far from being an objectively detailed historical study. What Tieck does again is to set psychological problems of passion and self-mastery against a background of chaos and death. Images and themes from earlier works play their part in the careful structuring of the novel; but the supernatural is little more than a device to balance normality. History itself is grim enough.

---

[19] Stamm (1973), for instance, claims that Tieck consciously introduced the marvellous into the Novelle in order to raise the status of the form.

[20] Edward, the hero, at one point excuses Christine's outburst against the cruelties of Marshal Montrevel on the grounds that her reason must have suffered. Indeed it must, she replies, 'I have looked into the pain of the world and the loathsomeness of man' (*WTh* IV, 53). Fanaticism may affect even the sane.

Scant justice has been, or is here, done to this novel or to *Der junge Tischlermeister*, planned about 1796 as a pendant to *Sternbald*, begun in 1811 and finally published in 1836. This long Novelle, circling around the problems of marriage and of a social structure in upheaval, places the worlds of appearance and reality, the question of the role we have to play, against a background of detailed discussion of stage performances. Tieck, in his own way, is challenging Weimar. He has survived and is now arbiter and reconciler. Through him Romanticism flows into Biedermeier and Poetic Realism.

3

Profusion and Order:
The Brothers Schlegel

'Do you know that Friedrich actually once sold one of his bright ideas to his brother Wilhelm, in return for a flannel bed-jacket?' Schleiermacher's item of gossip, retailed to Eleonore Grunow in a letter of 19 August 1802, may be apocryphal, but it suggests the relationship as contemporaries saw it and as most since then have assumed it: Friedrich had the ideas, August Wilhelm organized them and made them comprehensible and generally acceptable. It is not a wholly unjust picture, though the breadth of August Wilhelm's scholarship, his technical mastery and his experiences as a translator all add a good deal that is distinctive.

August Wilhelm Schlegel

August Wilhelm (1767–1845) studied at Göttingen, where he came into close and fruitful contact with the great classical scholar Heyne and with the poet Bürger, both of whom thought highly of him. After four years as tutor to a Dutch family he married Caroline as a kind of rescue operation and moved with her to Jena, where he lectured in aesthetics and made ends meet by reviewing. In 1801 he went to Berlin to lecture on literature and art, and the series of lectures he delivered there between then and 1804, although not published as a whole until 1884, may be said to have schematized and tamed Romantic doctrine for the educated German public. He had been divorced from Caroline in 1803 and in the following year he was persuaded by Mme de Staël to become tutor to her son and to join her at her home at Coppet near Geneva and on her wanderings around Europe. He appears to have been part literary adviser, part resident lion, part henpecked lover, but came into his own during a visit to Vienna in the spring of 1808, when he delivered a course of lectures, *Über dramatische Kunst und Literatur*, that made his name throughout Europe. Published in 1809–11, and in a second edition in 1817, they were almost immediately translated into French, English and Italian, and somewhat later into Polish, Dutch and Russian. Their influence may be traced in Coleridge and Hazlitt (who reviewed them in the *Edinburgh Review* in February 1815), in Hugo and Manzoni, Mickiewicz and Pushkin; more than any other single book they disseminated Romantic aesthetics among the general public. Mme de Staël's own *De l'Allemagne* (1810, but not effectively issued until 1813) helped to draw attention to the Vienna lectures but, in fact, contains rather less about August Wilhelm's ideas than one might have expected.[1]

Schlegel became increasingly patriotic and anti-French, going well beyond Mme de Staël's feud with Napoleon, and between 1812 and 1814 he attempted to make his mark as a diplomat and political publicist, mainly in the service of Bernadotte in Sweden. Still following Mme de Staël he visited England and then, after Napoleon's fall, Paris, where in the winter of 1814–15 he became one of the first to give proper attention to the Troubadour manuscripts. After further travels and the death of Mme de Staël in 1817 he returned to Germany, where from 1818 he was Professor of the History of Art and Literature and then of Indology at Bonn. His scholarly activities in the study of medieval literature, particularly the *Nibelungenlied*, and in the virtual founding of German Sanscrit studies, now took first place in his life—closely followed by his personal vanity. Students called him the 'Herr Pariser', and it is not easy to forget Heine's description in *Die romantische Schule* of Schlegel lecturing in Bonn, perfumed, wearing kid gloves, referring to 'my friend the Lord Chancellor of England', accompanied by a liveried servant to trim the candles in their silver stands. When foreign visitors came he would ask them whether they wished to converse in Latin, English, French, Italian or German. Thus his life ends on a note of pedantry and farce.

Yet the solid achievements of August Wilhelm Schlegel are quite remarkable. His scholarly initiatives, never wholly developed by him, were imaginative and scrupulous. His creative work, though without depth of commitment, was not wholly negligible. Its main value lies in the introduction of new metrical forms (among the innovations are iambic rhythms in the sonnet and a widespread use of Romance strophic sys-

[1] For Mme de Stael see: Countess Jean de Pange, *August Wilhelm Schlegel und Frau von Stael. Eine schicksalhafte Begegnung*, Hamburg, Goverts, 1940, 496 pp. (originally Paris, 1938, as *Auguste-Guilleaume Schlegel et Madame de Stael*), and her introduction to *De l'Allemagne*, Paris, Hachette, 5 vols, 1958–60. The life at Coppet emerges vividly from Benjamin Constant's *Journaux Intimes*, full of jealousy and denigratory asides. For a wide-ranging account of August Wilhelm's influence see Chetana Nagavajara, *August Wilhelm Schlegel in Frankreich. Sein Anteil an der französischen Literatur 1807–1835*, Tübingen, Niemeyer, 1966. The basic study of the influence of the Vienna lectures is, however, still Josef Körner's *Die Botschaft der deutschen Romantik an Europa*, Augsburg, Benno Filser, 1929, 152 pp.

tems). Even in his own day the poetry was considered to be too artificial, too verbose, too contrived; but Goethe and other contemporaries were ready enough to learn something from his formal mastery. A drama *Ion* (1803) is certainly a lifeless adaptation of Euripides and owed its initial success almost exclusively to Goethe's interest and staging,[2] and most of the satires and parodies now seem stilted and predictable. But there is some bite to the parody of Schiller's 'Würde der Frauen' ('Ehret die Frauen! Sie stricken die Strümpfe, Wollig und warm, zu durchwaten die Sümpfe... Flicken zerrissne Pantalons aus') and a remarkable persistence about the long piece *Ehrenpforte und Triumphbogen für den Theaterpräsidenten von Kotzebue bei seiner gehofften Rückkehr ins Vaterland* (1800). Kotzebue was then in prison in Siberia and Schlegel is getting his own back for the attack on him and his brother in a one-act drama *Der hyperboreische Esel* (1799), in which one character speaks solely in phrases pieced together from Friedrich's Fragments and from *Lucinde*, a device also used by Friedrich Nicolai in his anonymous satirical novel *Vertraute Briefe von Adelheid B** an ihre Freundin Julie S*** (also 1799).

The attack on Kotzebue, marginally interesting in itself, does however suggest one of Schlegel's chief virtues: a rigid insistence on standards. Although his critical position is much closer to Herder than to Lessing, in its stress on the danger of establishing despotic norms and the necessity for universality and flexibility in a critic, he avoids a shapeless relativism. A work is to be understood in its context and from within its own structure, and there are different kinds of achievement; neo-classical exclusiveness is rejected. Nevertheless value judgements are possible and necessary, and the frivolities of Kotzebue and Iffland, the conventional lyrics of Matthisson, the idylls of Voß or Pfarrer Schmidt of Werneuchen, the sentimental novels of A. H. J. Lafontaine or Friederike Unger all require rebuke. It is a feature of the three hundred or so reviews written by Schlegel for the *Allgemeine Literatur-Zeitung* of Jena between January 1796 and his final break with the periodical in October 1799 that the claims not merely of the Romantics but also of Weimar Classicism and of idealist philosophers are constantly upheld against fashionable *littérateurs* and against the blinkered representatives of the end of the Enlightenment. This constant stream of elegant, epigrammatic, learned publicizing ensured that the 'new school' could not be permanently dismissed as the ravings of hot-headed visionaries, but had to be taken as a serious subject of debate.

The Berlin and Vienna lectures thus systematized Romantic doctrines within a historical framework. In the Berlin series, which moves from an exposition of a new poetic through a polemical analysis of the decay

[2] See Uwe Petersen, *Goethe und Euripides: Untersuchungen zur Euripides-Rezeption in der Goethezeit*, Heidelberg, Winter, 1974, 235 pp.

of modern culture (partly an attack on the Enlightenment's limitations, partly regret at Germany's political situation, partly a sketchy condemnation of Gutenberg, gunpowder and imperialism) to a historical account of medieval literature, we may distinguish three important elements. First the recognition of the antinomy of ancient and modern taste and the critic's obligation to be impartial as between them, in that they both represent the unfolding of the poetic spirit under their own particular conditions. Then the rehabilitation of 'romantic' literature from the *Nibelungenlied*, here compared with the *Iliad*, to Calderón. What Schlegel does is to create a Romantic mythology from medieval material, tracing Christianity and chivalry through the Arthurian legend, Charlemagne and the Spanish Romances to Dante's allegorical representation of the universe, and not wholly avoiding the impression that the new mythology is an eclectic compilation of exotic subjects. The third and perhaps the most influential formulation is that of the relationship of the poet to nature. Poetry as imitation of nature is only meaningful if we recognize that everything is in a continual state of becoming, an incessant creation. The poet must become aware of this creative power at work within himself, as in nature, and his work must display the same organic properties. The distinction between mechanical form, arbitrarily imposed from without, and organic form, unfolding from within according to the requirements of the whole, was elaborated in the Vienna lectures. It was by no means new but, formulated with as much precision as can be expected in these matters, it had a great deal of influence, though the belief that Coleridge's concept of organic form was entirely dependent on it is still the subject of vigorous debate.[3] In these various echoes of Schelling some distinctions become blurred, notably that between conscious and unconscious activity; and we find ourselves faced, too, with the 'Infinite' and with the nature of the 'Idea'. To impart meaning to things the artist must present those ultimates that form the foundation of the phenomenal world. This can only be done in signs or pictures, 'art is a continual symbolizing'. Language itself has a symbolist function; when this becomes petrified, poetry must restore it and must re-establish that 'mutual linking of all things by an unbroken process of symbolizing' (*KSB* II, 83), which was the first basis of the growth of language. The importance of this associative process, both for the Romantics and in later literature, scarcely needs stressing.

Otherwise the Vienna lectures do not add a great deal, except in his-

[3] For the Coleridge controversy see Thomas McFarland, *Coleridge and the Pantheist Tradition*, Oxford, Clarendon, 1969, pp. 256–61, and Norman Fruman, *Coleridge, the Damaged Archangel*, New York, Braziller, 1971, and London, Allen & Unwin, 1972, pp. 158–61 and 209–14, with subsequent refutation of Fruman by McFarland in *Yale Review*, lxiii (1974), 252–86, and a splendid row in countless journals.

torical exemplification and in relating the whole development of drama to the contrast between classical and romantic, the former finite, the latter yearning for the infinite, Greek tragedy concerned with man's struggle with fate, modern 'mixed' drama portraying the development of character towards that which transcends human life, ancient tragedy resembling a sculptural group, romantic drama to be viewed as a large picture. The whole of ancient art and poetry is 'as it were a rhythmical *nomos*, a harmonious proclamation of the immutable laws of a world already set in order and mirroring the eternal archetypes of things. Romantic poetry, on the other hand, is the expression of the secret attraction to the chaos that is continually striving to produce new and marvellous creations' (*KSB* VI, 112). Feeling (Gefühl), the motive force of romantic poetry, holds the parts of the universe together and grasps the most subtle and shifting relationships.

The historical demonstration of these philosophical propositions gives due weight to Greek tragedy but essentially consists of a glorification of English and Spanish drama, particularly Shakespeare and Calderón. Schlegel's translations from Romance literatures (notably Dante and Petrarch in Italian and Calderón in Spanish) were of considerable importance;[4] and one may add the impact of his critical appreciations— evident also in his praise of Cervantes, of whom he planned a complete translation, though only Tieck's *Don Quixote* emerged, apart from a fragment of the play *Numancia*.

In both his translations and his criticism, however, the permanent revelation is Shakespeare. The main critical discussions are in two essays in Schiller's *Horen:* on *Hamlet* in 1796 ('Etwas über William Shakespeare bei Gelegenheit Wilhelm Meisters') and 'Über Romeo und Julia' in 1797. The *Romeo* essay attempts to demonstrate the inner unity, the artistry of form in this apparently formless play; Shakespeare is a supremely conscious artist. Schlegel is here fighting on two fronts: against what remained of the rationalist view of Shakespeare as hopelessly formless and the Storm and Stress glorification of him as an artless intuitive genius. Working with the concepts of organic form and self-conscious reflection, he provides in the Vienna lectures remarkable analyses of the individual plays, and places Shakespeare at the rich and exuberant juncture of the medieval and modern worlds. His plays are the highest expression of romantic poetry (the term is still, of course, being used typologically). August Wilhelm is not free from some absurdities in his glorification of Shakespeare, and we must not forget that Lessing and Herder had prepared the ground for adequate appreciation and that Goethe

---

[4] The Italians principally in the *Blumensträuße italiänischer, spanischer und portugiesischer Poesie*, Berlin, 1804. Spanish drama in *Spanisches Theater*, Berlin, 1803–9, edited by Schlegel and with five of Calderón's dramas translated by him.

had sustained an enthusiasm for the plays. Yet, for all that, Schlegel's Shakespeare criticism is a substantial achievement and one which remained influential in Germany and England throughout the nineteenth century.

The translation of Shakespeare goes beyond that; it is his incomparable monument. His first attempts at translating one of the plays date from his student days at Göttingen 1799, where he worked with Bürger on a translation of *A Midsummer Night's Dream*. A recent comparison of this version with that of 1797 shows clearly how, by the year in which the publication of his translations began, he had overcome the disparities of style inherent in the linguistic patterns of the Storm and Stress, the Anacreontics and Sensibility, and had evolved his own coherent picture of Shakespeare and thus a unified imagery and rhythm.[5] Schlegel's translations appeared regularly until 1801, by which time thirteen plays (sixteen if one counts the parts of the histories) had appeared, and in 1810 he added *Richard III* to these. Then, after a long interval, Tieck's daughter Dorothea and Graf Wolf von Baudissin completed the translation (1825–33). Tieck himself had some supervisory part in the more difficult ones.

The translations were not without their critics. Neither Wieland's translations nor those of Eschenburg retained their hold, but Voß and his sons produced their own versions between 1806 and 1829, with lively accusations of plagiarism against the others. Yet the Schlegel–Tieck translations were the ones that convincingly established themselves. Why was this so? Part of the answer, no doubt, lies in August Wilhelm's astounding technical mastery and the breadth of his vocabulary. Although there are innumerable minor errors (some, in the early plays, apparently the result of Caroline's emendations) they are, in the last analysis, insignificant. What matters is that it is a valid re-creation of Shakespeare and not an interesting exercise. Shakespeare was alive for the Romantics in the way that the Bible was alive when the Authorized Version was produced and, in both cases, the translation came just when the language had leapt to life. Without the linguistic achievements of

[5] See *A. W. Schlegels Sommernachtstraum. In der ersten Fassung vom Jahre 1789 nach den Handschriften herausgegeben* (by Frank Jolles), Göttingen, Vandenhoeck & Ruprecht, 1967, 248 pp. (= Palaestra, 244); Peter Gebhardt, *A. W. Schlegels Shakespeare-Übersetzung. Untersuchungen zu seinem Übersetzungsverfahren am Beispiel des Hamlet*, Göttingen, Vandenhoeck & Ruprecht, 1970, 265 pp. (=Palaestra, 257); Margaret E. Atkinson, *A. W. Schlegel as a Translator of Shakespeare: A Comparison of Three Plays [Hamlet, Twelfth Night, Julius Caesar] with the Original*, Oxford, Blackwell, 1958, ix, 67 pp. For Shakespeare and Schlegel generally one should still consult Friedrich Gundolf, *Shakespeare und der deutsche Geist*, Berlin, Bondi, 1914, viii, 359 pp., and in many subsequent editions, and R. Pascal, *Shakespeare in Germany 1740–1815*, Cambridge, C.U.P., 1937, x, 199 pp. An interesting and relevant study in detail is Hans Georg Heun, *Shakespeares 'Romeo und Julia' in Goethes Bearbeitung. Eine Stiluntersuchung*, Berlin, Erich Schmidt, 1965, 86 pp.

Weimar Classicism the Schlegel translation would not have been possible. One could go on to say that, without August Wilhelm's own additions to the language, the Tieck–Baudissin translations are barely conceivable. Schlegel took the new resources of German and harnessed them to his own exceptional knowledge of levels of speech, shifts of vocabulary, speech rhythms, syntactical forms and metrical patterns. He was thus able to achieve what Schleiermacher, in another context, called 'parodistic' (as opposed to 'identifying') translation; he brought the reader to the language of Shakespeare, he magnificently altered German to fit the demands of the Renaissance Englishman. The translation has been criticized for being too lyrical, not sinewy enough, and there is some truth in this; but any strictures are heavily outweighed by the new understanding of the play of the imagination and wit in Shakespeare, by the feeling for his great variety and use of contrasts, and by the ability to sense the movement of the line and the scene.

August Wilhelm Schlegel made Shakespeare part of the German experience. He was also one of the first modern literary critics, producing formulations that we have now come to take for granted.[6] He was the most universal of scholars and readers, the first European comparatist. And for Jena Romanticism, that most philosophically abstruse and élitist clique (to use the disobliging language of their adversaries) he performed the incalculable service of making sense of their doctrines and anchoring them, revolutionary though they were, in the Western literary tradition. What he could not do, though, was to arouse in us the intellectual excitement that comes from reading Novalis or Friedrich Schlegel. August Wilhelm casts a clear light; they burn.

Friedrich Schlegel

If one had to chose a year for the birth of German Romanticism, it would be 1797. By then Friedrich Schlegel and Novalis were far advanced in their correspondence; in June of that year Friedrich moved to Berlin where he met Tieck and Schleiermacher; and, in the autumn, Friedrich and August Wilhelm formulated their plan to produce their own periodical, *Athenäum*. The first number appeared in May 1798 and the sixth and final one in August 1800. The group character of early Romanticism, the notion of collective creativity (Symphilosophieren), appears in the quasi-anonymity of the contributions—the use of initials or pseudonyms and the complete suppression of the author's identity in the collections

---

[6] For an unenthusiastic view of his contribution to modern literary theory, however, see Klaus Lindemann, 'Theorie—Geschichte—Kritik. August Wilhelm Schlegels Prinzipienreflexion als Ansatz für eine neue Literaturtheorie?', *ZDP*, xciii (1974), 560–79.

of fragments. Total knowledge must be sought communally; the encyclopaedic view needs friends to complement one another.[7]

The position of women in the nexus was crucial. The *salon* came to Germany with Henriette Herz, and later Rahel Varnhagen, in Berlin and, pre-eminently for early Romanticism, Caroline Schlegel in Jena. Movement across social classes was still problematical enough in the Jewish circles of Berlin, but did exist. Emancipation, however, moved a stage further in the brisk change of sexual partners, though it could be argued that what this showed was women dissatisfied with contractual status but still dependent on men. Dorothea left her husband for Friedrich Schlegel; Sophie Bernhardi left hers, partly as a result of a passionate interlude with August Wilhelm; Caroline, the young widow, lived with Georg Forster under his family roof, became August Wilhelm's wife, was wildly admired by Friedrich and in 1801 went to live with Schelling, whom she later married. These three carried on an intensive correspondence and, for a few short years, the whole group moved around them and particularly around the strong-willed and warm-blooded Caroline, the cause of much friction but also of what we should now call creative unrest.

The male centre of the group was, without doubt, Friedrich Schlegel, the restless initiator of so many projects, the unsystematic schematizer and programmer of life and art. It is perfectly possible to explain the attraction of communal production for Friedrich in terms of his own psychological needs; Caroline speaks of him, with his passionate desire to be sociable, as living in perpetual isolation. He quarrelled with most of his friends and yet needed them in the exploration of his own mind. He found them, and himself, infinitely fascinating as men placed in a revolutionary situation, the world to be made new, history to be reclaimed for the present, modernity to be defined and lived, the infinite or the divine to be seized in phenomenon and event.

Friedrich's early years were deeply unsatisfactory. He seemed intellectually and emotionally inadequate to bear the distinguished Protestant and literary heritage of his father Johann Adolf (1721–93), poet, hymn-writer and translator, or of his uncle Johann Elias (1718–49), critic and dramatist, one of the main channels for the introduction of Shakespeare into Germany. Of the five brothers and two sisters (the third son joined the British Army and died in Madras in 1789) August Wilhelm was the bright star, and it was perhaps in emulation of him that Friedrich made extraordinary efforts to catch up on his education. He read frantically and in all directions, and at Göttingen and Leipzig became an excellent classical scholar and a competent handler of problems in

[7] See Inge Hoffmann-Axthelm, *'Geisterfamilie': Studien zur Geselligkeit der Frühromantik*, Frankfurt a.M., Akademische Verlagsgesellschaft, 1973, 217 pp.

mathematics and medicine (later extended to the natural sciences generally), law, history and philosophy. Later, in Dresden, he became interested in the fine arts, about which he wrote a good deal,[8] and still later, in Paris, he learned Persian and Sanscrit, to add to his perhaps limited knowledge of English, Portugese, Hungarian and Danish. He read widely in French, Spanish and Italian and had some limited acquaintance with Russian and Czech literatures. Only after his move to Vienna in 1808 did Friedrich have any settled employment, and then for a relatively short period. His life was thus one of constant financial strain and the concentration on lecturing rather than writing was partly because he needed the money. He gave many series of public lectures at Jena, Berlin, Cologne and Vienna on history, philosophy and literature, and published a good number of these. In addition there were private series, such as those given to Sulpiz and Melchior Boisserée and their friend Bertram in Paris from November 1803 to April 1804, partially repeated in public in Cologne from June to September 1804. These survive in notes taken probably from Friedrich's own lecture notes and were first published in 1958. They form the basis of the *Geschichte der alten und neuen Literatur*, lectures given in Vienna in 1812 and published under the above title in 1815. These were then further revised for the collected edition of 1822, mostly by adding material. These later lectures are certainly more polished and comprehensive versions, but they are also more tendentious and less excitingly self-revealing.

The history of this one work, probably Friedrich's most influential, illustrates two of the problems confronting scholars. Much material is still unpublished or has only become available in the last fifteen years or so as the great collected edition gets under way. The importance of this for the ordinary reader is that much of Friedrich's own intellectual exploration is conveyed in notebooks and drafts, which circulated within the group of friends, and that the progressive growth of his thought is both practically interesting for the literary revolution of the period and theoretically justified by his own view of his philosophy as always in process of becoming, always in flux. The other difficulty lies indeed in the extent of the revisions he made to his earlier works for the collected edition of 1822–5. By then, as the leading representative of Catholic mysticism, he needed to accommodate substantial changes in his views on history and philosophy, although he was not concerned so much to repudiate his youthful speculations as to bring them up to date, to renew rather than to hide. The whole process of revision, of which this is only an extreme example, does however mean that he was constantly and

---

[8] The description of the paintings in the Louvre in *Europa*, written in Paris in 1802–3 and Cologne 1804, with their emphasis on the Italian primitives and the early German painters, had a considerable influence on the Nazarenes (*KA* IV, xxvi–xxx).

confusingly changing his terminology in a struggle towards adequate forms of expression, and the terms of his youth often acquire a new meaning in his later writings. But, in spite of this, it is now possible to see an organic unity in all the shifting phases of his thought; he varies and develops his opinions, but tends to absorb previous views rather than to reject them.

Friedrich's early work is markedly coloured by Kant and Winckelmann and by his intensive classical studies; a recurrent oversimplification has been to call this the period of his 'Graecomania', after Schiller's mocking epigram 'Die zwei Fieber' in the *Xenien*:

Kaum hat das kalte Fieber der Gallomanie uns verlassen,
Bricht in der Gräkomanie gar noch ein hitziges aus.[9]

A number of essays written in 1794 and 1795 culminate in 'Über das Studium der griechischen Poesie', completed and sent to the publishers in December 1795 but not published until 1797, as the main section of his book *Die Griechen und Römer*. (The dates are of some significance in that Schiller's 'Über naive und sentimentalische Dichtung', with its very similar arguments, was published in three numbers of *Die Horen*, of which the first appeared on 25 November 1795.) Antiquity is the first model in Friedrich Schlegel's search for harmony, both in his own life and as a reconciliation of the dualistic view of human nature so characteristic of the eighteenth-century heritage, whether it took the form of Kant's ethical dualism or Rousseau's contrasting of natural and civilized man. India and the Middle Ages later performed a similar role, though Antiquity was never wholly rejected.

Still in the tradition of Winckelmann the Greek period is seen as one of beauty, harmony, order; its poetry is an expression of the totality of being (the argument will be recognized as continuing as late as Lukàcs's *Theorie des Romans* in 1920) transcending all limitations, free, 'disinterested' in the Kantian sense, objective, part of the cosmic rhythm. Modern man, however, is confused; his culture lacks unity, his faculties are exercised in isolation from one another. His poetry, similarly, allows one element to predominate at the expense of others; instead of the generalized harmony of beauty we have some one characteristic feature, the intentional, the interesting, the didactic, the imaginative, the ugly, the terrible, the dissonant. Modern poetry has remarkable qualities, exemplified at their highest in Shakespeare; all it lacks is beauty. Schlegel looks forward to a development of modern poetry, foreshadowed in Goethe, in the direction of a new objectivity, a new recognition of the autonomous claims of art. This is to be achieved by true imitation of

[9] 'The Two Fevers': 'Scarcely has the cold fever of Gallomania abated than, heaven help us, a hot fever of Graecomania breaks out.'

the Greeks which, in this context, means creative understanding and study of the models of antiquity and certainly not a subservience to Aristotelian prescription. Providing the new historical interpretation that will make all this possible is what Friedrich regards as his purpose, and modern poetry gains in importance from 1796 onwards as his concern with the philosophy of history grows. He becomes aware of the special conditions, and thus of the limitations, of antiquity; and a 'progressive' view of the historical process brings with it a sense of infinite aesthetic perfectibility.

The changed emphasis is to be seen in the Fragments published in Reichardt's periodical *Lyceum* in the autumn of 1797 and number 93 may serve as an example: 'In the ancients we see the perfected letter of all poetry; in the moderns, we sense the spirit coming into being' (*KA* II, 158). It was here also that he had published his essays on Georg Forster and on Lessing, two masterpieces of critical characterization. In these essays, and particularly in the *Geschichte der alten und neuen Literatur*, Schlegel abandoned normative poetics and exploited Herder's ideas, even if unconsciously, by examining literary works and figures in a way which we now take for granted: a combination of historical understanding and critical judgement. They are characterized as organic wholes, but are understood in the context of their time and as part of the general development of poetry, which is itself part of the history of culture.

The *Lyceum* and *Athenäum* Fragments and the *Gespräch über die Poesie* (1801) contain the germ of Friedrich Schlegel's programme for Romantic poetry, though it must be remembered that the aphorisms, drafts, working hypotheses and paradoxes of the notebooks, which are only now being published, had doubtless been circulated a good deal at the time. The fragmentary form of much of the material is both significant and potentially misleading. It has led many to argue that Friedrich's thought was wholly unsystematic. This may indeed be the case, but the fragmentary form itself conveys not so much want of system as the potential of the subject, which it deliberately leaves open-ended. The nature of his thought lies in its constant flux and in the daring of its associative leaps, the mind exploding with ideas, sparks flying from its own incandescence. The danger of all this, of course, is that assertion takes the place of argument, and paradox is handled with an indulgence exceeding its theoretical justification. 'Friedrich', said Novalis, 'goes in for poetic trifling with speculation', a sentence which Schlegel is now suspected of having tried to erase (*KS* III, 652, and IV, 547).

In his criticism and theory Friedrich had hitherto been using the term 'modern' both in a chronological and an ideological sense, rather in the way we now speak of the 'modern' novel. This was as unsatisfactory then as it is now and he needed a new term, one that could be divorced from strict chronology and, if necessary, extended to become coincident with poetry itself. The term to hand was 'romantic', with the rich but ambivalent background we have already sketched. It is a pleasing irony that the term used to escape from chronology has now become almost meaningless without its chronological status. Friedrich excused himself from sending August Wilhelm his definition of the word 'romantic' on the grounds that it was a hundred and twenty-five sheets long (letter of November 1797), and, indeed, he found he could make use of most of the echoes thrown by the word.

Chief among these is the relationship to 'Roman'. One is tempted at times to believe that this etymological coincidence has contributed too greatly to German theories of Romanticism, particularly since the commitment to the norms of the novel genre is often so ambiguous. It has been argued[10] that the term 'Roman' had a wider connotation in the eighteenth century: Herder, for instance, called Shakespeare's dramas 'philosophische Romane' and A. W. Schlegel referred to them as 'Romanspiele'. Friedrich himself certainly spoke of Dante's, Shakespeare's. Ariosto's and Tasso's 'Romane'; and indeed he claims that 'many of the finest novels are a compendium, an encyclopedia of the whole spiritual life of an individual of genius; works of which this is true, even if they are quite different in form like *Nathan*, acquire thereby a touch of the novel' (*KA* II, 156; *Lyceum* Fragment 78). Any linguistic loophole would, that is to say, be exploited: 'Roman' would mean what he wanted it to mean; its various historical types would be amalgamated in the absolute novel, combining poetry, history, criticism, philosophy, science. *Wilhelm Meister* certainly played a part in this obsession with the novel, though references to it in the notebooks are a good deal more critical than the brilliant expository essay 'Über Goethes Meister' in the *Athenäum* (1798), where he admires particularly its irony, its movement towards the unity of the individually reflective and the universal, its symbolic overtones.[11]

'Romantic poetry is a progressive universal poetry' (*KA* II, 182); this lapidary programme of Romantic poetry is, in fact, only the first sentence of Fragment 116, and what follows makes it plain that the basis for the definition is the novel. Indeed many of the provisions relate clearly enough to points we have already indicated: the new poetry is to reunite the separated genres and to bring poetry into contact with philosophy; it is to mix poetry and prose and to achieve an interplay between art and life; it is to present, as only the novel can, an objective picture of

---

[10] By Eichner, *KA* II, lvii, and V, lviii–lix, and in his essay in '*Romantic' and its Cognates*, 1972, pp. 109–11.

[11] See Raymond Immerwahr, 'Friedrich Schlegel's Essay on Goethe's *Meister*', *Monatshefte*, xlix (1957), 1–21.

an age or a world, while at the same time mirroring its author; it allows countless reflections, on both senses.

What did Schlegel mean by 'a progressive universal poetry'? Friedrich, 'tortured by the chaos of his thoughts' (as Schleiermacher wrote to Brinkmann on 4 January 1800) and set at the Fichtean point where the unifying creativity of the human mind was installed at the centre of things, made the desire for universality the mainspring of his thinking. Goethe was a universal genius; Friedrich wanted to be one. In him and in Novalis we find a last great attempt to unify nature and mind, art and science. An aspect of this is the importance he, like Novalis, gives to the concept of 'encyclopaedia', or 'the textbook of universality' as he terms it (*KA* XVIII, 252). Through it he hoped to transcend Fichte's limitations and to include the practical side of life: society, culture, economics. Yet it is interesting that he regards its ordering as primarily a semantic problem: 'Encyclopaedia is just philology, intensified by philosophy and poetry' (*KA* XVIII, 361). Words will do our living for us, perhaps.

The uniting principle changes at various periods in his development; later it becomes history or religion. In the early and decisive years it was poetry, though 'Poesie' has here a meaning beyond literature, becoming the all-pervading creativity in nature and self, the productive faculty of imagination. Universality, though, is not a state but a process and Fragment 116 goes on to speak of Romantic poetry as always in process of becoming, always incomplete, always, that is to say, 'progressive'. This contrasts with the Classical state of perfection and completion, the closed cycle of Greek history, and with the 'given' nature of reality in which rationalists and empiricists appeared to believe.

Romantic poetry must bring together the universal, the infinite, the absolute and the approximations and contradictions of the world (one thinks ahead to the game in Hesse's *Glasperlenspiel*). It must comprehend the two poles of infinite abundance in infinite unity; only when it senses the infinite in everything does the imagination liberate man from the limitations of the self. The power that enables the poet to make the associative leaps that suggest infinite abundance is that of wit. Schlegel rescues the term 'Witz' from the associations it had come to have with humour and restores the joint meaning of 'esprit' and 'intelligence' current earlier in the century. He derives it, to some extent, from Leibniz's *ars combinatoria*, and calls it the principle of combinatory art (*KA* XVIII, 259). Wit discovers similarities; often it is 'like two friendly thoughts meeting each other again after long separation' (*KA* II, 171; *Athenäum* Fragment 37). It opens out onto new recognitions and brings together all kinds of scattered insights; it is, one feels, tailor-made for Friedrich Schlegel. Wit is the 'synthesizing imperative' (*Literary Notebooks*, 537); it is mind analysing and synthesizing in a chemical way. It operates through intuition, and is thus divinatory and prophetic. It is related to arabesque, a term used by Schlegel in various senses, from the ornament of painting to the ideal romantic genre, but centring on the blending of heterogeneous elements, notably chaos and system. The artistic ordering of chaos is indeed one of the poet's main functions and, in the sixteenth paragraph of the *Rede über die Mythologie*, Cervantes and Shakespeare are singled out as having in their work 'this artfully arranged confusion, this charming symmetry of contradictions' (*KA* II, 318). The same section concludes that poetry's initial task is to suspend the laws and processes of rational thought and to plunge us again into that 'beautiful confusion of imagination, that original chaos of human nature, for which I do not as yet know of any more beautiful symbol than the motley throng of the ancient gods' (*KA* II, 319). Modern man is in need of a new mythology, a new bible. This is not, however, to be a renewal of ancient myths, though Christianity, the Middle Ages and the Orient have much to offer, but a system of connexions and correspondences, a 'hieroglyphic expression of nature around us' (*KA* II, 318). Mythology in the past provided a common foundation for poetry; the new mythology must achieve universality by expressing the poetic structures of the universe, and these are to be derived by the imagination from the new speculative physics, or Naturphilosophie. As nature was animate for the Greeks, so the new Romantic physics show nature as a free and living organism speaking to us in symbols, an enciphered poem. One can see the painful construction of this kind of mythology taking place in Klingsohr's Märchen in Novalis's *Heinrich von Ofterdingen*, but even there it is difficult not to share Schleiermacher's puzzlement, 'I cannot see how a mythology can be *made*' (letter to Brinkmann, 22 March 1800). An exemplary contrast may be found in Hölderlin's handling of the mythological.

To what extent Schlegel's interpretation of mythology is influenced by Schelling remains unresolved; what is clear is that this stress on mythology as a system of symbols is very similar in both. The symbol for Schelling unites and for Friederich Schlegel, working from Fichtean premises, brings together in approximation the finite, earthbound reality of history and the infinite, unconditional truth of the absolute. The importance of myth for the Romantics can scarcely be overstressed and we shall return to it in considering Görres. But we may mention here the interpretation of myth from the point of view of the collective imagination of a nation, a group, or humanity as a whole, and thus its supra-personal aspect as a mediated instinctive expression of the God–nature complex; and its primitivistic content, namely the Golden Age, the secularization of paradise. Myth in Romanticism becomes Rousseauistic.[12]

[12] The relationship between myth and symbol is reinforced by Friedrich Creuzer, *Symbo-*

In the creation of myth, this organization of symbols that can represent infinite abundance, the poet is working by intuition, by divinatory creative power and enthusiasm. He is pointing beyond himself to something he cannot fully comprehend; because the abundance is infinite it cannot be wholly grasped and must therefore be the subject of yearning (Sehnsucht). How is the poet to address himself to this situation? How should he present the tension between infinite idea and finite phenomenon? Is his position irremediably paradoxical, aware of the need for synthesis but also of the impossibility of achieving it, and conscious of the provisional and relative nature of all experience? The first consideration is that he must be aware of his own position; he must be *self*-aware, conscious of being conscious. His attitude must be ironic.

What has come to be known as Romantic Irony has been much maligned, partly, no doubt, because the use made of it degenerated into a device, a mechanical and sometimes patronizing destruction of illusion. Its intellectual origins are, however, respectable enough. Friedrich Schlegel, in his various formulations of it, starts from the Fichtean philosophical position that the ego both posits the objective world and is limited by it. But this limitation is overcome when, to simplify the terminology, the ego recognizes what is going on and remembers that the non-ego is indeed its creature. Intelligence recognizes that all its creations are relative. The poetic act analogous to the Fichtean process is that the artist, through his intelligence, frees himself from the limitations of what his enthusiasm has created. Thus there is 'a constant alternation between self-creation and self-destruction' (*KA* II, 172; *Athenäum Fragment* 51).

Three points seem to follow. First, the artist's supreme freedom is emphasized. That this can lead to unbridled subjectivism is true enough and this was Hegel's main objection.[13] Friedrich Schlegel may seem to confirm this danger by his stress on 'Willkür', but he generally used the term not in the modern sense of 'caprice' or 'arbitrariness' but in the sense of 'operation of the free will'. The artist's freedom should be complemented by self-restraint. By distancing himself from his work he avoids the excessive commitment that can destroy a poem—no doubt an implied criticism of the Storm and Stress writers.

lik und Mythologie der alten Völker, 4 vols, Leipzig and Darmstadt, 1810–12. See Klaus Ziegler, article 'Mythos und Dichtung' in Merker-Stammler, *Reallexikon*, 2nd ed., vol. II, Berlin, 1965 [i.e. 1959–64], pp. 569–80, and Dieter Schrey, *Mythos und Geschichte bei Johann Arnold Kanne und in der romantischen Mythologie*, Tübingen, Niemeyer, 1969, ix, 264 pp.

[13] For Hegel see Ernst Behler, 'Friedrich Schlegel and Hegel', *Hegel-Studien*, ii (1963), 203–50; and Otto Pöggeler, *Hegels Kritik der Romantik*, Bonn diss., 1956, pp. 66 ff. It may be added that Hegel seems mainly responsible for the mistaken view that Friedrich just misunderstood Fichte and transferred the creative power of the absolute ego indiscriminately to the artist's finite ego.

The second point is that the poem has its own aesthetic reality, of which the ironical intervention of the author may form a part. The novelist standing outside his work, regarding it as an object, may transfer his attitude to the novel back into the world of the novel. (Historical examples are to be found in Cervantes and Sterne and, to a lesser extent, in Diderot and Jean Paul.) Thus the novel may be raised to a higher power ('potenziert'), become as it were a 'Roman des Romans', and unite poetry and criticism. This was certainly one intention of *Lucinde*.[14]

Finally, the poem itself achieves symbolic value; it is open-ended, growing from the dialectical tension created. The recognition of its own finite nature points forward to the unattainable infinite; it exists in an ever-changing approximation to totality. We are back to 'progression'. The poem is no longer a finished statement, but an insight into a dynamically expanding range of possibilities.

Friedrich Schlegel's theory of Romantic Irony is developed in a slightly different philosophical direction by K. W. F. Solger and by Adam Müller; though Solger, at least, substantially misunderstood Schlegel. The effect on literature itself is, however, less than some accounts might lead one to believe. Tieck's dramas and Brentano's *Godwi* probably owe little to the philosophical side of the theory and E. T. A. Hoffmann is some way removed. Not until Thomas Mann is there a major exemplification of Friedrich Schlegel's approach to irony. In *Tonio Kröger* the artist's distancing of himself from his work is discussed; in *Der Zauberberg*, and later in *Doktor Faustus*, we can see the whole range of irony and combinatory wit—Hans Castorp, we may remember, is the 'small lord of contradictions'; and in *Joseph* a new mythology is almost brought into being.

This is perhaps the place to mention, sadly, that Schlegel's own poetic productions are more interesting than effective. His poems, ranging from once popular patriotic songs, through love poems to parodies, reveal an enthusiastic interest in metrical forms but little more; though there is occasionally, as in the long 'Hieroglyphenlied' of 1824-7, a notable intellectual content, in this case a theology of history. The drama *Alarcos*

[14] The attitude of Friedrich Schlegel, and of the Romantics generally, to Jean Paul is ambivalent, as was his towards them. The form and freedom of his novels undoubtedly influenced *Lucinde*. The darker, grotesque elements reappeared later in Romanticism, but, for Schlegel, the exuberance of the imagery and the arabesque products of his humour are the most appealing characteristics. What is at first sight more surprising is that Friedrich criticizes him for being too subjective, lacking in control, deficient indeed in that ironic self-restraint that would have enabled him to stand back and objectify his work; thus, except for the interest of their form, his authorial interventions are trivial. Only in his idyllic pictures of provincial life does he seem to Schlegel to achieve a synthesis of the individual and the general, for in them the small country town becomes a symbol of the heavenly city. See Mennemeier, *Poesiebegriff*, pp. 264-83, and Polheim, *Arabeske*, pp. 138-47.

(1801) shows the influence of Calderón but is frankly muddled and dull, with the artificiality of the Spanish imitation unalleviated by any linguistic felicities. It was presented at Weimar on 29 May 1802 and, but for Goethe's intervention, would have been laughed off the stage. Some of the minor Romantics thought highly of it as the synthesis of classical and romantic that Schlegel had intended, but it has had no stage success in its own right.

Nor has *Lucinde* ever acquired many real admirers, though it was once the subject of much controversy. Equally minimal has been its influence on the theory of the novel, although it was written in the first five months of 1799 and its content is interwoven with most of Friedrich Schlegel's own views on the form. We have to bear in mind that the *Lucinde* we possess is only the first part; short extracts and a number of poems intended for the second part exist, and there was talk of a third. Märchen were also contemplated for both these. The original enthusiastic conception, indeed, was of a vast, all-embracing work, the new bible to which we have already referred. No doubt the intermingling of genres would have been more evident as the work progressed, but what we have now is a narrative core surrounded by prose improvisations in the form of letters, fantasies, allegories, idylls, reflections, dialogues. What is represented in 'this mad little book', 'this fantastic novel', is 'romantic confusion', 'the most beautiful chaos' (*KA* V, 22, 24, 14, 9). The epic continuity is broken in order to concentrate attention on the intellectual and spiritual content, on the process of love. In practical terms it also seems clear that Friedrich could only manage narrative when it was partly autobiographical.

The novel's reputation as a glorification of sensuality was always more dependent on autobiographical connexions (particularly the knowledge that Lucinde was to be equated with Dorothea, with whom Friedrich was living) than on study of the text. Gutzkow and the Young Germans misunderstood the work when they seized upon it as a sensualist manifesto, as exaltation of the flesh; they would have done better to pick Heinse. (It is, incidentally, instructive to compare English reaction to the sensual descriptions in Shelley's *Epipsychidion*.) *Lucinde* is, in fact, a fairly moral work in spite of its depiction of Friedrich's wild-oats period in the figure of Julius. What it presents is a view of woman, love and marriage (of the common-law variety) substantially different from the prevailing eighteenth-century ethos in which women were regarded as procreative machines or sexual objects; intellectually and spiritually they tended to be thought of as rather inferior men. Love's basis and achievement, the novel says, is harmony; lovers complement each other. There is, in the ideal union, no separation of sexual and spiritual love. A mystery is achieved between two people, and the analogy between love and religion is close. Love is also one of the chief components of the novel form and of Romantic poetry in general, in that it gives a glympse of infinity. It is an 'intimation of the higher, the infinite, a hieroglyph of the one eternal love, of the sacred life-abundance of creative nature' (*KA* II, 334; *Gespräch über die Poesie*).

Lucinde is a clear failure as a work of art, and serves Schlegel's theories ill. Yet, though his own poetic production lacked bite and the intentional chaos remained chaotic, poetry was undoubtedly of overwhelming importance for him. It was a supreme integrating power that was to place man in his new world and to divine the future. Schlegel's hopes were bright; he projected into the future an idealized Golden Age from the past, though one modified by his and Schiller's 'naive-sentimental', 'classic-romantic' distinction. He inherited a theory of perfectibility, a prophetic certainty of a coming age of fulfilment; in the *Gespräch über die Poesie* he speaks of 'the Golden Age, that will yet come' (*KA* II, 322). Achieving it is the goal of Romantic Poetry: 'The revolutionary desire to realize the Kingdom of God is the point of elasticity of progressive development' (*KA* II, 201; *Athenäum* Fragment 222). There was an original human state in which God was thought and felt; this was the Golden Age. If the poet can imaginatively combine it with the richness of the present's phenomena and his intuitions of the future, then this indeed is the fulfilment of time, is eternity (*KA* VI, 276-7).

Implicit in all this is a philosophy of history and an ethical commitment dependent on it. In Schlegel we have the paradox that he provides the philosophical justification for Sehnsucht (yearning for the unattainable) and at the same time affirms a future harmony. Friedrich felt himself to be at a revolutionary point and wished to use revolution. Looking back in 1804 he sees only the bleakness of failure: 'The greatest period was that in the eighteenth century—Rousseau, Buffon, Lavoisier, Robespierre—something new and great could have arisen; magic [by which he means the mystical understanding of the Godhead] might indeed have emerged as the ruling principle of all human actions. *From this sprang Novalis's and my love for revolution*' (*KA* XIX, 14).

There is no sudden change in Friedrich's views, but circumstances crowded in upon him. In 1801 the close circle of friends began to break up. Though in that year, in the poem 'Herkules Musagetes', he was still implying confidence in his own creative literary powers he must have been having some private doubts, not diminished by his desperate financial circumstances. His search for a new mythology had led him increasingly to history, including the history of religion. His translations from Sanscrit and the epoch-making studies of Indian thought (*Über die Sprache und Weisheit der Indier*, 1808)[15] not only hardened his views on

[15] See Ursula Oppenberg's scholarly *Quellenstudien zu Friedrich Schlegels Übersetzungen aus*

language, the stuff of poetry, but had led him to think of mythology more exclusively in terms of religion. The experience of Paris, to which he had moved at the end of June 1802, had opened up a new idea of Europe, the richness and variety of whose culture made it a fitting pendant for the Orient. This discovery of Europe, dramatically evidenced by the publication of his new periodical *Europa* (1803–5), more or less coincides with his disillusionment with revolution. Then, in the spring of 1804, he returned to Cologne with the brothers Boisserée and was profoundly influenced by Gothic architecture. In it he found the spirit of the Middle Ages, the idea of the infinite, the 'spiritual idea of the Church itself' (*KA* IV, 166).

Friedrich Schlegel had not abandoned poetry, but it had lost its primacy. For some years before the formal conversion to Catholicism in April 1808, he had been looking beyond literature for salvation and had come to see it as a subordinate element in cultural renewal; the search for oneness, for the organic whole, led easily to divine revelation. The conversion itself had the immediate effect of making all his publications suspect; Goethe was greatly disgusted by it and saw the nefarious influence of Catholicism in the Indian studies. And it was easy to hark back to 1796 to Friedrich's own criticism of Jacobi's *Woldemar* ending 'with a somersault into the abyss of divine mercy' (*KA* II, 77); or, like Heine in *Die romantische Schule*, to claim that Friedrich fled in mortal terror from the modern world 'into the shaking ruins of the Catholic Church'. Yet the conversion was logical enough and represented less a change of direction than a diminution of expectation. Ultimate hope replaced ardent yearning, revelation reinforced poetic divination, man's cultural goals became part of the workings of salvation.

The years from his conversion to his death in January 1829 were devoted to consolidating his new position. He committed himself to a multi-racial Austro-Hungarian state, a model for European unity, German reunification and Catholic order. His periodical *Concordia* (1820–3) brought together Viennese late Romantic criticism of contemporary culture (Baader, Adam Müller, Zacharias Werner) and contained, in the essay 'Die Signatur des Zeitalters' (*KA* VII, 483–596), the definitive statement of his conservative view of history and the state, and of his strictures on contemporary disorder. *Concordia*, in spite of its appeasing title, widened the breach between him and August Wilhelm, who saw

dem Sanskrit, Marburg, Elwert, 1965, 135 pp., which is also of biographical interest, and her essay (as Ursula Struc), 'Zu Friedrich Schlegels orientalistischen Studien', *ZDP*, lxxxviii (1969), Sonderheft, 114–31; A. Leslie Willson, *A Mythical Image: The Ideal of India*, 1964, and his 'Dichter-Priester. Bestandteil der Romantik', *CG*, 1968, pp. 127–36. Ernst Behler, 'Das Indienbild der deutschen Romantik', *GRM*, xlix (1968), 21–37, surveys the various studies and shows he believes Friedrich to have become dissatisfied with Indian thought, particularly its pantheistic traits. India is the whipping-boy for his own past.

Friedrich retreating into obscurantism. Friedrich was indeed attracted by mysticism, and from 1820 on there is a highly charged, esoteric correspondence with a fanatic of occult practices, Christine von Stransky; but the final form his philosophy takes is an attempt to re-establish the whole man, to break the tyranny of abstract thought, to point to God as the highest manifestation and origin of all life.[16]

The rehabilitation of the later Friedrich Schlegel is now well under way, and is a necessary corrective to the sneer that he sold out to Metternich, or that he became a mere publicist for clericalism. Yet we must not allow ourselves to be diverted from the achievements of his most brilliant period: the inauguration, with his brother, of new directions in literary criticism; the creation, in however fragmentary a form, of many concepts still potent in art and aesthetics; the establishment of a theory of Romantic art, with all that implies; but, above all, the attempt to give meaning to the philosophical and scientific revolution of his time.

---

[16] For the late philosophy see particularly Günther Müller's introduction to his edition of the essay *Von der Seele*, Augsburg and Cologne, Benno Filser, 1927, lxviii, 59 pp., and Ernst Behler's introduction to *KA* X.

4

Poetry in Metaphysics:
Novalis

'Why so violent against *metaphysics* in poetry?'
(Coleridge to John Thelwall, 13 May 1796)

The general nature of German Romanticism, particularly in the early writers, is non-mimetic; experience seldom crystallizes into form. The tension is in the action of the mind; the imagination wrestles with the absolute, fiction demands metaphysical verification. The writing often has an etherealized, blood-drained quality that does violence to common expectation and common sense. The writer himself may diminish in the vaporous air.

Novalis's poetic creations often seem, in these terms, inadequate to sustain what we sense to be the majesty of his genius—the German Coleridge, perhaps. Thus critics have either felt it necessary to overpraise the only intermittently powerful *Geistliche Lieder*, and to excuse the narrative deficiencies of *Heinrich von Ofterdingen*, or have taken the intention for the achievement in, for instance, seeing *Ofterdingen* as one of a proposed cycle of novels. In older criticism there is talk of a 'hectic' disposition and the early death at twenty-nine is both foreshadowed and used to palliate.

No excuses are necessary for Novalis. His *Fragmente* are as powerfully exciting as any plastically arranged poem or fiction; what is our objection to poetry in metaphysics? The sustaining interest in the reading of Novalis's works is the sense of contact with a mind of visionary intensity and total commitment. The poetic achievement is in the momentary glimpses of ideal reality: what, in other contexts, we should call epiphanies.

The life seems at first sight, to be dominated by one experience, the death of Sophie; but this impression is illusory. Friedrich von Hardenberg (1772–1801), brought up in an aristocratic but pious Moravian household, in training to become a mining engineer, became engaged to Sophie von Kühn in March 1795, the week of her thirteenth birthday. Two years later, after a lingering illness, she died: 19 March 1797. The depth of Friedrich's despair is undeniable; his wish to die with her is no mere conventional grief. Then at her grave, on 13 May 1797, he experienced a visionary exaltation that seemed to lift him out of time and space: 'In the evening I went to Sophie. There I was indescribably joyful—moments of enthusiasm blazed within me—I blew the grave away before me like dust—centuries were as moments—I could feel her presence—I thought she would appear at any instant' (*KS* IV, 35–6). This is the language of conversion; it bears, however unconsciously, the Moravian assurance, in their case the certainty of God's overruling that inhibits the fear of death. It leads to an intense cultivation of the inner life.

Recognition of the profound importance of the Sophie experience must, however, be tempered by two considerations. One is that there are earlier passages in which Friedrich appears to prefigure the annihilation of death and the recognition of a higher, timeless, non-sensory world within us (*KS* IV, 180). Then secondly one must accept that this intense existential experience slowly faded, more especially as he found personal contentment in his relationship with Julie von Charpentier. In the last two years of his life Sophie is an insubstantial symbol; she is his poetic shorthand. After the visionary experience, however, he had projected her figure onto the heavens, writing of 'Christus und Sophie' in his journal in June 1797 (*KS* IV, 48) and noting that 'what I have for Sophie is religion, not love' (*KS* II, 395).

He had also created a new persona for himself. The name Novalis first occurs in a letter to A. W. Schlegel on 24 February 1798, accompanying the fragments published as *Blütenstaub* in the first issue of the *Athenäum*.[1] The epigraph to the collection reads: 'Friends, the soil is poor, we must sow generously even to ensure moderate crops' (*KS* II, 413). Members of the Hardenberg family appear to have used the names 'von Rode' and 'de Novali' in the thirteenth century—'Rodung' corresponding to the old Latin substantive 'novalis', formed from 'novus' and mean-

[1] Novalis has traditionally been pronounced with a long 'a' and the stress on the second syllable, the normal Latin stress as an amphibrach. It appears, however, that the family tradition supports a stress on the first syllable with a short 'a' (i.e. as a dactyl), and that the poet himself may have pronounced it thus. It may well be that those close to the family stressed the first syllable, whereas the literary world used the long 'a'. For a partial review of the evidence see Ritter, 1967, pp. 75–7 and 328–9; *KS* I³, 2, and IV, 989; and Preitz, *Friedrich Schlegel und Novalis*, 1957, p. 200. A puzzling feature not hitherto noted is that the theologian Richard Rothe, in two poems on Novalis written in 1815, uses the dactylic stress, and he would have heard the name in literary circles, not in the immediate family (*Gesammelte Vorträge und Abhandlungen Dr Richard Rothe's*, Elberfeld, 1886, pp. 201–3).

However this may be, it seems sensible now to cling to the Latin stress, with its rich associative background.

ing 'cleared land', 'fallow land'. Novalis, then, was to sow this new ground, to raise up things new; and it is difficult not to think in New Testament terms of the 'new man' sowing 'a natural body' which 'is raised a spiritual body'.

If the mission and the apocalyptic religious vision found their catalyst in the Sophie experience, what were the elements already existing in Novalis's thought? It should first be said that his earliest poetry is anacreontic imitation and that the reading of Gleim, Uz, Gotter, Geßner and Wieland served as a counter-balance to the pietistic paternal legacy. Nor indeed did the adolescent grace of the rococo ever entirely leave him, even at his most serious. Friendship with Schiller and Karl Leonhard Reinhold during his two semesters at Jena appears to have moved his thoughts in the direction of idealist philosophy, but principally its aesthetics. Then at Leipzig in 1792 he met Friedrich Schlegel, who wrote to August Wilhelm in January: 'Fate has delivered into my hands a young man from whom everything may be expected' (*KS* IV, 571). Thus begins the process of 'Symphilosophieren', that mutual enrichment by meetings and correspondence that is one of the chief features of both their lives.

There seems, however, to have been a gap in their correspondence, or it may merely be in its survival, from 1794 to 1796. When it resumes, both have been overwhelmed by Fichte. The copious notes of Novalis's wrestling with the new philosophy are now dated between the autumn of 1795 and the summer of 1796, with much 'Fichtisieren' in his personal contacts with Schlegel in the second half of that year. From April to July 1797 he returned to Fichte and on 29 May there is a laconic diary entry: 'Between the turnpike and Grüningen I had the satisfaction of discovering the real meaning of the Fichtean Ego' (*KS* IV, 42).

Novalis took from Fichte a sense of the overwhelming creative power inherent in the Ego, but in his case there was a substantial transference of this to the empirical self. What the Fichtean system did for him above all, however, was to unleash the questionings of his own mind. We see a continuing battle with Fichte's terminology, in an attempt to refine and to reform it, to achieve in language what logic has left undone. For Fichte's preoccupation with rational consciousness has left gaps that human experience cries aloud to fill; especially painful for Novalis is the absence of love from Fichte's system. In the autumn of 1797 he renewed his acquaintance with the works of the Dutch philosopher Frans Hemsterhuis (1721–90), and above all with his dialogue *Alexis, ou de l'âge d'or*. The modified sensualism of Hemsterhuis presupposes a former golden age when man had direct intuitive rapport with the universe through the senses. These have now atrophied but, in their place, certain 'higher' organs or abilities have developed. One of these is the moral sense, which manifests itself in the different forms of love, and which reinforces the continuing efforts of things, and especially of the self, to recreate the original unity of the universe. But we remain separate and only after death will complete unity be possible. (The significance of this for the Sophie experience need not be further emphasized.) On earth, the nearest approximation to harmony is attained through art; this is where the greatest number of different phenomena can be combined in one organic whole. In art there is intuitive recognition of unity and totality, and of the richness deriving from coincident sense impressions and associations. Art has a synthesizing role.

The brevity of Novalis's active life and the uncertain chronology of his writings have, until recently at any rate, made it all too easy to think of his philosophical formulations as static, as part of an elaborate and stable intellectual framework. The counter danger is to seize on all his reading as 'influence' and to regard him as a chameleon. Novalis, it is clear, had an extraordinarily alert and receptive mind; he read with astonishing range and vigour; he was immersed in the philosophical speculations of the day—many of his intimates had as their small talk the Ego and the Absolute. What one must do, therefore, is to recognize that there are stages in his development, as he wrestles with Fichtean terminology or encounters Naturphilosophie, and that he transforms assimilated material into bricks for the metaphysical house he may some day build. In 1797 he had also undergone two intensely disruptive emotional experiences, Sophie's death and the vision at the grave, which channelled his thought in the direction of willed synthesis, a reorientation of the relationship between psyche and soma. The first fruits of this intellectual struggle are contained in *Blütenstaub*, the only general collection of fragments he published, though many others were clearly intended for eventual publication.[2]

The fragmentary form has seemed to some to represent a characteristic attitude but, in Novalis's case, the influence of Friedrich Schlegel's enthusiasm may have been decisive. Both see the fragment as being something more allusive, more open-ended than the rather sententious aphorisms of the eighteenth century. Novalis's fragments in particular are more confessional, more speculative, depth-charges rather than constructs. In a letter to Schlegel he calls his own attempts 'fragments of the continuing dialogue with myself—cuttings [in a horticultural sense]' (*KS* IV, 242). Fragments are provisional and hypothetical in character and the earlier critics rather felt that Novalis outgrew the form. But, as he says in a dialogue of about the same period as *Blütenstaub*, 'hypotheses are nets

---

[2] *Blütenstaub* was probably written and assembled from August 1797 on; a copy *Vermischte Bemerkungen* from the turn of the year 1797–8 survives in manuscript and shows a number of variations from the version published in 1798 in the first issue of *Athenäum*.

and only if we cast will we catch. Was not America itself discovered by hypothesis?' (*KS* II, 668).

The new ordering of material in the collected edition shows that much that previously appeared fragmentary had been wrenched from its context in more ambitious studies (and often, as in Kamnitzer's edition of the *Fragmente*, excitingly but misleadingly reassembled). But his conscious choice of the form should still not be underplayed, and the astonishing breadth and agility of his mind, the daring and beauty of his analogies, the creativity and novelty of his language, make the fragments the most breathtaking of all the products of German Romanticism.

The most striking fragment in *Blütenstaub* is the sixteenth, which reads in part: 'Is not the universe within us? ... The way of mystery leads inwards. Past and future, eternity and its realms, these lie within us or nowhere. The external world is the world of shadows; it projects its shadows into the kingdom of light. Now indeed everything within us seems dark, lonely and without form; but how different all will appear when this darkness is gone and the shadow-body has passed away' (*KS* II, 419). An important aspect of Novalis's experience is suggested here. The fragment combines reminiscences of Hemsterhuis and Schelling; it hints at complexities and depths beyond Fichte while still acknowledging the primacy of the Ego; it carries the dark personal experience of Sophie's death and, as it closes, its cadences prophesy the annihilation of space and time, partly in the language of Pietism.

In December 1797 Novalis entered the mining academy at Freiberg, then one of the greatest scientific institutions in Europe, and we now see him assimilating both scientific and pseudo-scientific information at an ever more bewildering pace. The increased expectation of coincidences between the spiritual and the natural world fed on his reading of alchemistic works, on John Brown's medical theories and on Ritter's more high-flown speculations. At the same time the possibilities of systematization were sharpened for him by the example of the Academy's head, Abraham Gottlob Werner, geologist, mineralogist, linguistic historian, philosopher, encyclopaedist, the originator of what now seems the curious 'Neptunist' doctrine that all rocks had been precipitated from a common fluid.

Without aiming at too great a precision of dates, we might now consider what the principal strands in Novalis's thought were by about the spring of 1799, taking his own definitions.[3] For it is now that the winding

---

[3] By then there were two unpublished collections of fragments, the *Logologische Fragmente* of early 1798 and the *Teplitzer Fragmente* of July–August 1798. The *Allgemeine Brouillon* and the scientific notebooks can also now be seen to be much less fragmentary in character than the traditional selections had suggested.

stairways of his thought reveal their particular fascination, and now that the poetic power of his sometimes contradictory formulations becomes evident.

One term used by him is 'magischer Idealismus', probably the 'very great, very fertile idea, throwing a ray of light of the highest intensity on the Fichtean system' of which he wrote to Friedrich Schlegel in May 1798 (*KS* IV, 254). There are some obvious dangers in trying to subsume all his thoughts under this heading (a fashion Heinrich Simon set in 1906 in his book of that title), but it remains more significant than some recent critics allow.[4] Novalis uses the words 'magisch' or 'Magie' in a good number of senses and often pejoratively, but in 'magic idealism' we may take the meaning as approaching the neutral one given in a fragment of early 1798: 'Magic is = the art of using the world of the senses in one's own way' (*KS* II, 546). We are all potential magicians, but the poet is the realized Magus. The magic vision transcends the normal world, raises it to a different pitch, rather as in Brown's medical theory of excitability.

The Ego itself performs miracles, makes its own magic. It moulds the world of the senses; but it also liberates the world by discovering mind in it. The crucial operation is 'to make the abstract sensory and the sensory abstract' (*KS* III, 299); or, more pointedly, 'if you cannot turn thoughts into external things, then turn the external things into thoughts' (*KS* III, 301). Novalis was not, at first, propounding a poetic programme; the initial impulses were philosophical and perhaps biographical. The attempt to spiritualize matter, to annihilate time and space, will, however, tend to find meaning in poetry or religion, if anywhere. The principle of synthetic unity has, after all, as its most potent exemplar the poetic symbol.

It is here that Novalis, no doubt following Friedrich Schlegel, speaks of romanticizing the world: 'The world must be romanticized. Only thus will we rediscover its original meaning. Romanticizing is no more than a qualitative involution.... If I give a higher meaning to the everyday, a mysterious aspect to the ordinary, the dignity of the unfamiliar to the familiar, the appearance of infinity to the finite, then I am romanticizing it' (*KS* II, 545). The synthesizing element implicit in this intensification of the normal world releases new meanings from both world and self. A whole series of new relationships comes into being. We recognize our-

[4] See Manfred Frank, 'Die Philosophie des sogenannten "magischen Idealismus"', *Euph*, lxiii (1969), 88–116, and the rather unsatisfactory article by Karl Heinz Volkmann-Schluck, 'Novalis' magischer Idealismus', in *Die deutsche Romantik*, ed. Hans Steffen, 1967, pp. 45–53; also Haering, 1954, pp. 364–81, and Dick, 1967, pp. 223–77. None of these really takes account of the way Baader made mysticism and magic respectable again and tried, more comprehensively than Novalis, to reconcile Fichte and Schelling with older systems of magic. For 'Magie' and 'Willkür' see Heftrich, 1969, pp. 135–40 and 176–7.

selves in innumerable unsuspected guises and meet ourselves constantly in the natural world (in stones and flowers, for instance, as we shall see in *Ofterdingen*). This is only to be expected as man is 'a source of analogies for the universe' (*KS* II, 610). Novalis was almost obsessed by analogies and their symbolism; they are his version of Friedrich Schlegel's 'wit' as the principle of combinatory art.

Poetry still does not have the primacy it achieves later. Two other interests weigh heavily: the encyclopaedic project and religion, with indeed some suggestion of combining them. The preliminary work towards the encyclopaedia is to be found in the Freiberg notebooks and the 356-page general rough-book, the *Allgemeine Brouillon* written between September 1798 and the beginning of March 1799. Novalis's intention was not just to gather material from the various disciplines, though this was a necessary preliminary. His chief aim was to lay a foundation for all knowledge, to write by analogy, to show relationships and influences, to create a 'living' instrument of thought, to reconcile. When he spoke of a 'moral astronomy (moral in the Hemsterhuis sense)', or of 'a religion of the visible universe' (both in a letter of 20 July 1798 to Friedrich Schlegel; *KS* IV, 255), or of 'the sacred road to physics' (*KS* IV, 276), he was reflecting the joint status of encyclopaedia and religion in the achievement of harmony. We must now see how this overriding desire is reflected in his more consciously literary works: the *Lehrlinge zu Sais* with its interpretations of nature; the personal, religious, mystical *Geistliche Lieder*, with the added mythical overtones in the *Hymnen an die Nacht*; and *Heinrich von Ofterdingen*, with its attempt at synthesis through symbolism.

Die Lehrlinge zu Sais seems to have begun as a series of fragments and then to have developed in the direction of the novel. The Märchen of Hyazinth and Rosenblüte, the kernel of the work, was written towards the end of 1798 or the beginning of 1799. Then there were notes in that year suggesting further plans, and in early 1800 Novalis was proposing to take up the work again once he had finished *Ofterdingen* and to make it a 'genuinely symbolical novel of nature' (letter to Tieck, 23 February 1800; *KS* IV, 323). Nothing came of these later proposals and the work remains an unfinished agglomeration of fragment, essay, Märchen, dialogue and narrative. Strenuous attempts have been made to discover formal groupings, chiefly triadic in character, within the work as we have it; but, apart from elements of repetition between some sections, little of this convinces.[5]

The stimulus for the *Lehrlinge* was the renewed contact with the natural world, tangible and mystical, in practice and reading at Freiberg. The

[5] See Jury Striedter, 'Die Komposition der "Lehrlinge zu Sais"', *DU*, vii (1955), 5–23, and Klaus J. Heinisch in his *Deutsche Romantik—Interpretationen*, 1966, pp. 85–98.

theme of the veiled goddess at Sais, weaving the world on her loom, was well known through Schiller's use of it; for Novalis the veil conceals the profoundest secrets of the natural world. The master, based on Werner, initiates the disciples into the secret hieroglyphic language of nature by revealing how he himself had traced the connexions of all things, the harmonious whole in disparate phenomena. In a past, a golden age, not perhaps measured in years, man had intuitively responded to this unity, but the present offers a multiplicity of more conscious efforts—poetic sympathy, religious communion, sensual enjoyment, ethical model-making, intellectual subjugation—to bridge the gap between man and nature.

What higher mode of perception can the future offer? Novalis exemplifies with the Märchen of Hyazinth and Rosenblüte. Hyazinth, too, loses his original harmony with nature but, as he journeys towards the veiled virgin, the fruits become more aromatic, the heavens a deeper blue, the air milder and he finds himself again able to converse with the flowers. In this correspondence of mood and landscape, receptiveness and harmony, Novalis created the one valid sustained symbol of the *Lehrlinge*; but when Hyazinth is led in a dream to the goddess, lifts the veil and Rosenblüte falls into his arms we are far from certain what we should believe. The crux has been interpreted in a number of ways: as showing that love is at the heart of all being, as creating a personal relationship out of Fichtean theory (the non-Ego becomes 'thou'), as portraying union after death and, with the aid of a couplet of May 1798, as showing that only through self-knowledge can we know the world, and only through love unite with it: 'One was successful—he lifted the veil of the Goddess at Sais—But what did he see? He saw—wonder of wonders—himself' (*KS* I^3, 110).

Novalis aims in the later sections at a Messianic interpretation of nature and has difficulties with the stages towards it. His troubles would, no doubt, have multiplied had he gone on, as the last plan suggests, to incorporate Greek and Indian gods, ancient cosmogonies or a journey to the pyramids. (*KS* I^3, 11–12). The master himself was to die, but the child (who had earlier lived for a while among the disciples and made them strangely happy) was to return with his John the Baptist, as a Messiah of nature, inaugurating a new testament, a new nature, a new Jerusalem. The *Lehrlinge*, that is to say, was to develop on chiliastic lines. As we have it, however, it is a haunting but deeply flawed work: on the one hand a mishmash of Fichtean activism, flirtation with Schelling's world-soul, echoes of Rosicrucian literature and of the alchemists, with shadowy characters wilting under the burden of their own eloquence. On the other hand it is a construction of great rhythmic beauty, an exercise in the imaginative heightening of metaphysical concepts, a determined attempt to grasp the material world as a unity, to spiritualize and redeem it.

The visionary, chiliastic nature of Novalis's imagination is very clearly seen in his political writings.[6] *Glauben und Liebe*, which we tend to think of as a collection of fragments, but which Novalis himself always called an essay, was written in the early months of 1798, soon after Friedrich Wilhelm III and his bride, Luise, had come to the throne of Prussia. Novalis undoubtedly idealized the young couple and transferred to them something of his own Moravian emphasis on the family; and Queen Luise is, in some ways, a surrogate for Sophie. But the work is not a piece of vulgar monarchical propaganda and, when the king first read it, he found it difficult to understand and vaguely disquieting. The unease is not surprising. What Novalis is doing is projecting a myth onto the royal pair, often using images from the physical or the mystical sciences. The state is an organic structure, it is personal, a 'Macroandropos' (*KS* III, 286), a family, a unit bound together by love; and the king, if he is a good man, is a symbolic expression of this in the way that the dead letter of a constitution can never be. It was really rather too obvious that this utopian vision bore little relationship to the Prussian state.

Novalis himself would, at bottom, have been well aware of this. The royal couple were a poetic symbol of a mythical golden age. It is in this light, too, that we must approach *Die Christenheit oder Europa*, written mainly in October 1799 but not published, except for a few extracts, until the fourth edition of his works in 1826. History is, for Novalis, a poetic creation rather than an academic discipline, and mythologizing the early Middle Ages provides him with an extended poetic symbol to underpin his visionary prophecies. Briefly the argument is that, in the Middle Ages, Europe was happily united under the hierarchical order of the Catholic Church. The Protestant Reformation destroyed this unity by associating religion with nation states and by subjecting Christianity to the judgement of the profane science of philology. The Jesuits succeeded in re-establishing the hierarchical sense, but the Enlightenment

---

[6] His own indirect political activity in the Electorate of Saxony is examined by Hans Wolfgang Kuhn, *Der Apokalyptiker und die Politik: Studien zur Staatsphilosophie des Novalis*, Freiburg in Br., Rombach, 1961, pp. 94–5 and 170–8, showing that he was not a reactionary in the usual sense and that his concept of the ideal state had little connexion with everyday politics.

Recent attempts to recruit Novalis as a forerunner of modern radicalism in virtue of his utopian constructs do not convince; an extreme example is Richard Faber, *Novalis: Die Phantasie an die Macht*, Stuttgart, Metzler, 1970, 104 pp. A somewhat more measured consideration of the chiliastic elements in Novalis's thought is to be found in Jürgen Kreft, 'Die Entstehung der dialektischen Geschichtsmetaphysik aus den Gestalten des utopischen Bewußtseins bei Novalis', *DVLG*, xxxix (1965), 213–45.

developed hatred of the Catholic religion into a hatred of Christianity, of all belief, of enthusiasm, of poetry. Now there are signs that a new age is about to be born, a new church, a new humanity, a new history, where Christianity will mediate between political powers and usher in perpetual peace.

Die Christenheit oder Europa was written when Napoleon was returning from Egypt to overthrow the Directory and when the Coalition was stepping up its activities against France, although Russia withdrew from it in that month. The struggles of nation states, the bloody wars of modern man were certainly in his mind; but his remedy for them is essentially timeless and removed from the practical world. The 'new Jerusalem' of which he writes is no earthly paradise; it is a poetic vision, an echo of eighteenth-century utopianism and millenarianism, and an oratorical flourish appealing primarily to the reader's emotions. The whole is grotesque history, but magnificently ordered sermonizing, compelling in its vivid over-simplifications, its occasional memorable image (such as the Enlightenment's supposed view of the universe as a self-grinding mill), and in the prophetic assurance of its judgements. What influence the work had is a matter of dispute. Adam Müller had a sight of the manuscript at the publisher Reiner's in Berlin in 1809 and may have taken something from it; in general, though, what it seems to have done to the close friends who read it was to confirm an enthusiasm for the Middle Ages and the Catholic Church rather than to convince by its arguments.

The markedly Christian stress in *Die Christenheit oder Europa* certainly owes something to the reading of Schleiermacher's *Reden*, which Novalis received in mid-September 1799. Older criticism also made the *Reden* almost wholly responsible for the *Geistliche Lieder*, but it has now been shown fairly conclusively by Ritter that some were written before this.[7] They must therefore be taken as growing equally out of his new intellectual interest in religion, indirectly stimulated by Friedrich Schlegel. One of the poems has been shown to have a model in an old Catholic Advent hymn, first published in 1631; but the form of the *Geistliche Lieder* as a whole grew from the Moravian background and from the hymns of Zinzendorf, with their emotional colouring, their quasi-erotic devotion to the Saviour and their sometimes grotesque imagery. Although 'Wenn ich ihn nur habe' and some others have been adopted in hymn-books,

---

[7] See Heinz Ritter, 'Die geistlichen Lieder des Novalis. Ihre Datierung und Entstehung', *JDSG*, iv (1960), 308–42, and in his *Der unbekannte Novalis*, 1967, pp. 135–59. The conclusions may be summarized as follows: VII, July 1798; XII, IV, V, I, VI, II, III, March 1799; XI, VIII, IX, after Easter (24 March) 1799; X, XV, end of March 1800; XIII, August 1800; XIV, August–September 1800. But Sander L. Gilman, in *Seminar*, vi (1970), 225–36, dates XII between February and November 1800.

Novalis is not writing for a congregation but expressing mainly subjective, and sometimes sentimental, emotions.[8] The earlier group is perhaps the one in which the emotions are closest to the surface but, for all of them, the themes are interesting as recapitulations of Novalis's personal voyagings and speculations, rather than in themselves: the experience of being mystically reunited with Christ; his resurrection re-establishing the Golden Age; the return of the poetic spirit with him; God and man meeting again in the cosmic process, 'Er ist der Stern, er ist die Sonn', Er ist des ewgen Lebens Bronn, Aus Kraut und Stein und Meer und Licht, Schimmert sein kindlich Angesicht'.[9] Childhood, as suggested in these lines, and more clearly in 'Wer einmal, Mutter', represents faith and love in the Golden Age. The whole slightly cloying accent is certainly on love, to the almost total exclusion of sin, death, justice, or any other overpowering emotion. The formal simplicity of the poems is itself a factor in controlling the emotional tension. For poets like Charles Wesley or William Williams, Pantycelyn, such controls increase tension by resisting it; but Novalis's imaginative flights are seriously enfeebled when confined to set forms. The imagery evaporates in the rational requirements of stanzaic discipline.

The seventh poem belongs much more in form and spirit (and perhaps in date) to the *Hymnen an die Nacht*. The chronology of the hymns is disputed; probably all that it is reasonably safe to say is that they seem mainly to have been written between September 1797 and the end of the year, with revisions and additions, including the whole of the sixth hymn, at the turn of the year 1799–1800.[10] Most seem originally to have been in free verse, but they were printed as prose in the *Athenäum*, and there is no reason to doubt that this was with Novalis's approval. In spite of the lapse of time, the experience at Sophie's grave is clearly the motive force behind the hymns. A hasty reading of Young's *Night Thoughts* in April 1797, A. W. Schlegel on *Romeo and Juliet*, Herder's mythopeic poems on night, sleep and death, the reading of Eckartshausen and Jean Paul, all may have contributed something; but they are, in fact, little more than side issues. Nor does it help greatly to specu-

[8] See the article on 'G. F. P. von Hardenberg' in Julian's *Dictionary of Hymnology*; also those on Moravian hymnology and on Zinzendorf.

[9] 'He is the star, He is the sun, He is the fount of everlasting life; From plant and stone and lake and light, His childlike countenance glows' (*KS* I³, 174).

[10] Two versions of the hymns exist: a manuscript version now dated by Ritter as from the turn of the year 1799–1800, and the much altered printed version that appeared in the *Athenäum* of 1800. See Ritter, *Der unbekannte Novalis*, 1967, pp. 71–4, 94–101 and 176–8, and his *Novalis' Hymnen an die Nacht. Ihre Deutung nach Inhalt und Aufbau auf textkritischer Grundlage*, Heidelberg, Winter, 1930, with 2nd ed. 1974, vii, 308 pp. The dating in Henry Kamla, *Novalis 'Hymnen an die Nacht'. Zur Deutung und Datierung*, Copenhagen, Munksgaard, 200 pp., has been superseded by Ritter, though the latter's reliance on graphological evidence is not always wholly convincing, but Kamla's critical material is still of much interest.

late whether the quality of some of Novalis's experience—such as the sense of buoyant release from earth—owes anything to outside agents, notably opium.

Essentially what we have in the first four hymns is a mystical vision of a realm outside time and space. The empirical world is symbolized by light, and this too has its claims. (Light can suggest direct sensory perception, as in Classical Antiquity; or the hard glare of rationalism, as in the Enlightenment.) But night, mother of all things, the erotic fount of creation, slackens the grip of the world of objects; we retreat into dreams, which release us from the human condition. Then, in that prolonged dream we call death, we arrive at the realm of absolute freedom, total harmony. Night and death annihilate space and time, to return to a well-worn theme of Novalis's.

In the fifth hymn the symbols are related to the whole course of human history. There is clearly an intentional comparison with Schiller's *Die Götter Griechenlands*, revealing a sharp watershed between Romanticism and the spirit of the late eighteenth century generally and of Classicism. Human destiny, man's fulfilment, is now removed to another world (an aspect reinforced in the sixth hymn). The fifth begins by presenting an ideal picture of a golden age of antiquity, into which the fear of death introduces time and transience. The gods withdraw, nature becomes lonely and lifeless, imagination gives way to rationalism. The coming of Christ, through the Virgin Mother from the womb of night, sees the return of the gods; and Novalis goes to some trouble, by pointing the association with the Magi and by introducing a bard from Greece who makes his way to India, to associate Christianity with other religions. The crucifixion and resurrection then assign a new meaning to death; man can contemplate union with Christ and the Virgin. Unhappily, however, it has to be said that the vision of the new life is conveyed in rhymed stanzas, consciously imitating the congregational hymn, that are wholly inadequate to bear the weight of revelation. The great myth of redemption collapses in conventional banalities of devotion.

The *Hymnen an die Nacht* are of cardinal importance in German Romanticism's creation of its own mythology, where Christian symbolism is associated with natural phenomena and with human psychological states. That they are inimical to good sense has worried few critics, but some, notably Tymms, have found the nostalgic play with the idea of death and the marked element of self-pity actively displeasing. What is a perhaps more strictly literary criticism is that the poems operate too freely in generalities, or in images that are either conventional or subordinated to relatively unsubtle intellectual concepts. One misses the depth of imagery of Hölderlin in his dithyrambic verse; there is little allusiveness, no overpowering sense of composition either verbally or structurally. What does give vitality to the hymns is an impression of total personal involvement, a translation of pathos into a coherent philosophical stance. They move us, but nothing in them burns in our imagination.

Novalis now came to believe that the most complete fulfilment of the poetic function was to be achieved in the Märchen and the novel. Poetic activity is open to all, it is a universal characteristic of the human spirit and he speculates about its function in innumerable fragments. It is the expression of our inner world (*KS* III, 650), where all is united (III, 685); it takes possession of objects (II, 535) and, by doing so, releases them from their adventitious connexions (III, 685). Thus there arise innumerable new combinations (II, 534) and the laws of the symbolic construction of the transcendental world begin to emerge (II, 536). Poetry creates an intimate community of finite and infinite (II, 533). It operates with magic words, ringed with associations (II, 533), with hieroglyphs as yet not interpreted (II, 545); it is mystical and prophetic (III, 685–6), divinatory and magical (II, 533). It presents the world as a universal metaphor of the spirit (II, 600), as matter endowed with sensibility and thus poeticized (III, 640).

The Märchen is the supremely liberating form; it is, as it were, the canon of poetry, in which the poet worships chance (III, 449); it is a disconnected ensemble of wonderful things and events, a kind of musical fantasy (III, 454); it presents the true anarchy of nature (III, 438). By cancelling the order of the present, it can re-establish the harmony of the past, the total intermingling of the natural and spiritual worlds, and point the way to that future golden age in which nature will be spiritualized and redeemed (III, 281). The Märchen's apparent unreality is its significance, for it represents, unrecognized by us, that world of chance and mystery in which we are truly at home (III, 564).

The novel is a connecting stage on the way to Märchen. It has in it elements of the everyday world and of history, both elements foreign to the Märchen, and one finds Novalis making lists of human occupations and social situations, or turning over possible themes set at critical points in history: the destruction of Jerusalem, the Reformation, the discovery of America, the Crusades (*KS* III, 563 and 682–3). The everyday and the historical are, however, no more than stages, even in the novel. Novalis was greatly attracted by the techniques of *Wilhelm Meister* but, in early 1800, he reacted violently against what he came to think of as its 'unpoetic' nature, its 'abandonment of nature and mysticism' (*KS* III, 638–9). His own novel would be different both from *Lucinde* and from *Wilhelm Meister*; what would be depicted in it would be 'transitional years from the infinite to the finite' (*KS* IV, 281). It will be the 'mythology of history' (III, 668), and it was indeed as the creation of a new mythology that some of Novalis's friends prized *Heinrich von Ofterdingen*. Our twentieth-century difficulty is in seeing the result as mythology rather than as self-conscious allegory.

It comes as something of a surprise to learn that the landscape of *Heinrich von Ofterdingen*, at least in the early parts, was inspired by the real world, the scenery at Artern near the Kyffhäuser mountain in Thuringia. Novalis had paid visits there in 1799, when he found the story of the medieval poet, Heinrich von Afterdingen (the spelling Novalis himself always used), in chronicles in the library of an acquaintance, Major von Funk. It was on the second visit, in December of that year, that he began to make notes for the novel, and in less than four months he had finished the first part. The beginning of part two and the sketches for its development were probably written between July and October 1800, in the intervals between his work as a mining engineer. Then his illness worsened and he died in March 1801. Various manuscript notes, later complemented by Tieck's slightly dubious recollections, give some indication of the proposed further course of the novel.

The subject of *Heinrich von Ofterdingen* is poetry and its revelation of a higher world. It is the poet's imagination that can gather together loose connexions and associations and prophetically sense the future harmony of nature and spirit. Thus it is necessary for Heinrich to be, or to grow to be, a poet. He is also to be a full man and, in the second part, he was to become a general, a man of action. As counterpoint to the theme of poetic unity, Novalis, particularly in the early sections, attempts to grapple with the world of concrete situations. These are, however, always viewed symbolically; there is always an ideal purpose, a total rejection of the purely mimetic. There are so many correspondences with the invisible that the world of the senses is increasingly overlaid by them, and everything assumes a dreamlike quality; Novalis indeed makes a good deal of formal use of dreams in the novel. The work opens with a short realistic introduction (the sleeping parents, the clock on the wall, the windows rattling in the wind), followed by Heinrich's monologue, leading gradually to imaginative reverie, to sleep and to extended dream experience, erotically tinged, anticipatory or prophetic in some of its content, and heavily loaded with symbolic elements, particularly that of the blue flower. The subsequent sentimentalizing of the 'blaue Blume', and its indiscriminate application to all forms of romantic yearning, should not be allowed to obscure its importance in *Ofterdingen*. It inaugurates Heinrich's journey and it was apparently meant to be involved in the conclusion, if we are to believe the planning note: 'Flower conversations. Animals. Heinrich... becomes flower—animal—stone—star. Following Jacob Böhme at the end of the book' (*KS* I³, 341 and III, 672). There is no shortage of speculation about the origin of the symbol nor about its interpretation.[11] Correspondences with the magic flower of Thuringian legend, or the blue lotus of India, Dante's rose, Böhme's lilies or Goethe's theory of colour are less important than the general orientation of mysticism and Naturphilosophie towards a view of the natural world as a hieroglyph (*KS* I³, 329). Interpretation may begin at the simplest level by thinking of blue as the colour of infinity, of sea and sky and far mountains (*KS* I³, 205), of longing for something far off. The sense of longing is reinforced by the context in which Heinrich thinks of the blue flower in the first two pages of the novel: it is a longing both for the past, when the flowers could speak, and for a future world, which he has entered in dreams. In its centre it bears the mystery of a girl's face, and recalling this later in the story kindles his love for Mathilde. Part two, and the paralipomena to the novel, lead us into more complexity. Cyane, who partly takes Mathilde's place, represents the blue-flower by her name (cornflower: Greek 'kyanos'=dark blue); she it is who opens the mysterious vistas of confusion of identities, perhaps even of metempsychosis, and of a transcendental progress: 'Wo gehen wir denn hin?' (Where then are we going?), asks Heinrich; 'Immer nach Hause' (Always towards home), she replies (*KS* I³, 325), and the measureless dark blue spaces of heaven open. Heinrich eventually picks the blue flower (which is also Edda=Mathilde=Cyane). He becomes a tree, a stone, a golden ram; and finally, after the purification of sacrifice, a man again (*KS* I³, 348, and III, 678). Thus the flower itself fulfils the high mission of poetry and love, the uniting forces. It represents the mysterious correspondences of nature, through the recognition of which we become one with the natural order and thus, in truth, become ourselves.

This symbol, like many others, becomes progressively more complex, more committed to total synthesis of the most disparate elements, the more the novel advances, or was meant to advance. Much the same is true of the structural organization of the work. The first part operates relatively realistically, with Heinrich being introduced to love and poetry, to representatives of trade, war, the East, aesthetics, though the detail involved is somewhat shadowy. Novalis's picture of the Middle

[11] For the blue flower see: Jutta Hecker, *Das Symbol der blauen Blume im Zusammenhang mit der Blumensymbolik der Romantik*, Jena, Frommann, 1931, 93 pp.; Friedrich Hiebel, 'Zur Interpretation der "blauen Blume" des Novalis', *Monatshefte*, xliii (1951), 327–34, substantially contained in his *Novalis*, 1951, and 2nd ed. 1972, with an additional note in the latter, p. 376; A. Leslie Willson, 'The "Blaue Blume", a New Dimension', *GR*, xxxiv (1959), 50–8, and in his *A Mythical Image: The ideal of India*, 1964, pp. 155–69; Géza von Molnár, 'Another Glance at Novalis' "Blue Flower"', *Euph*, lxvii (1973), 272–86. For a more generalized discussion of flower motifs see Curt Grutzmacher, *Novalis und Philipp Otto Runge*, Munich, Eidos, 1964, pp. 12–25. For blue see Hans Hegener, 'Metaphysik des Blau bei Novalis', *Die Farbe* [Göttingen], xxiv (1975), 131–44.

Ages draws to some extent on Tieck and Wackenroder, but does not distinguish very clearly between the thirteenth and sixteenth centuries.[12] This, in itself, may not greatly matter (what is the date of the action in Kafka's *Schloß?*); Novalis is much more interested in an idealized picture of the Middle Ages as a period of universal productive experience, before knowledge became fragmented or men were parted by separate churches or by nation states. Nor does he intend his characters to be too sharply individualized. They are, rather, variations on given types (a feature he initially admired in *Wilhelm Meister*), representatives of the universal world. We have seen, however, that Novalis does not wish to disregard the world of objects or the common life of man, but vagueness and generality tend to take over in spite of himself. The devices for achieving symbolic depth—*déjà vu* situations, dreams, substitutions, recurring motifs—do indeed point the reader to the reality of Heinrich's inner life; but outwardly he does not engage us on any empathic or narrative level, and the resources of the novel form thus remain imperfectly exploited.

The work, as Novalis wrote to Friedrich Schlegel on 5 April 1800, was to change gradually into a Märchen but, in some respects, the whole novel has this transcendental character.[13] The reconciliation of the external world with the inner occurs through the power of poetry, and this power is prefigured by successive stages of explicit Märchen interpolations: the Orphic legend of Arion, whose sons possessed the direct magic that could create harmony between the elemental powers in nature and man; the invented Atlantis Märchen (although Novalis calls it a 'tale', a 'Geschichte' or an 'Erzählung') in which poetry and love together restore the golden age; and the set-piece complexities of Klingsohr's Märchen with its obvious intention of rivalling Goethe's *Märchen*. This grandiose attempt to symbolize the cosmic setting of man's activities and to show the interplay of past and future is highly characteristic of Novalis's mythic intent, and perhaps of the problematic nature of his achievement. Joyce shows the shadows of Agamemnon or Ulysses

[12] For Tieck see Robert L. Kahn, 'Tieck's *Franz Sternbalds Wanderungen* and Novalis' *Heinrich von Ofterdingen*', *SiR*, vii (1967), 40–64, in spite of the over-enthusiastic search for parallels.

[13] A note for the second part reads: 'Viele Erinnerungen an Märchen ... Wunderliche Mythologie. Die Märchenwelt muß jetzt recht oft durchscheinen. Die wirkliche Welt selbst wie ein Märchen angesehn' (*KS* I³, 343, and III, 674; Many reminiscences of Märchen ... Strange mythology. The world of the Märchen must now frequently shine through. The real world itself regarded as a Märchen).

Johannes Mahr, *Übergang zum Endlichen*, 1970, argues strongly that Heinrich develops towards the particular and finite on each stage of his journey; but to argue thus he has to ignore the fragmentary notes for part two, on the far from negligible grounds of Friedrich Schlegel's report (in a letter of 17 April 1801 to August Wilhelm) that Novalis, on the last day of his life, had told him that he had entirely changed his plans.

looming behind the citizenry in the bars of Dublin; Novalis sets deities and personified natural forces alongside human representatives. What tends to reduce Klingsohr's Märchen to ingenious allegorizing is the inhuman, totally abstract nature of the supposedly human figures. There is some mystification and contrived obscurity (references to 'dark connexions', 'dark speeches', 'dark—opaque—confused'; *KS* I³, 337, 341; III, 672), coupled no doubt with genuine puzzlement about the course of his own thoughts; but there are also, in the paralipomena and in a letter of 18 June 1800 to Friedrich Schlegel, numerous clues as to the significance of the characters. Thus their impersonality is confirmed and Novalis himself partially refutes those critics who insist that the Märchen should not be interpreted allegorically—though over-simplified equations must, of course, be resisted. 'Not too strictly allegorical' is his note for himself (*KS* I³, 342; II, 673). What is, however, beyond question is that there are many conscious symbols drawn from galvanism, alchemy, astrology and mineralogy, or developed from Jacob Böhme, Giordano Bruno, Indian and Nordic mythology, or the Revelation of St John.

Klingsohr's Märchen points to the development and planned apotheosis of part two of the novel. This is introduced by a series of couplets suggesting the transforming, poeticizing process that is to take place. 'A new world will break in; time and space will no longer order everything; God's image will be on plants and stones; the world will become a dream, and the dream the world' (*KS* I³, 318–19). As Heinrich experiences Antiquity, war, the East, the life of a monastery, a broad spectrum of human activities in history, we find time and space melting away. The characters of the novel become identified with those of the Märchen, the kingdom of the sun is destroyed and the seasons are united, as in Böhme's paradise. Heinrich has taken on the role of Fabel, the figure in the Märchen but also 'poetry', and has poeticized the real world; he has released the spiritual in the world of objects. All connexions are re-established, all limitations are annulled. That the scheme remained a fragment was not a consequence of the difficulty of portraying these mysterious correspondences; *Heinrich von Ofterdingen* remained unfinished because Novalis became mortally ill. Thus we can only dimly discern the outlines of what would have been his *Faust* Part Two.

In the years after his death, Novalis was imitated by some very bad poets, like Otto Heinrich Graf von Loeben, which brought forth sharp satirical reaction.[14] Both the admiration and the criticism were based on wrong assumptions about his work; ethereal and sentimental enthusiasm and reverie were the keynotes derived from the biography. What we now see behind the sometimes vague rhetoric and the conditioned

[14] See Leif Ludwig Albertsen, 'Novalismus', *GRM*, xlviii (1967), 272–85.

imagery of the period is a profoundly disturbing modern figure, attempting nothing less than a total reordering of experience. Novalis used mathematics to make daring speculations about functions and relationships, about the nature of infinity and continuity, about the present as the point at which past and future meet. In the physical world it is not wholly fanciful to find in his thoughts faint approximations to the wave theory of matter or even to the general theory of relativity. These scientific insights are then all related to the inner history of man and nature; one continually finds such statements as: 'Space spills over into time, like the body into the soul' (*KS* III, 458).

Novalis's scientific modernity is matched by the innovatory aspects of his poetic theory and, to a lesser extent, of his practice. 'The separation of the poet from the thinker is an illusion—and is to their mutual disadvantage' (*KS* III, 406). Werner Vordtriede[15] has shown how the French Symbolists were his legitimate inheritors in the descent into the inner life, in the correspondences with nature, in the attempt to express the inexpressible, as well as in the employment of particular motifs and symbolic forms. The magical function of poetry; the deliberate creation of chaos, or of an alogical sequence; the role of chance and of abstraction; the conscious mathematical constructs; the associative techniques; the decipherment of the world by transposing into the transcendental—many of these possibilities the modern poet has learned indirectly from Novalis.

What must seem odd is that the claims made for Novalis are accompanied by serious reservations about his poetic productions. The very difficulty of the intellectual exploration, it may be said, exposed the inadequacies of his attempts at also reforming and developing the genres through which he tried to express it. He could not both change the world and the novel. So he remains the vivid creator (with Friedrich Schlegel) of a new, revolutionary and still only partly accepted form, the fragment.

---

[15] Werner Vordtriede, *Novalis und die französischen Symbolisten. Zur Entstehungsgeschichte des dichterischen Symbols*, Stuttgart, Kohlhammer, 1963, 196 pp. See also, but treat with some reserve, Hugo Friedrich, *Die Struktur der modernen Lyrik. Von Baudelaire bis zur Gegenwart*, Hamburg, Rowohlt, 1956, 214 pp.

5

The Legacy of Myth:
The Grimms, Brentano and Arnim

The rejuvenation of the University of Heidelberg in the years immediately following the city's transfer to the Grand Duchy of Baden in 1802 created a new centre for Romanticism. The so-called 'Heidelberger Romantik', less rational and encyclopaedic than the Jena group, more physically aware of the seductions of the past and of the natural world, should perhaps be defined as Brentano, Arnim and Görres, with the Grimm brothers as absent friends. The most eloquent evocation of the golden period around 1808 is that by Eichendorff, looking back in later years, but he is the inheritor of the group rather than one of the close circle.[1]

In the Heidelberg years the great unifying experience is that of folk culture, whether expressed in song or chapbook, Märchen or myth, superstitions or customs; and one can see how, sharpening Herder's equation of folk or 'natural' poetry with genuine poetry, they wished to authenticate the national spirit in the shadow of French domination. Arnim's short-lived periodical, the *Zeitung für Einsiedler*, April to August 1808 and republished as a book *Trösteinsamkeit* later that year, Joseph Görres's *Die teutschen Volksbücher* (1807) and the *Deutsche Sagen* of Jacob and Wilhelm Grimm (1816 and 1818) are important evidences of both the creative and the scholarly-antiquarian concern with folk culture; but we must confine ourselves to the two most influential and widely known collections: *Des Knaben Wunderhorn* (1805 and 1808) and the Grimm *Kinder- und Hausmärchen* of 1815 and 1819.

The origins of the *Wunderhorn* may well lie in the singing that Arnim and Brentano heard on their Rhine journey in 1802; certainly there is

[1] Eichendorff's essay *Halle und Heidelberg* (1857). See also Herbert Levin, *Die Heidelberger Romantik*, Munich, Parcus, 1922, 153 pp., and Richard Benz, *Heidelberg—Schicksal und Geist*, Constance, Jan Thorbecke, 1961, 480 pp.

a suggestion that tunes were at first intended to accompany the poems.[2] A freshness and spontaneity, a poetic expression of primitive unity and freedom from the complexities and greyness of modern life, shine through the folksong for them. Yet the stress is on the poetry, and the collecting process is far removed from the niceties of scholarship. It is now clear that very few of the songs were taken from oral sources by Brentano and none by Arnim. No more than about one song in six was included unaltered and about the same number were wholly written by one of the editors. Very many of them are versions from old chronicles, or of folksong fly-sheets, or of popular poems from the sixteenth and seventeenth centuries, from Opitz, Spee, Gerhardt and others. What the two were primarily interested in was the poetic impulse, which they felt beating in themselves as in the folksongs and other poems of their collection. Brentano, in particular, was concerned with imaginative reconstruction, with absorption into his own poetic creativity. Arnim also saw the individual poet's imaginative power breaking out at all periods and available to reinforce that of any other true poet, so he was able to appropriate and adapt as he wished; but he was more conscious of the nationalist, patriotic background to his editorial activity. In both, however, the intention behind this ordering of hymns to nature, love songs, riddles, drawing-room ballads, apprentices' and hermits' songs and the like, was less a folkloristic one than an attempt to create a work of art.

The brothers Jacob and Wilhelm Grimm have, in theory and to a certain extent in practice, an altogether sterner view of the claims of folk literature. In friendly but firm correspondence with Arnim, Jacob Grimm maintained that folk literature was composed collectively, in a way not wholly explicable but dependent on its status as the heir of myth, itself related to divine revelation. The further we move from the mythical, paradisal past, the greater the deterioration, and the obvious corollary is that the closer we can get to origins, the better. However sceptical modern scholarship may be of this view, it did undoubtedly lead the Grimms to an attempt at scholarly reconstruction that extends from lexicography and grammar, to collecting legends and folktales, and to the editing of a great number of early German and other texts.

The brothers started collecting folktales as part of their contribution to *Des Knaben Wunderhorn* and, indeed, were prepared to have Brentano publish what they had assembled. When he failed to do so, they went ahead themselves and the first volume appeared in 1812, furnished with

[2] Brentano's letter to Arnim on 15 February 1805, suggesting a folksong collection, mentions the musician Johann Friedrich Reichardt as a possible collaborator; see Erich Stockmann, *Des Knaben Wunderhorn in den Weisen seiner Zeit*, Berlin, Akademie, 1958, p. 8. Anything written about the *Wunderhorn* must, however, remain provisional until the two volumes of notes by Heinz Rölleke are available in the new Brentano edition.

scholarly notes. Most, though by no means all, of the tales were taken from oral tradition and, in circulars distributed to possible collectors, Jacob stressed the need for authentic reproductions. (His Vienna circular of 1815 is the founding document of modern folklore studies.) After the second volume in 1815 Jacob, the more precise scholar, withdrew to his other work and Wilhelm not only added but revised quite considerably for the second (1819) and subsequent editions. Even Jacob, however, had not reproduced the tales word for word as transmitted; there were, after all, many variant versions—mere fragments, as they thought, of the mythological past.

What the brothers did was to put the content into a literary form which was partly based on the two tales in Low German that the painter Philipp Otto Runge had taken down from some fishermen in Pomerania, and partly their own invention, following, it would appear, some of their own speech habits. Wilhelm went rather further in the direction of embellishment, psychological motivation, the elimination of over-specific space and time indicators, clarifying the narrative structure, heightening the effect and, to some degree, adapting either to the prevailing mores or for children.[3] In detail, he stylized by frequently substituting the imperfect for the present tense or direct for indirect speech or by transposing into dialogue, by eliminating foreign, and often also dialectical, expressions, by introducing proverbs and popular sayings, by repetition of words and phrases and the use of alliteration and onomatopoeia. Thus, in succeeding editions, there was created that childlike and limpid narrative style that so influenced later Romantics, and that set the tone for all future Märchen. Far from being a routine compilation the *Kinder- und Hausmärchen* are a careful aesthetic construct.

Brentano

Whipped by the gales of the imagination, Brentano reached out for human warmth, fled to the protection of faith, or longed for a renewal of wholeness, not least within his own psyche. His life is a wavering between magical feelings of endless possibilities, religious enthusiasm bordering on mania, sarcastic and malicious *jeux d'esprit*, deception and self-deception, and the profoundest melancholy. In a draft of a letter to Fouqué in 1812 he compared his past life to a harp played by the wind, untuned by shifts of weather, and played so passionately *forte* by love that the strings are all torn (*Briefe* II, 157; *W* I, 1208). Mother

---

[3] Though the Märchen were not initially designed for children, the Grimms were pleased that children (for instance, those of Savigny and Görres) enjoyed them, and the 'little edition' of fifty of the tales, first issued in 1825, became an enormously popular children's book.

figures, harlots and a stigmatized visionary obsess him; a confining marriage is followed by a disastrous one; and even his love for his sister Bettina (shown in all its tenderness in the *Frühlingskranz aus Jugendbriefen ihm geflochten*, which she published to his memory in 1844) was clouded in later years. There is, at least in youth, something of the charming but malevolent child.

The biographical details are significant not only in themselves, but because they have coloured critical views of Brentano ever since. Born in 1778 into a wealthy merchant family, he toyed with trade and the professions but never really needed to earn his living. Friendship and literary collaboration with Arnim, an ambivalent but powerfully influential acquaintance with the Jena group, close association with Tieck (who had never met anyone who could improvise so well, nor lie so graciously and charmingly) and Görres—these provide the male acccompaniment to the female friendships. Towards the end of 1815 he had a crisis of language and poetic imagination, and this was followed by a return to the Catholicism of his childhood and a renunciation, for the time being, of poetic production. Then came the years spent at Dülmen, a small town near Münster, as scribe for the visions of the nun, Anna Katharina Emmerick, five astonishing, weary but exalted years at her bedside; then, after her death, a wandering life and a continuing conflict between the old scornful, passionate, satirical, capricious, worldly Brentano and the religious propagandist, dispenser of alms, historian of the Sisters of Mercy, friend of cardinals, consciously resisting the daemonic forces still throbbing within. The world itself had moved on, from the faintly rococo atmosphere that still surrounded his youth to the grim and earnest utilitarianism of the Restoration period. Recent criticism has attempted to show how his versions of A. K. Emmerick's visions, published as *Das bittere Leiden unsers Herrn Jesu Christi* (1833) and *Leben der heiligen Jungfrau Maria* (posthumously in 1852), have in them elements of social and political criticism, as for instance of the Metternich formula 'Ruhe und Ordnung' (civil peace and good order).[4] At all events, there is now a readiness to see in these highly popular, if for most readers anonymous, works an imaginative and mythologizing power still in action, as it undoubtedly is in the late versions of the Märchen and the religio-erotic lyrics inspired by a new love, Emilie Linder, painter and patron of the arts. Certainly the 'liberal' view that his later years were those of a simple-minded religious fanatic, of no interest to literature, is no longer seriously entertained. Nor indeed does the pious interpretation fostered by his friends after his death in 1843, with every effort made to show him growing to spiritual perfection, arouse any greater response.

[4] See Wolfgang Frühwald, 'Clemens Brentano', *DDRW*, p. 298.

What is to be seen, rather, is the wound in his life, forming and re-forming as the outer world and the movement of history dictate.

One other word before we come to the works themselves. A very great deal remains unpublished: many thousands of diary papers from the Dülmen period but also much in the way of letters, drafts of creative works, early plays and other material. Any picture of Brentano's achievement must therefore to some extent remain provisional until the new critical edition in some fifty volumes has made further progress.

The novel *Godwi oder das steinerne Bild der Mutter. Ein verwildeter Roman* was written between 1798 and 1800 and published in two parts in 1801 under the name 'Maria'. It shows clearly the effects of reading *Wilhelm Meister*, Heinse, Jean Paul and Tieck, but is essentially an attempt to write a novel from Friedrich Schlegel's recipe. There is certainly some influence from *Lucinde* itself, particularly in the general atmosphere of erotic freedom, but the challenge of Schlegel's poetics of the novel, notably in *Athenäum* Fragment 116, is more potent. The artist's freedom to distance himself from his creation, to break in and out of illusion, to create a chaotic but systematic whole, these are the structural principles underlying *Godwi*. It is the theory of the 'arabesque', that apparently capricious and confusing form of ornamentation that is nevertheless controlled by the most careful artistry. The confusion is in the tangled web of relationships (the wild, uncultivated garden implied in the subtitle); the structure lies in the perspectivism that is explicitly discussed in the novel. Godwi indeed defines the romantic as being a perspective, an optical glass or as lying in the colours of the glass, in the refractive process (*W* II, 258–9).

Thus the work is, in its first part, an epistolary novel with many of the letters written by Godwi or his friend Römer; but, in the second part, Maria, who had been given the correspondence to edit by Römer in order to earn the hand of his daughter, visits Godwi to ask for advice in continuing the story. Römer, the prospective father-in-law, is not happy with the way in which Maria, the author, has arranged part one. Godwi and Maria then pass in review much of what we have seen in part one, clarifying as required ('This is the pond into which I fall on page [146] of the first volume', *W* II, 307); that is to say, a character explains matters to the fictive author and tells him how to proceed. Then, in a fragmentary continuation, Maria dies and Godwi gives an account of his death (the name Maria being masculine here), while Brentano identifies himself with Maria in an addendum. Undoubtedly these changes of perspective cast different light on persons and images; and the interweavings combine with an attempted use of the non-literary arts (as in descriptions of paintings or statuary) to create, or to attempt to create, a synthesis, a reflection of the totality of existence.

The structural experiments have, however, no real metaphysical commitment; the themes remain thin and isolated; the characters are as wooden as they are elaborately confusing; the plot is deeply uninteresting. The discussions are endless and, though the prose is supple, the descriptions of the natural world are too often pallid and generalized. What nevertheless makes the novel more than a theorist's plaything is precisely the inter*play*. Tempestuous though Brentano's moods were, and autobiographical though the erotic pilgrimage to different manifestations of womanhood in *Godwi* may be, and however conscious the attempt to re-establish lost paradise in motif and allegory, what finally emerges is the playful, marvellously disengaged atmosphere of the lyrical novel, shot through with poems of great evocative power, including 'Sprich aus der Ferne' and his 'Lureley', the poem that really created the legend.[5]

Two dramatic drafts from the *Godwi* context remain unpublished, but by 1800 he had already seen his drama *Gustav Wasa* in print. This is more Tieckean than Tieck, labouring under devastatingly unfunny puns and general word-play, and is now of interest only as a rather dud fusillade in the Romantics' war with Kotzebue. *Ponce de Leon* (dated 1804, though appearing in 1803) deserves more attention, if only for its influence on Büchner's *Leonce und Lena*, and for Ponce's claim to be one of the earliest exemplars of disharmony, that fruitful strand in later nineteenth-century literature. A shortened version had one performance at the Burgtheater in Vienna in 1814, but the conflict between the demands of language and the necessities of drama disqualify it for the stage. The characters are puppets playing with words, often sparkling in themselves, but seldom advancing action or establishing personality. The relentless stream of puns, false etymologies, comic homonyms, double meanings, deformations of proverbs and any conceivable form of word-play eventually deadens the spirit. The verbal fireworks fail to illuminate, the words respond to the author, not to the character.

One other drama may be mentioned here *Die Gründung Prags* (1814) written after a period spent on his family's property in Bohemia. First impressions are of a laborious, lengthy and bookish reconstruction of the Libussa legend, in rhymed iambic pentameters and forbiddingly complicated into the bargain. But Brentano is also exercising a prophetic role and attempting to recreate a unifying Slav myth, incorporating nature mysticism, fate and divination, pre-feudal social structures and the impact of Christianity. The sweep of the intention has captivated some critics, but the achievement has interested few readers and no spectators, and the play remains a great quarry of antiquarian detail and symbolic

[5] A note on the various versions of the legend may be found in Jürgen Kolbe, *Ich weiß nicht was soll es bedeuten. Heinrich Heines Loreley*, Munich, Hanser, 1976, 48 pp. See also Heinz Politzer, 'Das Schweigen der Sirenen', *DVLG*, xli (1967), 444–67.

reference impossible to stage. Its loosely related scenes hover in their effect between opera and oratorio; heathen festivals, visionary prophecies or folk traditions take on a musical, sometimes almost incantatory form.

No mythic or harmonizing purposes underlie Brentano's Märchen, at least in their early form. The original intention to collect German Märchen in the same way as folksongs soon gave way to invention (most of the Rhine tales) and adaptation (the Italian tales of Basile's *Pentamerone*). Brentano thought little of Grimm's Märchen, many of which he considered carelessly told, their simplicity spoilt by gracelessness, in contrast to Runge's Märchen. The Grimms, on the other hand, found his over-decorative and not faithful to the spirit of the folktale. There is, for that matter, no reason why they should be. Brentano certainly uses plenty of motifs from the folktales: kings and princesses, stepmothers, talking animals, magic rings, earth spirits; his Märchen, too, tend to open with the formulaic narrative statement of time or place ('Es war einmal' or 'Once upon a time'); but, in between, the exuberance of language takes over: baroque metaphors or word clusters, innumerable rhetorical devices, sensuous imagery, sometimes synaesthetic, or grotesque correspondences. All is child's play; into the stories he unloads all his own childlike extravagances, but he also recreates the magic of a child's untroubled eye.

His own attitude towards the Märchen was profoundly ambivalent: rather half-hearted attempts at publication before the Dülmen period and rejection of their playfulness afterwards. In two instances, rejection is cancelled by rewriting. *Gockel, Hinkel und Gackeleia* was written as *Gockel und Hinkel* in 1815 or 1816, but this early version remained unpublished until 1846 (the manuscript, discovered in 1923, has since allowed the establishment of an improved text). After 1835 Brentano greatly expanded the Märchen, weaving complex patterns around events and ornamenting the plainest descriptions with rich detail, but above all providing a religious dimension, both in running additions with a devotional or Biblical flavour and in the loosely connected *Blätter aus dem Tagebuch der Ahnfrau* that appeared with the new version on its publication in 1838. The *Tagebuch* repeats several times and then ends with the couplet that has become a Brentano motto:

> O Stern und Blume, Geist und Kleid,
> Lieb, Leid und Zeit und Ewigkeit![6]

Elisabeth Stopp has convincingly shown this to be a subtle and emb-

---

[6] 'O star and flower, spirit and garment, love, sorrow and time and eternity!', *W* III, 930, and I, 619. See Elisabeth Stopp, 'Brentano's "O Stern und Blume": Its Poetic and Emblematic Context', *MLR*, lxvii (1972), 95–117.

lematically charged expression of meditation on the meaning of Christ's redemptive activity. Thus it sums up what Brentano had earlier wished to achieve in *Die Romanzen vom Rosenkranz*, the restoration of paradisal unity. The *Romanzen* were written between 1804 and 1812, twenty of the planned twenty-four being completed, but not published until 1852. He had wanted to issue them with lithographs by Runge, and his letters to the painter in 1810, the year of the latter's death, are important documents for his poetic intentions. He wished Runge to allegorize the feelings the poems aroused in him, to provide arabesque ornamentation that would be hieroglyphs of the poet's purpose.[7] This purpose, one may gather, was to exemplify the unifying powers of Christian myth (though often expressed somewhat narrowly in the Catholic guise of candles, holy water, splinters of the cross and, of course, the rosary). The ostensible subject-matter is the lifting of an old and hereditary curse, a consequence of an incestuous relationship; but superimposed on this there is, or was meant to be, a web of fable (Tannhäuser), history (the pilgrimages and the crusades), astronomy, magic and cabbalism, autobiography, religiosity and eroticism, reminiscences of Calderón and Goethe's *Faust*. Good and evil, God and the devil, the dualism after the Fall, these are the structural basis of the labyrinthine plan with its myriad combinations, scholarly extravaganzas and flowering of imaginative language. Of the poetic power of isolated passages there can be no doubt and what will later be said of his lyrics applies equally to the *Romanzen*; it is the whole that seems less than the sum of its parts.

Before we turn to the lyrics, on which his reputation chiefly rests, we must say something about the Novelle that is still his best-known prose work. The *Geschichte vom braven Kasperl und dem schönen Annerl*, written in 1816 or 1817, is at first reading an uneasy combination of two strands. The genesis may have been, as tradition indicates, two stories told by the mother of Luise Hensel (the eighteen-year-old girl with whom Brentano fell in love when he first saw her in October 1816 and who later became a lyric poet of some achievement). To these must be added suggestions from folksongs and popular anecdotes. The effect is of a Storm and Stress infanticide horror-story laced with considerations of honour reminiscent of Lessing's Tellheim but also of Corneille or Spanish drama. Some have claimed to see in the story the first German Dorfgeschichte or village tale; but though there may at times be something of a rural atmosphere and some degree of interest in peasant life these are

[7] 'einem solchen Künstler [clearly referring to Runge himself], glaubte ich, könne es lustig sein, mit freien Federzügen aus einzelnen festen Gestalten dieser Lieder jene Beziehungen zu Heiligerem symbolisierend herauszubilden und hindeutend zu begleiten', *Briefe* II, 23, and p. 55 in the usefully annotated *Clemens Brentano, Philipp Otto Runge Briefwechsel*, ed. Konrad Feilchenfeldt, Frankfurt, Insel, 1974, 119 pp.; anticipated in his 'Clemens Brentano und Runge: Aus ungedruckten Briefen', *JDSG*, xvi (1972), 1–36.

secondary features. Nor are the numerous attempts to fit the work into a normative Novelle pattern in any way illuminating.

The story's power lies in its own inner coherence, strained though that may be in its ending. Brentano creates, in the dual narration by the grandmother and the 'writer', a model of his own dualistic experience of the world. The framework is provided by the 'writer' (who is so uncertain of himself that he can, when questioned by the old woman, only dare to call himself a 'scribe'—Schreiber) and when he takes a decisive part in the action there are signs of strain, confusion and rush in spite of all his good will.[8] The grandmother, however, brings into the present both echoes of a primitive past and a gaze fixed on eternity. Everything runs together in her world: superstition and myth, fate and daemonic forces, the everyday and the supernatural, the fear and the hope of death. Alewyn's glittering exegesis of the work shows how everything in her world is repetition, how the story contains a whole network of correspondences and assonances, not least the recurring motifs: rose, veil, apron, teeth. The coexistences of time are intimately reflected in the structure of the story; the shock of recognition of the approaching execution swings the perspective from the past to the future, and that future converges on the day of judgement.

The ending has convinced few; does it harmonize or emphasize the different views of life? Is the statuary a Romantic prop, an evocation of Catholic Nazarene art, or an ironic criticism of contemporary 'artistic' doctrines? It is difficult not to feel that the rapid denouement, from the grandmother's opportune death at the grave (with all the neatness of her joining Kasperl and Annerl at this junction of heaven and earth) to the likenesses of the Duke and the Princess on the monument, comes perilously close to trivializing the whole.

To turn to the lyrics is to enter a world in which the life of language is all. Many, of course, are too easily achieved, too dependent on fluency and a remarkable sense of sound pattern, too diffuse or, in the later poems, too bland. It is also useful to distinguish between periods of his poetic production, particularly as one needs to recognize the extent to which he remoulded his own work, both in the pietistic Berlin period around 1816 and in the period after Dülmen, in order to invest the poems with new layers of religious significance. Nor must one tear poems from their context in narrative or drama.

Some characteristics are nevertheless fairly generally applicable to his

[8] John M. Ellis, *Narration in the German Novelle. Theory and Interpretation*, 1974, p. 31, has a tart comment on the relationship between the narration and the thematic structure. There is none, because the thematic content is crude, a monotonous handling of the concept of honour. 'Having given us a story with this rather uninteresting thematic content, Brentano overlays it with artistic effects (notably the narrative scheme) to keep our interest. Superficial artistic gloss is introduced to make up for lack of real content.'

poems, though almost defying precise identification. It is not difficult to say that some of the poems ('Lureley', for instance) have affinities to the folksong in their apparent simplicity of diction. Similarly one can point to frequent echoes of earlier German poems. Goethe, Spee, Middle High German poetry, Hölderlin, the list is as extensive as his reading. Then there are the complexes of images that refer back to emblem books or sideways to the visual arts. The Romantic view of music as the integrating force synthesizing all the arts has also been traced in some detail in its working out, whether consciously or unconsciously, in Brentano.

If one takes as an example 'Der Spinnerin Nachtlied' from *Aus der Chronika eines fahrenden Schülers* (1818, though the first draft dates from 1802) one can see the motifs, the restricted vocabulary, the repetitions and simple emotional states of the folksong reinforced by the rhyme scheme and the colour of the vowels—the recurring 'a' tonality expressing remembrance of happier days and the 'ei' evoking abandonment and sorrow. The poem, that is to say, is a highly conscious production aiming at a naive effect:

> Es sang vor langen Jahren
> Wohl auch die Nachtigall,
> Das war wohl süßer Schall,
> Da wir zusammen waren.

It seems, as critics have said, really to sing itself, to be pure lyric substance.[9]

Yet how can this be? What is it that forms the special quality of 'Sprich aus der Ferne' or 'Säusle liebe Mirte' or 'Hörst du wie die Brunnen rauschen'? How can they mean so much and say so little? Certainly they neither describe nor represent, except in the vaguest and most detached way. They depend on sound largely divorced from reference, yet they are surely more than ' 'Twas brillig, and the slithy toves'.

Hans Magnus Enzensberger has attempted a solution showing how words torn from their customary meaning become newly available for poetry and reveal fresh and significant associations (the process is one he calls 'Entstellung'). These new evocations serve a hermetic world, with its own laws, where multiple meaning and the dissolution of boundaries between subject and object take over. Brentano thus becomes the precursor of much in modern poetry that relies heavily on grammatical distortion, syntactic shock and associative identification.

One may not give wholehearted assent to this view of Brentano's totally innovative role,[10] but the concept of a deliberate attempt to create

---

[9] 'Many years ago the nightingale must have sung, and it would have been a sweet sound, for we were together' (*W* I, 131, and II, 525–6 and 613).

[10] Enzensberger has come in for some rough handling, especially since the unrevised

a poem whose laws—including those of acoustic-semantic identification—lie within itself is reinforced by the deliberately enigmatic character of some of the lyrics. Their enciphering, hieroglyphic nature both reveals and conceals. They are to be understood from within themselves; though it must be added that critics who most urgently emphasize this do manage to import a good deal of Brentano biography into their interpretations. This is natural enough; Brentano knew he was operating on the frontiers of language, where tonal values, associative echoes and cognitive function meet. Thus his recurrent linguistic crises, his despair of communication, his panic as to whether words in themselves can be enough; these provide much of the energy and of the haunting character of his work.

Arnim

It is now widely accepted that Arnim is the most unjustly neglected of the Romantic writers. His achievement as co-editor of *Des Knaben Wunderhorn* has, of course, always been recognized, perhaps even exaggerated; but, like Percy's *Reliques*, the *Wunderhorn* is now literary history rather than living literature. His novels and dramas, and most of the Novellen, have long been damned by praise of the intention and condemnation of its formless execution. Many saw in him a clash between the romantic and the realist, between fantasy and history. His contemporaries marvelled at his facility and the range of his imagination, but they too were disconcerted by the apparent extravagance and carelessness of construction, by the heterogeneity of the formal patterns and the confusion of character and myth. Indeed the most widely appreciated of all his works has generally been the agreeable but relatively slight Novelle *Der tolle Invalide*.

For a century and a half it was customary to think of Arnim's literary problems in biographical terms. Ludwig Achim von Arnim had been born in 1781 in Berlin into an aristocratic Protestant family with property at Wiepersdorf in Mark Brandenburg. University studies in the law and natural sciences, with a modest but respectable book *Versuch einer Theorie der elektrischen Erscheinungen* (1799), yielded in Göttingen to literary interests and friendships. Here in the late spring of 1801 he met Brentano, whose sister Bettina he was later to marry. *Hollins Liebeleben* (1802), with its echoes of *Werther* and *Lucinde* rather toned down in an

---

reissuing of his study, on the grounds of textual errors and also of inadequate examination of the sources of some of the apparent linguistic dislocations. See, for instance, Siegfried Sudhof, 'Brentanos Gedicht "O schweig nur Herz!... Zur Tradition sprachlicher Formen und poetischer Bilder', *ZDP*, xcii (1973), 211–31, and Gajek at many points in his *Homo Poeta*, 1971.

epilogue, followed as his first novel. Nearly three years on a Grand Tour showed him not only Europe at a crucial point in history but introduced him to the natural splendours and folk history of Switzerland (*Aloys und Rose*, 1803) and the picturesque landscapes and history of Scotland—partly mediated through Walter Scott—and Wales, to which he much later returned in two Novellen, *Die Ehenschmiede* and *Owen Tudor*. One other consequence of his visit to Scotland was an acquaintance with Scott's *Minstrelsy of the Scottish Border*, the collection of ballads into which a good deal of Scott's own creative work went during the process of editing.

Arnim was always conscious of standing at the crossroads of history, and under the dome of heaven. His Prussian patriotism, in some sense an extension of his concern for the German past, expressed itself in his *Kriegslieder* (1805) but also, coupled with his conservatism and anti-semitism, to the founding of the 'Christian-German Dining Club' in Berlin in 1811,[11] with Adam Müller, Brentano, Kleist and Fichte among its members. Yet the society's primary purpose was probably social and Arnim's conservatism was by no means that of a plain aristocratic reactionary. His withdrawal in 1814 to his estate in Wiepersdorf, where he remained until his death in 1831, is evidence of his distaste for policies aimed merely at the restoration of the status quo. It was on the interplay of tradition and renewal that Arnim based any hopes for the future. He wrote of the new as surgery and the old as medicine, both necessary,[12] and it is the organic growth of a new order that forms the subject of his two ambitious, if flawed novels, *Gräfin Dolores* (1810) and *Die Kronenwächter* (1817 for the first volume; the fragmentary second volume was not published until 1854).

Armut, Reichtum, Schuld und Buße der Gräfin Dolores takes the marriage of Graf Karl and Dolores and makes of it an image of society's sickness and the possibilities of therapy. An opening scene of remarkable beauty shows two residences near each other, one a turreted, black, forbidding castle, the other a light, airy, Italianate palace in a green garden. On closer inspection, however, the palace where Dolores and her sister live is seen to be neglected and defaced, ransacked by the mob and commandeered by soldiers. The old castle gives the narrator 'what people are accustomed to call a romantic feeling; it removes us from the sharp clarity of daily life to that dawn of history to which in secret we still

[11] The essential documents dealing with the 'Christlich-Deutsche Tischgesellschaft' are handily assembled in *Heinrich von Kleists Lebansspuren. Dokumente und Berichte der Zeitgenossen*, 2nd edition by Helmut Sembdner, Bremen, Schünemann, 1964, xiv, 557 pp., see pp. 404–9.

[12] 'Mit einem Bilde gesagt, jene neuere Zeit ist die Chirurgie zur Besserung der Welt, jene ältere Zeit die Medicin. Aber beyde sind nothwendig.' From the 1806 essay 'Was soll geschehen im Glücke', edited by Jörn Gores in *JDSG*, v (1961), 196–221.

cling' (*SRE* I, 11). The mood is set for the confrontation between consciousness of the past, binding us to a universal world of harmony and order, and the forces of disintegration in the age of revolution. Dolores is unfaithful to her husband for the first time on the fourteenth of July, the day the French Revolution may be said to have started with the storming of the Bastille. It is easy enough to represent this as a plea for feudalism and a rejection of progress; the new palace, after all, burns to the ground later in the novel and its ruins lie there in sight of the old castle, 'like those of some frivolous age in decline, penitent and apologetic face to face with the more permanent, recurrent and unassuming' (*SRE* I, 373). The individual marriage, too, is seen as creating and mirroring the structure of society; the revised version of *Hollins Liebeleben* incorporated in the novel extols the laws of God and man, the virtues of civil order.

Nevertheless there is another dimension in the novel, implicit in its form rather than directly expressed. There is, it is true, room for some caution here. It is known that most of this long novel was written, or in some sections cobbled together, in little more than two months, immediately after the publication of Goethe's *Wahlverwandschaften*. Arnim's contemporaries thought the novel characteristically chaotic: he works almost entirely without plan, putting in anecdotes and episodes as they strike his fancy, with no thought of the whole (Tieck); the disorder in his books is the same as that in all his affairs (Brentano); a lunatic confusion ... a hell from which there is no redemption (Goethe).[13] *Gräfin Dolores* has some twenty interpolated anecdotes, retold legends or folk-tales, dramatic pieces, even a novel; and then there are sixty or more poems. It is all distinctly unpromising.

Yet this confusion is not purposeless; the meaning of the novel cannot be divorced from the sum of its richness and variety, even if we grant readily enough that not all interpolated scenes are judiciously fitted and balanced and that sheer exuberance is sometimes the uncomplicated progenitor. The form is not that of a patchwork quilt, still less the mosaic that some have called it; the principle is accretion. Arnim himself justifies his departure from a straight narrative path with the claim that what is important in a story is contact with everything, 'so that every event becomes our own, and lives on in us, a perpetual witness to the fact that all life stems from the one and returns to the one' (*SRE* I, 425–6). However strange and varied the forms may be, the very heterogeneity is itself reconciling.

[13] Rudolf Köpke, *Ludwig Tieck*, 2 vols, Leipzig, 1855, II, 203; Brentano letter of 2 November 1810 to the brothers Grimm, *Briefe* II, 53; Goethe letter to C. F. von Reinhard, 2 October 1810, *Goethe und die Romantik*, ed. Carl Schüddekopf and Oskar Walzel, Weimar, 1899 (=Schriften der Goethe-Gesellschaft, 13–14), II, 343.

In the earlier part of the novel Karl and Dolores live out the old and new values; around them disturbing contemporary figures, often satirically based on recognizable models, represent arid or destructive trends in modern life. Figures from the past emerge with greater difficulty, in visions, myths, fables or songs, to support the reconciliation of husband and wife. When Karl finds Dolores again in the monastery chapel they are brought nearer each other than ever before by their 'contact with that higher world that draws to itself thousands who here remain separated from one another' (*SRE* I, 323). Arnim's concern is to introduce this higher world into the stream of history and he attempts to do this by reaching back to a primitive past for universal, unifying models. His purpose is no less than to give meaning to the present. The interaction of the old and new has been shattered by the French Revolution, a re-enactment of the Fall. Yet, as he writes of Dolores, 'every sinner carries within himself a lost paradise';[14] so also do society and history. The poet, as he draws into one net the rich variety of things, begins to restore paradisal integrity.

Echoes of Schelling on history and mythology may well be heard here, and they recur in the preface to *Die Kronenwächter*, where the permanence of 'spirit' shines mysteriously through history into poetry. Literary creation does more than reproduce the kind of truth we expect from history; it is an insight born of the past's spilling over into the present, a reminiscence of the spirit as it once took form on earth, a vehicle to lead the world back to communion. What Arnim would have claimed he was trying to create was a condition in which visions of the past, when man was nearer to spirit and was able to read the signatures of the Creator more clearly, can illuminate the present. What he writes is not a historical novel but a work in which real and ideal can mingle, in an attempt at the spiritual regeneration of his own age, a parallel perhaps to the role he assigns to music in his essay on folksongs, 'healing the great laceration in the world, through which hell gapes at us'.[15]

Die Kronenwächter, unfinished though it is, is his most ambitious attempt at using the past; its very ambition may indeed be the reason why it was never finished. He seems to have started preparing for it as early as 1805, reading very widely and questioning his friends, and the first volume appeared in 1817. The intention had been to complete the novel in four volumes, but though he had decided by 1816 to reduce this to

---

[14] 'jeder Sünder trägt in sich ein verlornes Paradies', letter to Wilhelm Grimm, 2 November 1810; *Achim von Arnim und die ihm nahe standen*, ed. Reinhold Steig, vol. III, *Achim von Arnim und Jacob und Wilhelm Grimm*, Stuttgart and Berlin, 1904, p. 87.
[15] Music's angels 'heilen den großen Riß der Welt, aus dem die Hölle uns angähnt' (*Des Knaben Wunderhorn*, dtv, 1963, III, 249).

two, the actual second volume published by Bettina in 1854 consisted of drafts related mainly to the first plan. There are thus inconsistencies that were once thought to have been introduced by Bettina herself, who certainly had to cobble the volume together.

Anyone trying to show Romanticism shading off into Realism has a fine buttress for his argument in *Die Kronenwächter*. He can point to set pieces of cultural history on the one hand, to descriptions of medieval buildings or meals or dress, to the depiction of groups of figures from the life of the people, popular customs and superstitions, historical figures (Luther, Dürer, Cranach) or half-historical, half-legendary characters like Faust—here a roistering shyster and brilliant quack. Impressionistic though some of the descriptions are, the figures in the landscape frequently remind us, as they did Wilhelm Grimm, of paintings and drawings by Altdorfer, Cranach or Dürer. The style, in the sections set in the old towns of Swabia, is sober and exact. The background has a different order of solidity from that of *Sternbald* or *Ofterdingen*; the language has a concreteness and sensuousness absent from Novalis and Tieck. Yet the fairytale elements, the mysterious dreams, the role of fate and magical coincidence, the grotesque, the subconscious, the supernatural, these are readily explicable as legacies of Romanticism, echoes often of the trivially Romantic tales of knights, robbers and Gothic horrors.

The novel, like Arnim, is more subtle than this. The interpenetration of myth and medieval reality is intended to realease for us the spiritual forces of the past, though the symbolism may well not succeed in all cases and the coincidences can startle and irritate. One may also have reservations about his re-creation of the psychological motivation of medieval or Renaissance characters, as distinct from the surface atmosphere of the late fifteenth or early sixteenth centuries.[16] The mythologizing inventiveness does, however, produce potent images of the mysterious unity underlying all being, images of increasing resonance.

The secret society of the Kronenwächter, the guardians of Barbarossa's old Hohenstaufen crown, watch over the descendants of the royal tribe from Kronenburg, their crystalline palace somewhere near Lake Constance. The castle is never seen by the reader but always described, sometimes at one remove, by a character, and doubt is even then cast on the truth of the story.[17] The foundling Berthold, of Hohenstaufen blood,

[16] Two other testimonies are worth noting. Eichendorff in his *Geschichte der poetischen Literatur Deutschlands* (*HKA* IX/III, 337): 'die Darstellung der verhängnißvollen Wetterscheide zwischen dem Mittelalter und der neuen Zeit... ist historischer, als viels geistreichverzwickte Geschichtswerke'. Then Fontane, in a note written in 1872, admires 'die vollendete Synthese der Geistesfreiheit mit volkstümlicher Einfachheit, Naivität und Talent' (quoted in his *Schriften zur Literatur*, ed. Hans-Heinrich Reuter, Berlin, Aufbau, 1960, p. 469).
[17] The Prior, after listening to the story by the stranger (who turns out to be Berthold's

hears how his father penetrated the castle to recover the crown. The description, magical and overwhelming, is of great beauty, from the snow-capped peaks around him like the walls of paradise, to the carpet of alpine flowers, the sun floating towards him on the lake like a burning ship, the rainbows cast by the glass towers of the castle (*SRE* I, 577–8). Within there are constantly singing birds, flocks of butterflies, flowers that seem to know no winter, but also a lion carrying a baby in its mouth. He kills the lion, but, when he has to choose between letting crown or baby fall into the rushing waters, it is the baby he involuntarily releases. Love and paradise, cruelty and power shine through; the castle as an ideal must relate to humanity. The symbolic pattern is a complex one; innocence and guilt, self-knowledge and hereditary memories shine through Berthold as he hovers between civic virtues and the claims of aristocracy. Faust's transfusion of Anton's blood into Berthold's veins (the surgery of modernity?) is as ultimately fatal as it is temporarily successful. Countless interrelated characters, often with their story narrated as they appear, authorial comments, the parallels and rhythmic repetitions in the interpolated Hausmärchen, all these point forward from the depths of history into the contemporary world, as do many of the motifs: the well, with its social function and its access to the deep secret worlds that are also represented by the miner; weavers and tapestries with mysterious patterns; the Strassburg Minster as the religious spirit outstretched towards heaven; the crown as the object of united longing. German past and the linked aspirations of its people are, as it were, messages left over from Napoleonic domination; but there are also warnings against a blind faith in inheriting an unchanged past. 'Only through the education of the spirit can the crown of Germany be won again', says a sketch for the second volume (*SRE* I, 1040).

Arnim had intended to include in this second part the work we now know as the tale *Isabella von Ägypten, Kaiser Karls des Fünften erste Jugendliebe* (1812). Bella's Gypsy people wander the earth, driven from their native Egypt for their unkindness to the Virgin Mary; the son she bears the Emperor will lead these our unhappy human representatives back to their home, their promised land. The love between Bella and Charles is, however, marred by dark forces erupting grotesquely into the story, pulling the Emperor down into the thrall of power and possessions. The fantastic figures that incorporate these forces have been a stumbling-block for many readers, though not for the characters within the story, as Wilhelm Scherer noted at the end of the last century; the coexistence of the mythological characters, creations of madness, alongside realistic historical people does not arouse terror in them, but they accept them

mother), says: 'Hält sie mich wirklich für so einfältig, daß ich das Märchen glauben soll, ich war so oft am Bodensee, und habe nie von solcher Felsbucht gehört' (*SRE* I, 580).

readily, seeming to find nothing odd. For the reader, this casts doubt on the very existence and reality of man himself; we often do not know whether we are awake or dreaming.[18] Heine, in *Die romantische Schule*, later draws attention to the grotesque horrors of the company in the carriage leaving Buik: an old witch; a dead 'Bärenhäuter' (the word means 'idler', 'lazybones', but originates in the reproach of lying on a bearskin and retains its corporeality here) whom greed has brought up out of the grave to sign a paltry contract as a servant; a golem in the shape of Isabella—that is to say, a figure made of clay that is indistinguishable from the real person but which will collapse if the Hebrew letters for 'truth' are wiped from its brow; and a young man made from a mandrake root torn from the ground at the foot of the gallows. Arnim himself follows this listing by an ironic invitation to think of our own times and our contemporaries in these terms; if we knew we were only dreaming, our anger at them would vanish (*SRE* I, 512).

Yet, in the story, we do not know that we are dreaming; and these figures, rising up from the depths of the unconscious, take on a life of their own. Scholars may tell us that they come from Grimmelshausen, from a Jewish legend related by Jacob Grimm, from material collected by Brentano for the *Zeitung für Einsiedler*. We can deduce that they have a symbolic force: the mandrake—erotic, earthbound, avaricious; the Bärenhäuter—savage, unredeemed nature; Golem Bella—earthly sensuality, deception, the Lilith figure. In the sweep of narrative invention, however, they carry us along unreflectingly and it is when they have gone that the tale rather limps to its close.

Die Majoratsherren, which appeared in 1819, is of all Arnim's Novellen the one that owes most to mesmerism, clairvoyance, somnambulism and similar twilight states seen even more clearly in E. T. A. Hoffmann. In a closely plotted story, almost classical in its disciplined structure, he sets fevered states of mind against a background of the recent past, with the rise of materialism and the decay of the old order and old families as prominent elements. Images from Jewish legend jostle with those from contemporary history and thought: Adam and Eve, Lilith, the Angel of Death, but also Kantian philosophers, Napoleon's Continental System, or a sal-ammoniac factory. The thread of an eighteenth-century plot, with babies exchanged in secret, is invested with mystery (by Esther's apparent Jewishness), social criticism (of the laws of inheritance, of the foppery of Frenchified aristocracy, of the dominance of money), wit and grotesque foolery (particularly in the case of the Lieutenant), but above all with hallucinatory experiences that are psychologically motivated but are also indicative of the special insights of

[18] Wilhelm Scherer, *Kleine Schriften*, vol. II, 1893, pp. 118 ff., quoted in A. Best, 'Arnims Kronenwächter', in *Jahrbuch der Kleist-Gesellschaft 1931 und 1932*, Berlin, 1932, pp. 122–97.

the imagination.[19] This probing of the unconscious with its associative technique is what commended Arnim to André Breton and the French Surrealists in the 1920s; but the search for deep significances is also, for the Romantic writer, a religious one.[20]

Der tolle Invalide auf dem Fort Ratonneau (1818) is the most accessible of Arnim's works, and the one constructed with most fidelity to the form of the Novelle. Its powerful polarities are reminiscent of Kleist; the daemonic is, however, viewed ironically if not grotesquely. The motifs flicker from the elemental to the comic, from the threat of consuming fire through fireworks to the burning of a wooden leg, from the devil as metaphysical despair to his function as a common swearword. Events and persons have a double meaning here too, but the ambivalence is securely carried by the strong characterization and the firm narrative lines.

The ingredients of Arnim's dramas are very similar to those of the novels and tales, but the gap between intention and achievement is greater. His interest in the theatre was undoubted and he certainly thought at first in terms of plays for the stage; but few prolific dramatists can have had so meagre a representation in the theatre—scarcely half a dozen performances in over a hundred and fifty years. It is not surprising that he should eventually have recognized, though even then not consistently, that he was writing for the reader rather than the spectator, so that some of his stage directions read like miniature short stories. And many of his dramas even remained unpublished until after his death.

The great disappointment to him was that he had counted on getting directly to the common people through drama; he had seen how this happened in puppet shows or shadow plays in carnivals and folk festivals and had adapted a number of old German pieces of this kind in his collection *Schaubühne* (1813). The intention was to comment in this way on contemporary problems and to present an ideal picture of man's place in a world made whole. Possession of such a world through the freedom of comedy, of play, is a characteristic of *Das Loch oder wiedergefundene Paradies*.

His most ambitious play is *Halle und Jerusalem* (1811), which was originally intended as little more than an adaptation of Gryphius's *Cardenio und Celinde* (1657) but which grew into a two-part work set in his own day. The first part contains colourful reminiscences of his own

[19] 'und es erschien überall durch den Bau dieser Welt eine höhere, welche den Sinnen nur in der Phantasie erkenntlich wird' (*SRE* III, 63).

[20] Janette Caton Hudson, *Achim von Arnim und André Breton*, University of Illinois at Urbana-Champaign dissertation, 1973. Breton contributed an introduction to *Achim d'Arnim, Contes bizarres*, Paris, Édition des Cahiers Libres, 1933, a reissue of the translations by Théophile Gautier fils. See also Anna Balakian, *Literary Origins of Surrealism. A New Mysticism in French Poetry*, 2nd ed., London, Univ. of London Press, 1967, xi, 159 pp, especially pp. 37-40.

student days in Halle and introduces the Halloren, the workers in the saltmines, with their own dress, customs and songs. More fundamental is the introduction of Ahasuerus, the Wandering Jew, who leads into the second part by guiding Cardenio and Celinde to the Holy Land.

A Shakespearian profusion of events and characters, without the inner discipline to organize them, marks the *Halle* play. In *Jerusalem* there is superimposed on this a clear debt to Calderón's religiously didactic mythological plays. Arnim mingles the real and fantastic, dream sequences and battle scenes, pilgrim songs and life in a harem, visions and temptations in the wilderness, Jesus on the Cross and an idealized Sir William Sidney Smith, defender of Acre against Napoleon in 1799. The scenes, often of considerable power, are unrelated, except in a very general way by the theme of redemption. The mood changes from exaltation to criticism of contemporary event, from mystic visions to obscure literary satirizing. It is all of a piece with his attempt to redeem his own time by infusing it with poetic and supernatural ideals incorporated in mythical and historical event. He is constantly importing symbols into inadequately realized, though richly described worlds. Yet the grandiose conception has an effect even in its final failure.

Wilhelm Grimm said of Arnim's works that they were like pictures framed on three sides but still being painted on the fourth, so that eventually the outlines of heaven and earth can no longer be told apart; from this there arose a painful uncertainty for the reader.[21] The criticism is not unjust, but the openness of form now also conveys for us an openness to the world that attracts and excites.

---

[21] 'Sie [Arnim's works] glichen Bildern, die von drei Seiten einen Rahmen hatten, an der vierten aber nicht, und dort immer weiter fortgemalt waren, so daß in den letzten Umrissen Himmel und Erde nicht mehr zu unterscheiden waren, woraus eine ängstliche Ungewißheit für den Leser entsprang', Wilhelm Grimm, *Kleinere Schriften*, vol. 1, Berlin, 1881, p. 299.

6

Natural and Supernatural:
Eichendorff, with Görres

For the common reader Eichendorff has long been the typical Romantic writer, garlanded with tributes to his evocations of German landscape and to his portrayal of the German character. The classic representation of this view is that by Wilhelm Kosch, then in 1921 editor of the critical edition of the works: 'Eichendorff is not only the most popular but also the most German of German writers. In him is reflected in its present form the old spirit of the German people, German faith, hope and love, the German soul, honest manly German pride, fervent German delight in nature, childlikeness and longing' (*HKA* I/1, viii). Vague impressions of forests and nightingales, moonlight and hunting-horns, wandering apprentices and artistic aristocrats both recognize and veil the relationship of Eichendorff to the earlier Romantics. They catch the surface connexions but miss the rigorous inner structure of his aesthetic and religious intentions.

Eichendorff would, from about 1830 until his death in 1857, have been accustomed enough to hear himself spoken of as 'the last Romantic'; later this becomes 'the last knight', 'der letzte Ritter der Romantik'. The great popularity of the later years was, though, almost an anonymous one, in the sense that the poems had become a part of popular tradition, sung and recited without much reference to an author. They seemed to be a continuation of *Des Knaben Wunderhorn*, bridging the gap between naive poetry and conscious art. Where the personality of the poet was recognized it was found to be upright, firm, helpful, pious—a warrant for the sincerity of the poetry.

His life had not been very eventful. The son of landed Catholic gentry in Upper Silesia, he had been brought up at the main family seat of Lubowitz and the days and the place shone idyllically through the rest of his life. About 1850, when preparing notes for what might have been his version of the *Prelude*, he saw Lubowitz in the context of the revolutionary period in which he grew up. Lying in the garden in the sultry noon shade he looks up at the clouds and imagines mountain ranges and islands with deep gorges. The view stretches over the Oder to the blue Carpathians and into dark forests ... The valley was still like an island of bliss, untroubled by the storms of the new age ... An officer rides through the cornfields with the news of the execution of Louis XVI ... 'But I looked towards the Carpathians, as if with a presentiment of new times, heralded by thunder.'[1]

Such a powerful evocation of childhood, rarely encountered before Proust even in direct autobiography, recurs in slightly fictionalized form in many stories and poems, particularly the earlier ones. What is noteworthy is that the intense longing for his childhood home (the family's financial straits had culminated in the sale of Lubowitz on his mother's death in 1822) is regularly accompanied by a sense of the dangers lurking in the garden, dangers of unbridled imagination, of sensuality, of negation of the divine order. Eichendorff is reading back into his childhood experiences the metaphysical and theological schema of his later years.

His university experiences plunged him into Romantic thought. He heard Schleiermacher and Steffens at Halle, and Görres at Heidelberg. Both his diary entries and the essay *Halle und Heidelberg* (1857) testify to the crucial impact on him of the personality and prophetic vision of Joseph Görres (1776–1848), and something of this needs to be conveyed.

Görres

It is not Görres the campaigning journalist (though campaigning for very different causes at various stages in his life) with whom we are concerned here, but rather the manipulator of large ideas. The transcripts of the Heidelberg lectures are still unpublished (*GS* IV, 331), but the subjects included philosophy, psychology, cosmogony, 'organopoie', physiology and aesthetics, and it is a reasonable assumption that they depended for their undoubted effect more on their rhapsodical improvisation and their imagery than on the coherence of their argument. At this time Görres was still flushed with the Naturphilosoph's enthusiasm for an organic view of life and creation as a totality, but was also moving through theological historiography (*Wachstum der Historie*, 1807) to the detailed system-building of *Mythengeschichte der asiatischen Welt* (1810). One can do little more than pick out some of the threads in this process.

Before the emergence of spiritual, ethereal experience (the realm of

[1] In Hubert Pohlein, 'Die Memoirenfragmente Josephs von Eichendorff. Texte und Untersuchungen', *Aurora*, i (1929), 83–116; partly corrected in Hermann Kunisch, 'Die Frankfurter Novellen- und Memoiren-Handschriften von Joseph von Eichendorff", *JFDH*, 1968, pp. 328–89.

light and the sun), primitive man was earth-bound, vegetative (the dark, living forces of nature), wandering somnambulant through the world, unselfconsciously happy. One part of modern man reaches back to this state through dreams and emotions, and through all within us that we neither understand nor control. An underlying unity does nevertheless exist, and is revealed most completely in myth, by which Görres means the collective unconscious underlying and preceding particular mythologies. Myth is the language of nature, the hieroglyph of creation, the innocent human response both to the one creator and to his world. Out of it grows history, in the development of different peoples, religions, cultures and states; but all, whatever forms the cyclical or alternating rhythm of growth have imposed, begin with the one world homeland around Hindu mythology's Mount Meru, north of the Himalayas. From this single fount spring all religious forms, all legend, all poetry.

This relentless, dithyrambic universalism expresses itself in imagery of great power and richness, in sweeping, confident sentences and daring imaginative leaps. All this can also be found in his article on Runge's 'Times of Day' cycle of drawings ('Die Zeiten', 1808), no doubt based on a lecture to which Eichendorff refers enthusiastically in a diary entry of 9 July 1807. Runge's own iconography is heightened as the symbolic values of the four periods of the day are related to the mystery at the heart of all things, to divine and human creativity, to the stages of history and, specifically, to the mysteries of religion. Echoes of these hieroglyphic interpretations sound through Eichendorff's work and the motifs themselves are ones to which we shall need to return.

Görres did more than plunge Eichendorff into nature mysteries, religious cryptograms and hymnic fusion of cosmogony and anthropology. He also provided a presence of the past, both generally and the past of Germany. For him the profundities of the past hold supra-personal truth. Echoes of the eternal mystery come from folksongs, snatches of 'that dark language that the gods speak' (*GS* III, 10). Past and future interweave: 'as the distant future stirs darkly and silently in the woman's womb, the intuition [Ahnung] of the past lies like a hidden seed within us' (*GS* III, 278).

Eichendorff

One further experience must be mentioned before Eichendorff's life settles down to blameless bureaucracy. He and his brother went to Vienna in 1810 to prepare for civil-service examinations and, during their two-year stay, they came, even if only temporarily and with reservations, under the spell of Friedrich and Dorothea Schlegel. The measured historical view of literature in its ethical, philosophical and cultural contexts that characterized Schlegel's 1812 lectures no doubt determined the course of Eichendorff's own critical activity in much later years. But it is the general Catholic atmosphere and the ethical emphases that, together with individual motifs, pass over immediately into his creative work. Of Schlegel's earlier 'Romantic' theory very little can be traced in Eichendorff.

He testifies to the encouragement of the Schlegels during the writing of his first novel, *Ahnung und Gegenwart*, between 1810 and 1812. (It was not published until 1815, five weeks after Napoleon's return from Elba, when people's thoughts were somewhat diverted from novels.) Dorothea seems indeed to have made a number of now unidentifiable corrections to the manuscript, and the title is said to have been suggested by her.

The title defines the novel. There is a clear intention that it should be about the present (Gegenwart), that is to say the confused, expectant period of Napoleonic domination ('ein getreues Bild jener gewitterschwülen Zeit, der Erwartung, der Sehnsucht und Verwirrung', he calls it in his draft preface, later taken over almost word for word by Fouqué; *HKA* XVIII/1, 72). It is a present that attempts to convey atmosphere and mood rather than historical or geographic specificity, and whenever the novel seeks to satirize contemporary society its vagueness means lack of bite. The present is related to both past and future by 'Ahnung'. The word means 'presentiment', 'foreboding' or 'intuition' and, as we have seen, it is used by Görres to connect with the mystery of the past; the same Görres passage also refers to 'eine dunkle Ahnung' that seizes us when we try to decipher the meaning of figures on ancient sarcophagi; it is as if those stars appear to us again that shone in the darkness when our childhood was emerging from night. It is also a favourite word of Friedrich Schlegel's, associated with dreams and with the infinite abundance of the divine.[2] Resonances of this kind, a reaching out towards some mysterious absolute, give the novel its haunting power. The Silesian homeland provides much of the formal imagery and the atmospheric richness against the background of which the action moves. For movement is a dominant structural element; wandering is the occupational hazard of the Romantic hero, whose good fortune it is not to have to earn his living. Eichendorff's story-line is firmer than we expect in a Romantic novelist, but it proceeds by addition, by accident and coincidence, and it achieves its suspense and narrative drive by small mystifications within episodes.

Attempts have been made to demonstrate that *Ahnung und Gegenwart* is constructed on a strictly allegorical basis. This seems to be going too far, but typical or allegorical significance certainly attaches to some of

[2] 'Die Vorstellung der unendlichen Fülle ist besser *Ahndung des Himmels* zu nennen', Friedrich Schlegel, *Philosophische Lehrjahre* (1805), *KA* XIX, 57.

the characters, whether based on living persons or literary predecessors, and critics have excelled themselves in the variety of their attributions. These contribute to a central meaning and purpose of the novel that can be fairly easily summarized, namely the relationship of art, religion and life. The Romantic aesthetic represented in poetry—and most of the main characters are poets—fails to respond adequately to the modern world. Natural song cannot comprehend the new complexities of society, and aspects of Romanticism reveal the emptiness of an art resting merely on religiosity (Eichendorff clearly has Loeben in mind here). Friedrich, the main character in the novel, moves from poetry to action and then to religion. He resists seduction by Romana (the Venus-Loreley figure) and thereby rejects the world of unbridled imagination. The natural world and poetry must both be redeemed by a religious renewal that has strong commitment and moral content. Thus, whereas his friend Leontin leaves at the end of the novel to find his utopia in America, Friedrich retires to a monastery to prepare for the regeneration of Europe.

The argument is summed up in an exchange between Friedrich and the dedicated craftsman poet Faber in the closing pages. Faber believes that poetry has no business to attempt to mould events; 'it does not wish and is not meant to be of any use' (*HKA* III, 330). Instead of replying directly, Friedrich sings a song. The poet is at the heart of the world ('Der Dichter ist das Herz der Welt') and God has given him the ability, through the power of love, to uncover the Lord's tracks in the earth, to set free the unassertive will of all creatures, and to venture to give a name to what is darkest, as well as to the serious and devout aspects of the variety of life (*HKA* III, 331–2).

Eichendorff has thus arrived at a theocentric art with much less agonizing than Brentano. Yet the ethical preoccupations implicit in this are relatively pallid when compared with the presentation of the natural magic that is meant to have been subjugated. More positively, the tension between nature and the Cross is presented in symbols that acquire great power throughout his work.

His one other novel, *Dichter und ihre Gesellen* (rather oddly described as a Novelle on its publication in 1834), is usually thought of as a later version of *Ahnung und Gegenwart* and it is difficult to deny this. What is interesting is that the place of the poet in the world is still occupying him; a letter of 1833 says it is to be a novel 'portraying the various courses of a poet's life' (*HKA* XII, 44). And although the events and the poetic characters are drawn in rather more exaggerated terms than in the earlier novel, the conclusions are similar.

Contemporary critics were by no means wholly captivated by *Dichter und ihre Gesellen*, but the Young German writers Gutzkow and Laube both find it charmingly redolent of their youth, even if the latter does describe it as a nightingale beating itself to death (*HKA* XVIII/1, 260–4 and 282–3). It is regarded as a disarming anachronism, a reminder of the real qualities of Romanticism in the midst of its decay in a welter of worthless imitations.

The similarity between these two novels, written at an interval of over twenty years, suggests a remarkable unity in his writing. It is, indeed, generally very difficult to assign a passage or a poem of his to a given period from internal evidence alone. The building-blocks are not interchangeable, but they are recognizably of the same material.

Eichendorff's works, prose and poetry, express a theology of landscape that frequently contains within itself a theology of history. The natural world is objective and given, it is God's creation, not ours. Fichtean subjectivism is odious, as it makes nature depend on the self. Indeed all subjectivism is a form of hubris, and the great sin of the Christian West comes with its triumph in the Reformation. Early Romanticism continues the evil, which fatally flaws its achievement: 'the arrogance of the subject, through which even the angels once fell, also caused the downfall of Romanticism' (*HKA* IX/3, 473). This distrust of the subjective, which also manifests itself in a particular dislike of pietism and associated areas of enthusiasm and sentimentality, allows little in the way of psychological investigation or analysis of motive. The outline of characters is no sharper than that of the external world in Eichendorff.

This external world, to which we are constantly exposed in Eichendorff, is a hieroglyph awaiting decipherment. As for Böhme, Herder and Görres, it is God's manifestation in terms that can be partly apprehended by man. It is 'the great picture book that the good Lord has spread out before us' (the *Taugenichts*, chapter nine; *W* II, 633), but the wind blows the leaves of the book into such confusion that it is difficult even for the poet to interpret them (*Ahnung und Gegenwart*; *HKA* III, 27).[3] The creator's will expresses itself mysteriously, and nature in many of its aspects is still unredeemed, full of danger, capable of drawing man into its own vegetative rhythms and away from the realm of duty and morality. Eichendorff is anything but a pantheist.

[3] Eichendorff frequently expresses this concept in terms of a song slumbering at the heart of all things, the song of nature waiting to be redeemed; e.g. in the poems 'Wünschelrute' and 'An eine Tänzerin' (*HKA* I/1, 134 and 264); in *Halle und Heidelberg* (*HKA* IX/3, 275, 289, 342); in the essays 'Zur Geschichte der neueren romantischen Poesie in Deutschland' and 'Brentano und seine Märchen' (*HKA* VIII/1, 22–3 and 61); of Calderón and Shakespeare in 'Zur Geschichte des Dramas' (*HKA* VIII/2, 296 and 306). On this theme see Robert Mühlher, 'Natursprache und Naturmusik bei Eichendorff', *Aurora*, xxi (1961), 12 35; Luthi, 1966, pp. 14–19 and 242–5; and Stein, 1964, pp. 151–5.

On the hieroglyph see Bormann, 1968, *passim*, and Liselotte Dieckmann, *Hieroglyphics. The History of a Literary Symbol*, St Louis, Washington Univ. Press, 1970, x, 246 pp.

There is little doubt that these theological purposes are consciously present in Eichendorff's poems and fiction; they are explicit in his literary criticism in the later years. So it is proper to see in the theology an examination for much that appears stereotyped and formulaic in the motifs and stylistic forms. Many of the themes are derivative, material lying to hand at the end of the Romantic epoch, and Eichendorff is well enough aware of this. On occasion he even satirizes his own use of them.[4]

It has been convincingly argued, particularly by Kohlschmidt, that formalized recurring expressions very generally in Romanticism serve to provide some anchor in stability, some counter to subjectivism, a reinforcement of the will to universality. The reader, too, is everywhere at home amid the innumerable echoes. Much recent Eichendorff criticism devotes itself to arguing whether the repeated motifs are of this rather generalized kind, whether they are symbolic, or whether they continue the emblematic tradition. In all this there is certainly too great a readiness to assume that all must conform to a similar pattern, whereas the problem is rather that of distinguishing between, on the one hand, atmospheric motifs and structural or linguistic formulas derived mainly from his reading and personal experiences and used fairly casually and, on the other, the more profound symbolic rhythms or hieroglyphic images that carry the theology. The modulation between these states, and the adaptation to the fiction or the poem, is achieved by slight variations within a limited vocabulary, or sometimes even by specific literary connexions.

What then are the main recurring patterns and motifs? emphasizing again that relentless decoding in all contexts is fatally removed from the normal, even instructed, reader's experience of an Eichendorff text. Sometimes the hieroglyphic sign holds its full value, sometimes there is no more than a faint associative trace. Almost always there is an inherent polarity, a dormant dialectic.

Space is the basic landscape experience, often mediated by sound—distant bells, posthorns, rushing streams, soaring larks. 'Out there', when we cross the rim of the self, there is both release and risk. Through this wide world the Eichendorff hero wanders towards his paradisal goal (a frequent motif expressing this is that of the meandering river), every achieved journey being only a part of his general pilgrimage. The garden, with its memories of youth (the decaying rococo park, artificial and unnatural but with an air of bygone splendour), or with its Eden-

---

[4] As in the Novelle *Viel Lärmen um Nichts,* probably written in 1831–2 and published in 1832; particularly the passage where he introduces Graf Leontin from *Ahnung und Gegenwart,* who is said to be immediately recognizable because he cannot even say he has had a meal without striking a chord on his guitar (*W* II, 663). The motif is one that can be seen elsewhere in Romanticism, notably in Dorothea Schlegel's *Florentin* (1801).

like echoes of the plan of salvation and the fatal enchantment of the senses, is a frequent point of departure and longing.[5]

Eichendorff's characters, in their equivocal relationship to the world of things, often isolate themselves physically. He accepted Loeben's criticism that there was too much tree-climbing in *Ahnung und Gegenwart* (*HKA* XIII, 61, and III, 478), but he went on using the motif. Rising above nature, the hero escapes from its hold and escapes momentarily from the stream of history. Eichendorff's general predilection for the view from above has been identified with the cosmic viewpoint suggested in seventeenth-century cosmological and encyclopaedic works; it is a symbol of elevation, of inner sublimity and ecstatic flight as in El Greco's paintings. More simply, it conveys an impression of breadth of vision and relative detachment and it is, in fact, almost impossible to separate the view from on high and the distant view.

Spatial relationships are nowhere more clearly expressed than in the figure at the window, and the archetypal Eichendorff poem 'Sehnsucht', from *Dichter und ihre Gesellen*, leads from it to many allied motifs:

> Es schienen so golden die Sterne,
> Am Fenster ich einsam stand
> Und hörte aus weiter Ferne
> Ein Posthorn im stillen Land.[6]

And there follow the two young journeymen singing as they go by, of ravines and rustling forests, plunging streams, marble statues, ruined gardens, palaces in moonlight, girls at the window listening to the sound of the lute, fountains murmuring in the glorious summer night.

The window is part of the house, the place of established order, security, comfort, home; but also the place where we are hemmed in, by society, history, our own weaknesses. Outside is freedom, danger, the mystery of the life of nature. Eichendorff's characters are at risk in this world: 'Oh God,' cries Florio in *Das Marmorbild* as he stands at the open window, 'let me not go astray in the world' (*W* II, 556).

'Die schöne Welt' is seductive, magical, the source of disorder and

---

[5] On the garden in Eichendorff see Walter Rehm, 'Prinz Rokoko im alten Garten. Eine Eichendorff-Studie', in *JFDH*, 1962, pp. 97–207, also in his *Späte Studien*, Bern, Francke, 1964, pp. 122–214; Oskar Seidlin, '"Der alte Garten"', *Euph*, liv (1960), 242–61, also in his *Versuche über Eichendorff*, 1965, pp. 74–98; Alfred Riemen, 'Eichendorffs Garten und seine Besucher', *Aurora*, xxx/xxxi (1970–1), 23–33. See also Eva Börsch-Supan, 'Das Motiv des Gartenraums in Dichtungen des 19. und frühen 20. Jahrhunderts', *DVLG*, xxxix (1965), 87–124.

[6] For the window in art and poetry see J. A. Schmoll gen. Eisenwerth, 'Fensterbilder. Motivketten in der europäischen Malerei', in *Beiträge zur Motivkunde des 19. Jahrhunderts*, Munich, Prestel, 1970, pp. 13–165. One thinks primarily of C. D. Friedrich's 'Frau am Fenster', but it is astonishing to find how widespread the motif has been.

confusion ('verwirrend', 'irren' are recurring words in the fiction and the poems). The daemonic attraction is personified in water-sprites, Loreley figures, enchanted minstrels (frequently associated with the spring), heathen goddesses—Diana and Venus. The rhythms of nature, its vegetative processes, its mysterious forces of renewal correspond to natural instincts in man, not least to the drive of sensuality. These life-creating elements are full of danger, but can be brought into harmony with man's moral imperatives through the mediation of Christian love. Profane love cannot do so, for it is itself part of the unredeemed natural process; Venus is herself a vegetative symbol. (She becomes a more negative figure, perhaps a hubristic representative when she is removed from nature into history in statuary—in a Marmorbild, in fact.)

One of the most characteristic of all of Eichendorff's groups of motifs is that of the rhythms of the day. We have already seen how the Görres interpretation of Runge's *Times of Day* drawings excited Eichendorff, but the symbolic weight to be attached to them varies constantly in his works. Morning scenes are invariably full of hope and expectancy and are presented as a complex of spatial and acoustic effects: cock-crow, receding tones of the posthorn, larks in the sky (a conventional morning effect of the eighteenth century and of the Romantic writers of the 1810s and 1820s, but also contributing to a picture of man and nature striving towards heaven). There are also undoubtedly overtones of Herder's description, deriving from Böhme, of dawn as a hieroglyph of the original creation.

At noon the sun beats down, the air is heavy, life drags along, the heart is filled with foreboding; nature is alienated from God. Evening is bathed in light, the eye is drawn to the far horizons of the setting sun, sounds carry clearly from great distances, the rivers run to the sea, and in its golden glow the golden age of harmony between God, man and the world is, for a while, restored. Night is not a metaphysical concept as for Novalis; it is mysterious, bathed in moonlight, often a time of confusion and unease, suggesting the daemonic in man and in the natural world. Nature at night is charged with history; the past stands still and is preserved in ruins, moonlit gardens under a cover of grass, flowers or ivy. But night can also bring peace and harmony by deadening the distinctions between things and showing the unity of the world.[7]

Two points should be stressed in this context. Eichendorff does not start from an idea and work to find pictures for it (his own definition

[7] One may think of the forest responding to its Creator's presence at night, while man closes his heart against the Lord, in 'Nächtlich macht der Herr die Rund' ('Der Wächter' from *Dichter und ihre Gesellen*), with its Gethsemane echo. Similarly the two 'Stimmen der Nacht' poems (1839 and 1840) with 'der Herr geht über die Gipfel' in the one and 'Nur der Mensch, dem Tod geweiht, Träumet fort von seinen Sünden' in the second.

of an allegory), but proceeds 'more organically' from contemplation of the richness and variety of the world to a symbolic beauty. This he calls Naturpoesie, as opposed to the Kunstpoesie of the former method (*HKA* VIII/2, 306). Secondly, as Peter Paul Schwarz demonstrates, the rhythm of the day, or the contrast between morning and night, conditions the narrative structure of some of the works, notably the *Taugenichts* and *Das Marmorbild*. The whole arabesque of Eichendorff's hieroglyphic is nowhere more exactly wrought than in *Das Marmorbild*, half Novelle and half Märchen, written in late 1816 and early 1817 and published in 1819. *Die Zauberei im Herbste*, written in 1808–9 but first published in 1906, may with certain reservations be taken as a preliminary study for it. The central theme is again the role of the poet, whose heightened imagination exposes him particularly to the fascination of natural, sensuous forces but also makes him a potential Christian mediator. Here we have the enchantment of the past welling up in the dream-world of natural magic. The heathen gods, and especially Frau Venus, persist even after the advent of Christianity as daemonic personifications of the lure of the finite, in nature and the senses. (The argument that *Das Marmorbild* represents Eichendorff's reaction against German Classicism's enthusiasm for Antiquity ignores the mythical development outlined by Görres.) The action takes place in Italy, home of the classical gods but also of the Holy City. An intricate mesh of motifs is woven through the action: colour symbolism, spring and regeneration, the ship of dreams on a moonlit sea, the figure of the circle, reminiscences of works of art, significant names (Bianca is clear enough, but is Donati the Greek god of death, Thanatos, or a Donatist, a fourth-century Christian schismatic?), the polarities of plants and stars, dark and light.

Aus dem Leben eines Taugenichts, probably written in the early 1820s and first published in full in 1826, has both suffered and benefited most from naive reading. It is undoubtedly the most popular of his works and the choice of the first-person narrator, half wanderer, half fool, corresponds to its picaresque and comic elements and sets a narrative tone of engaging innocence and the mildest irony. The Taugenichts can only express his emotions and reactions simply, and the result may appear trivial and superficial. But the alert reader recognizes that the very innocence of the presentation, the 'reine Tor' aspect, creates a narrative atmosphere that persuades us there is more in this than meets the eye, that lures us into accepting the picture of a providential world. There is a semi-allegorical framework, with the Taugenichts as man stripped to his essentials—disinterested, unencumbered, 'good-for-nothing' except to be God's creature. He is Christian moving through the world of transience and the senses, but linked in memory to his childhood home, his roots, and placed at last in his own private Eden where, in the formula of

Creation, 'Behold, it was very good.' This is the German Pilgrim's progress, robbed of any portentousness by gentle mockery, by echoes of the Singspiel and the Viennese popular theatre. Within this picture the complex of symbolic values we have already outlined operates almost independently. Eichendorff's overt intention emerges through the narrative tone and the half allegory, but his poetic understanding of the world also asserts itself enciphered in many hieroglyphs: Venus, heaths and heathens, lost cities, ruined gardens again, ghostly trees, the heat of noon, the rebirth of morning, the Stephansturm, the Danube as the river of life. The flavour of the *Taugenichts* is very special: a Mozart opera perhaps, décor by the Nazarenes and Blechen, libretto by Calderón and Grimmelshausen, on a theme by Bunyan.

The satire on philistinism in the *Taugenichts* is mild and oblique, but its bite, such as it is, is against materialism and self-satisfaction, not against bourgeois values as a whole. Eichendorff's political standpoint was broadly Conservative Catholic, but with a good deal of light and shade. His mistrust of particular reforms and of the general climate of rationalism, industrialization and economic materialism is evident enough in the Novellen *Auch ich war in Arkadien*, perhaps written in 1832 but not published until 1866, and *Libertas und ihre Freier*, 1849 but again not published until 1864. Yet the aesthetically most successful of the 'political' Novellen, *Das Schloß Dürande*, written between 1835 and 1837 and published in the latter year, is deeply ambivalent in its attitude towards revolutionary change. The need to overthrow the corrupt feudal system is recognized and, in the autobiographical *Der Adel und die Revolution* (1857), he speaks with some relish of the effect the explosion of the French Revolution had on the whole of Philistia (*W* I, 911). The Novelle, however, shows revolution as being also a source of the daemonic, an unleashing of catastrophe, of the wild beast in the heart of man (a phrase, from this most Kleistean of his works, that he later applies to Kleist himself).[8] Burning castles are a motif of the foundering not just of a class

[8] Applied to Kleist the phrase is found in the *Geschichte der poetischen Literatur Deutschlands* (*HKA* IX/3, 429): 'Hüte jeder das wilde Thier in seiner Brust, daß es nicht plötzlich ausbricht und ihn selbst zerreißt! Denn das war Kleist's Unglück und schwergebüßte Schuld, daß er diese, keinem Dichter fremde, dämonische Gewalt nicht bändigen konnte oder wollte.' Eichendorff places Kleist among the Romantics but nevertheless distinguishes him because of his inability to rise above the world and its phenomena to the transcendental (*HKA* IX/3, 422). More positively stated as the clash between absurdity and personality in a splintered society, this may indicate why Kleist appears in many ways closer to Büchner than to the Romantics.

Das Schloß Dürande is generally thought to have close affinities with Kleist's Novelle *Michael Kohlhaas*, but the appalling escalation of Kohlhaas's determination to achieve justice and revenge and the magnitude of his self-deception convey less a critique of society or a case-history of the lack of self-control (though both are present in this as in Eichendorff's story) than an agonized misgiving about the very nature of things. There is in

but of godly order itself, and it is the new task of the nobility to relate ordered change to eternal values. Nor was this an anachronistic as it may now sound. Both he and Arnim were reflecting some actual degree of achievement by the nobility of the post-Napoleonic period.

There is a considerable body of Eichendorff's work that we can do no more than mention: three other Novellen (*Eine Meerfahrt*, written perhaps in 1835–6 and published in 1866; *Die Entführung*, 1837 and published 1839; and *Die Glücksritter*, published in 1841), three epic poems, two historical tragedies (and fragments of a third), two dramatic satires, an incomplete puppet play, and a comedy (*Die Freier*, written over a number of years from about 1820 to 1829 and published in 1833) which is still played and which, in its misunderstandings and disguises, has something of the spirit of the *Taugenichts*. Then there are the translations from Spanish, notably of some fifteen of Calderón's religious plays; the historical, political and autobiographical pieces; and the literary criticism of the later years.

Yet it is as a lyric poet that his impact is greatest, and we have been in danger of subsuming the poetry in the totality of the work. There is, it is true, relatively little development in his poetry and not all that much variety, though there are some lighter poems and a few directly

Kleist's Novellen, as indeed in his dramas, a profound ambiguity, an uncertainty about the apprehension of, and still more the expression of reality. The arrangements of earth have failed, and chance reveals an apparently irrational universe; within this context man can do no more, and no less, than cling to that core of truth and reality that is himself.

Mehring and Lukács saw Kleist as a reactionary Romantic, but even Marxist criticism now tends to regard him more as an accelerated traveller through all the intellectual crises of the middle class at the turn of the century, metaphysically disorientated in an alienated world. Like the Romantics he looks back to a golden age, most movingly evoked in the valley scene in *Das Erdbeben in Chili*, but no real hope of harmony ensues. Nor is there the Romantic sense of the supremacy of poetics. Kleist's narrator is only rarely omniscient, more often he judges what he narrates from the perspective of his characters; an ironic mood may indeed be part of the narrative stance, but the arbitrariness of Romantic irony, the play of free will that is a re-creation of existence, these are lacking. The tight spring of action, the flavour of reality in psychological or social collapse, the gesture or symbol doing duty for the word, these are features of Kleist's Novellen that distinguish them from those of his Romantic contemporaries, whatever correspondences may lie in glimpses of dark forces within the human psyche.

So much that is contradictory has been written about Kleist—mirroring his own paradoxes—that it is useful to acquire a general picture before turning to any specialist study. To do this see: Eva Rothe, 'Kleist-Bibliographie 1945–1960', *JDSG* v (1961), 414–547; Helmut Kreuzer, 'Kleist-Literatur 1955–1960', *DU*, xiii (1961), 116–35 Manfred Lefevre, 'Kleist-Forschung 1961–1967', *CG*, 1969, pp. 1–86, a highly competent discussion of major contributions; and Robert E. Helbling, *The Major Works of Heinrich von Kleist*, New York, New Directions, 1975, ix, 275 pp. It is also worth looking back with Rolf Busch, *Imperialistische und faschistische Kleist-Rezeption 1890–1945. Eine ideologiekritische Untersuchung*, Frankfurt, Akademische Verlagsgesellschaft, 1974, 287: 136 pp.

There is now a thoughtful English introduction to the Novellen: Denys Dyer, *The Stories of Kleist*, London, Duckworth, 1977, viii, 205 pp.

related to contemporary ecclesiastical or political issues. Many of the songs are embedded in the novels and tales and are, indeed, *sung* by the characters. Yet though in detail the interpretation of them out of context may mislead, it is in general not unreasonable to see as one whole the only separate collection published in his lifetime, *Gedichte* (1837; there had been an appendix of poems in the 1826 volume containing the *Taugenichts* and *Das Marmorbild*, and the 1837 collection was slightly rearranged for the collected works in 1841). To remind ourselves of the lateness of the hour: 1837 was the year in which Büchner died, in which Gotthelf published *Der Bauernspiegel* and Dickens *Pickwick Papers*; Heine's *Die romantische Schule* had been published a year before. The formulas of Romanticism, ruins, moonlight, rocky landscapes, medieval knights and wandering minstrels, simple peasants, nature spirits, mill streams, posthorns, Waldeinsamkeit, childhood dreams, gypsies and the rest, had been worn thin not so much by the lesser poets of some significance, Wilhelm Müller, Kerner, Fouqué (particularly in his prose works) or Chamisso, but by the countless imitators of their work and that of Uhland. Romanticism had not died out, but it had been trivialized. Mörike, the Droste and Heine led it into very different directions; Eichendorff purified and deepened it.

The old motifs are, as we have already seen, given new vitality by context, by being related to a profound sense of the fragility of the phenomenal world and by a tension between the magic of the senses and the threat of the dark, between eternity and history. The very familiarity of these newly charged motifs is reminiscent of the folksong.[9] In his *Geschichte der poetischen Literatur Deutschlands* Eichendorff distinguishes the folksong from the art lyric: the former presents experience directly and in an apparently disconnected way; it is a hieroglyphic picture language. In the Naturlied (and, in this context, the reference is to a poem actually about nature) we are frequently surprised, as we are in children, by a warmly intimate understanding of external nature and its symbolism, and by the profound insight into the mysterious spirit-world of animals. Forest, springs, clouds respond to human emotions, the nightingale sings the inexpressible; everything is as fairytale-like as in dreams (*HKA* IX/3, 146–7).

Eichendorff equally appears to respond intuitively to the natural world and certainly to relate mood to landscape. His style, too, seems at first to be very close to folksong or, at any rate, to *Des Knaben Wunderhorn*. The diction is relatively simple, though the vocabulary is naturally

[9] Alexander Sydow, *Das Lied, Ursprung, Wesen und Wandel*, Göttingen, Vandenhoeck & Ruprecht, 1962, pp. 132–3, lists twelve Eichendorff poems that are current among the people ('voksläufig'), though one may surmise that this will be substantially less true for the post-war generations.

somewhat more extensive than that of the folksinger. The stanzaic forms are generally unadventurous and, although rhythmic patterns are sometimes used to provide speed or tension, there is little experimentation with form. The general impression is one of fluidity, and improvisation; but how much should we trust our first impressions? Would simplicity and improvisation have borne such powerful echoes into our own day? Did Schumann and Hugo Wolf, Mendelssohn, Brahms and Richard Strauss find no more in him?[10]

There have been recent attempts (Krabiel, 1973), based on the later poems, to prove that his handling of language is highly conscious and subtle, deforming accepted syntactical patterns and creating abnormal semantic relationships in order to point the hieroglyphic character of his motifs. This is partly convincing but, even without going so far, we may see looseness of grammatical forms, the impersonal use of verbs, devices to deprive nouns of their concreteness, synaesthetic connexions, carefully judged acoustic correspondences, that all belie the simple, unreflecting poet.

Wordsworth, in the 'Immortality' ode, took up the myth of pre-existence to idealize the child's state of grace, its total harmony with the universe. Eichendorff's point of reference is personal: the happy days at Lubowitz. But both are archetypal; we are dealing with the common childhood of humanity. Fortunato's song in *Das Marmorbild* is one 'that, like memories and echoes from some other world that is our homeland, comes to us through the little paradise garden of childhood' (*W* II, 562).

The garden of childhood had its thunderclouds, paradise is invaded by history; but the childhood vision, the 'freshness of a dream', is also the poet's re-creative power. On the level of simple theology, Eichendorff reintroduced the beauty of the world (as in the 1837 poem 'O Welt, du schöne Welt, du') into the scheme of grace. In socio-economic terms, he idealized the claims of preindustrialized life and paved the way for generations of innocents, and others, longing for the simple life. He held a remarkable balance between certainty and unease, sensuality and spirituality, Christian redemption and the darkness of the collective imagination, natural and supernatural.

What excites about Eichendorff is that, behind the apparent quiet conventionality, there combine in unusual strength the claims of sensuous natural beauty and of the transcendental. The aesthetic daemon is there all right, but under firm control.

[10] To this somewhat rhetorical question we ought probably to answer that some did, but others responded as conventionally as their contemporaries. For intelligent comments see Eric Sams, *The Songs of Hugo Wolf*, 1961, pp. 97–114, and *The Songs of Robert Schumann*, 1968, pp. 91–106, both London, Methuen. See also Eckart Busse, *Die Eichendorff-Rezeption im Kunstlied*, Würzburg, Eichendorff-Gesellschaft, 1975, 160 pp., dealing mainly with Schumann, Wolf and Pfitzner.

7

The Risks of the Imagination:
Hoffmann, with Chamisso,
Fouqué and Werner

E. T. A. Hoffmann

Only in recent years has Hoffmann's work been partly freed from his biography.[1] Interpretations may still take account of, but are not now dominated by, his alcoholism (doubtful), his schizothymic states (occasionally miscalled insanity), his ill-health (not now thought to have been syphilitic), or the tension between his professional and artistic selves. Hoffmann (1776–1822) was a lawyer, a very competent and conscientious one and, as far as he could be, a reforming civil servant. He was also a musician of great talent, composing many works that almost fought their way into the permanent repertory, and a draughtsman and caricaturist of skill and dash. He became a known writer slightly late in life, though he had completed a three-volume novel by the time he was nineteen and was writing another before the end of that same year, 1795. Neither has survived and they are known only by their titles, *Cornaro* and *Der Geheimnisvolle*. It is therefore an exaggeration to claim that his literary talent was fired by his passion for his young music pupil Julia Mark (he had also published *Ritter Gluck* before meeting the then thirteen-year-old girl), though the emotional upheaval in the years 1811 and 1812 was certainly acute. The experience, in any case, came at a period of great difficulty for Hoffmann. When Warsaw fell to the French in November 1806 the Prussian civil service in the city was disbanded, and he had found himself out of work. The next few years were therefore spent in attempts to earn a living, as a portrait painter, music critic and teacher, musical director of a theatre (in Bamberg, Leipzig and Dresden) and, eventually, writer. He started mainly with articles on music, but

---

[1] His life has proved infinitely fascinating to two scholars who have devoted most of their energies to it, Hans von Müller (1875–1944) and, more recently, Friedrich Schnapp. For the relationship between biography and work see especially Segebrecht, 1967.

by the time he returned to the service of the Prussian state in 1814 he was an established general author.

Yet, though none of this is decisive, there is no doubt that there are many autobiographical correspondences in the work. The idealized form of Julia Mark does recur in many of the female figures; friends and relations are pictured, often named, sometimes caricatured, in the fiction; and the locale (restaurant, theatre, picnic spot) frequently springs from personal reminiscence. The correspondences must, however, all be treated with some caution, as may be illustrated by comparing the dates of birth of Hoffmann himself and of Johannes Kreisler in *Kater Murr*. Hoffmann was born on 24 January 1776; Kreisler grudgingly reveals that he was born 'on St John Chrysostom's day, that is to say on the twenty-fourth of January of the year one thousand seven hundred and something' (Reclam, *Murr*, p. 93; *PW* V, 226). But St John Chrysostom's day is 27 January, which is also the birthday of Mozart, whose name Amadeus had been adopted by Hoffmann instead of his own third name of Wilhelm. Some mystification, not to say fooling, is at work. We are, in fact, dealing with a fiction. What is really misleading in Hoffmann's case is any attempt to reduce the fictions to exemplars of some autobiographical pathological state. For Hoffmann is the great storyteller of the Romantics and his meanings are as much in how he tells as in what is told. Indeed it is telling, creating, that represents the core of life.

Hoffman's two main definitions of his narrative theory are linked to the titles of two of his collections of Novellen and Märchen, and it makes little difference to the underlying principles that the introductory material containing the theory postdated some of the individual pieces, or that in the *Serapionsbrüder* the framework was something of an afterthought added for publicity purposes. The first two volumes of *Fantasiestücke in Callots Manier* appeared for Easter 1814, with a preface by Jean Paul, and they were followed by a third volume at the end of that year and a fourth at Easter 1815. Hoffmann had considered calling them 'Bilder nach Hogarth' (Pictures after Hogarth) but decided eventually on Jacques Callot (1592–1635), the French engraver, eighty or more of whose prints were to be seen at Bamberg. Hoffmann admired in Callot the great technical ingenuity, the thousands of figures and details in a confined space and yet each individualized, the audacity, power, life and naturalness of the depiction. (Towards the end of Hoffmann's life the sketch *Des Vetters Eckfenster*, 1822, gives a comparable and very moving picture of the dying man's loving gaze at the richness and variety of life as he looks through his window onto the market square.) Yet Hoffmann was equally attracted by the strangeness of the prints, by the way the most ordinary feature takes on a romantic, fantastic quality, by the grotesque deformations that allow mysterious allusions. For the writer the analogy with Callot lies in his receiving into his 'inner romantic imagination' (*PW* I, 63) all the myriad detail of the phenomenal world, and reproducing it in strange attire.

The procedure seems, at first sight, to be reversed in the 'Serapion principle'. *Die Serapions-Brüder. Gesammelte Erzählungen und Märchen* appeared in four volumes between 1819 and 1821, and the loose conversational links were certainly inspired by the regular informal gatherings of Hoffmann and his friends: the publisher Hitzig; Karl Wilhelm Contessa, a popular and not untalented narrative writer; David (Johann) Ferdinand Koreff, fashionable doctor and enthusiast for magnetism; and, less regularly, Chamisso and Fouqué. The opening tale is that of the supposed hermit Serapion whose fancies are so vivid and objective that they entirely replace reality for him. This becomes the 'Serapion principle' (das serapiontische Prinzip), according to which the more powerful the imagination, the more realistic the product. One can only bring effectively to life what one has seen within oneself; and one is reminded of Caspar David Friedrich's prescription that 'the painter should not just paint what he sees before him, but also what he sees within himself'.

Two works by members of the 'Serapion' circle call for brief attention here, Fouqué's *Undine* (1811) and Chamisso's *Peter Schlemihl* (1814), not least because they represent the two poles in the relationship of Märchen and reality.

Fouqué

Friedrich de la Motte Fouqué (1777–1843) was one of the most popular and esteemed authors of the first quarter of the century. His novels and dramas, with their exaggeration of Romantic motifs, their sentimentality and Germanic medievalizing, arouse little or no interest today, in spite of the eccentric but powerful advocacy of the important experimental writer, Arno Schmidt; but the Märchen *Undine* survives because of its apparent folktale naiveté. Undine is the water-sprite become woman, the incorporation of Paracelsus's nature-spirits, the link between innocent, unreflecting nature and conscious mind with its accompaniment of love, sorrow and the soul. The setting is abstractly medieval, resolutely exclusive of the real world, shadowy and lifeless.

Chamisso

Peter Schlemihl, though almost contemporary, seems much closer to Biedermeier; but it can also be seen as a turning from Naturphilosophie to the exact sciences. Adelbert von Chamisso (1781–1838) was eleven when his family fled from France, and the tensions of the subsequent decision to be German rather than French are undoubtedly reflected in *Schlemihl*. The flood of lyrics and ballads is competent enough and covers a great range, including some social and political criticism, partly in the style of Béranger, to which more attention is now being paid; but the poetry never seems to mean more than it says, the subject is presented not transformed. The attraction of *Peter Schlemihl* is in the way that narrative takes over from personal experience and conveys, through a deceptive naiveté, great subtleties of relationship between self and world.

The theme of the lost shadow, coupled to a subdued Faustian motif, was a *trouvaille* that might in itself have explained the immense popularity of the tale; but the clinching charm lies in the narrative tone, with innumerable Märchen motifs housed comfortably in a bourgeois setting (seven-league boots 'braked' by putting on slippers over them). The marriage of supernatural and everyday also occurs, in much more unsettling and daemonic form, in Arnim's *Isabella von Ägypten*; but the atmosphere of *Peter Schlemihl* is a good deal nearer that of the *Taugenichts*.

Interpretations of the shadow and of its loss abound: there is, most obviously, the loss of roots, of home and nation. Or it represents the sum of bourgeois standards, of the requirements of polite society, of what makes man a valid social being; and Thomas Mann saw Schlemihl as the romantic artist, the outsider, unable to meet the demands of society. Another explanation, however, presents the shadow as being the sum of all Romantic philosophy and art; or, again, it is the dark side of existence—night, sorrow, death.

More promising is the generalized recognition that the shadow is the product of a relationship between the solid self and an outside influence. Its absence shows this relationship disturbed. Schlemihl tries to take possession of the world (light) without its consequences (shadow). The shadow is also projected by the self, and there is indeed among some primitive peoples an assumed identity of 'shadow' and 'soul'; thus its loss indicates a serious failure of the self, seduced by its longing for ordering in society.

The outcome is a partial withdrawal from human relationships into a study of the earth sciences, cultivating his worldwide garden, living for his inner self; thus prefiguring to some considerable extent Chamisso's own voyage round the world (1815–18) and his increasing commitment to descriptive botany. So we see this eighteenth-century empiricist, shaken by the French Revolution and the literary impulses of Romanticism, settling resignedly into the role of a nineteenth-century liberal bourgeois.

Hoffmann

To return to Hoffmann. The Callot and Serapion principles are both aspects of the same aesthetic conviction: sensory observation is fired by imagination, and imagination must express itself concretely in the world of the senses. This productive tension between Hoffmann's capacity for myth-making and his evidential observation of the everyday ensures that an aesthetic echoing Novalis and Schelling does not lead to bloodlessness and insubstantiality. Creative energy in its unconscious working throws up images and forms (perhaps it is more than a soothing ploy when he keeps assuring his publisher that the next work is well on the way—in his imagination it no doubt is). Hoffmann's head one might irreverently describe as a nourishing compost-heap hot with speculatory novelties from magnetism to cabbalism, with frenzied personal griefs and disappointments, with raucous comedy—where else in Romanticism would one find an Irish joke? All this is then exteriorized in a much more deliberate way than has often been thought. The juridical mind creates its own patterns of witnesses' statements, of written and oral evidence, of logic and counter-logic, all within the courtroom, all safely in a frame. Thus, though Hoffmann's subject may be the irreparable dualism or heterogeneity of existence, his art-forms offer a reconciling prospect, somewhere on the edge of the real world.

We see this in his first published story *Ritter Gluck* (1809), which prefigures much of his later work. The narrator, in an exactly described Berlin in late August 1809, meets a stranger of unusual appearance and obvious musical gifts. The story ends with the stranger playing and singing from a blank score of Gluck's *Armida*, with embellishments that intensify the original; Gluck himself had died in 1787 but the stranger solemnly announces 'I am the Chevalier Gluck' (*PW* I, 77). Much ingenuity has gone into speculating whether the musician is mad, a reincarnation, a dream, an incorporation of the spirit of music, an expression of the duality of existence, of the coexistence of two realities. Two points may be more worth our attention: the ambivalent position of the narrator and the primacy of the realm of art. Doubt is the narrator's chief characteristic; we are never sure of his position and it seems more than just idiomatic that at the end he should be 'beside himself' (außer mir; *PW* I, 76). He is standing at some strange point which is and is not the Berlin of 1809, and is caught up in the creative power of an artist, who in a sense is also his creature. This creative power torments Gluck, his dreams unfit him for bourgeois life even as they break down the barriers between reality and illusion. Any harmony comes in the final artistic product, symbolized by Gluck's soft clasp of the narrator's hand and his strange smile.

Hoffmann's Märchen pursue the theme of the disjointed world and the possibility of aesthetic reconstruction, of redemption within the sphere of art. They are, in his new formulation, ideal vehicles in which to link the everyday and the supernatural, as implied indeed in the title of *Der goldne Topf. Ein Märchen aus der neuen Zeit*, written between July 1813 and February 1814 (a period, incidentally, during which he was presenting Mozart's *Magic Flute* at Dresden, but also a time of great personal unhappiness and stress).

The locale is modern Dresden, the student Anselmus's notion of happiness is a visit to the pleasure gardens outside the town ('the bliss of the Linke paradise', *PW* I, 278); we should note the term 'paradise' and perhaps also the apples he upsets and the curse placed upon him as a consequence: 'into the crystal thou shalt soon fall' (*PW* I, 277)—the Fall again. This is quickly followed by an awakening of the poetic, magical instinct in him through the crystal bells by which the little fire-snakes first call to him. Misleadingly his bourgeois love Veronika has a voice like crystal; but when Anselmus has blotted the magic hieroglyphs of nature that Archivarius Lindhorst has given him to copy, he finds himself stoppered in a crystal bottle. One ingenious commentator also suggests that Anselmus's lengthy absence from Dresden was caused by his suicide, plunging into the icy, and thus crystalline, waters of the Elbe; but Hoffmann is perhaps inventive enough without such aid.[2]

Precious stones, crystalline forms, have a fascination for the Romantics (one thinks of the carbuncle in *Heinrich von Ofterdingen* and in *Meister Floh*, Reclam, *Floh*, pp. 176–7, and *PW* VI, 180–1, as well as here, *PW* I, 297), as being on the frontier of organic life; but they represent also a threat to man in their cold perfection or their daemonic attraction, like the 'cherry-red sparkling almandine' of *Die Bergwerke zu Falun* (*PW* III, 245). In *Der goldne Topf* crystal is one motif of many through which the everyday world is penetrated by the energy of the poetic world. But the motifs are, until late on in the story, presented in an ambiguous light, so that the reader is kept puzzled as to the nature of reality. What Anselmus had taken for a fire-lily bush turns out to be Archivarius Lindhorst's dressing gown; when he seems to see the Archivarius fly away into the darkness a large bird of prey rises screeching before him—that is what it must have been, and yet how *did* the Archivarius disappear? Changes of perspective, half-concealed shifts of the narrative point of view, rationalizations by the characters themselves, matter-of-fact

---

[2] The Linke baths were on the right bank of the Elbe and a restaurant and theatre were attached to them; see Hoffmann, *Tagebücher*, 1971, p. 408. The connexion between the 'paradisal' aspect of their everyday attractions and the remembrance of ever-present evil in the Fall of Man is heightened also by the colloquial reference to the Devil: 'Ja renne— renne nur zu, Satanskind—ins Kristall bald dein Fall—ins Kristall.'

accounts of the inconceivable, all deliberately serve to confuse the reader.[3] Archivarius Lindhorst's brother has not gone to the dogs but to the dragons, as he relates, taking a pinch of snuff; he adds that he is in mourning for his father who died quite recently, three hundred and eighty-five years ago (*PW* I, 296). This naturally contributes to the comic effect which, in Hoffmann, has many facets other than the often cited grotesque and ironic; indeed in his letter to Kunz on 19 August 1813 giving a first outline of the Märchen he invokes the spirit of Gozzi with the buffooneries of the re-created *commedia dell'arte*. *Der goldne Topf* satirizes elements in contemporary philosophy, uses bureaucratic style for incongruous communications, sets the most philistine objects and professions alongside mythic projections, makes play with clumsiness and with other peculiarities of physique, teases the reader with hints or obfuscations, follows an impassioned argument about whether Lindhorst really is a salamander with a knockabout description of a morning-after hangover. Hoffman's comedy often reminds one of a grimace, a desperate manic grin. The surprise is that he generally brings it so well under control; well enough, for instance, to eliminate the original intention that the golden vessel should be a chamber-pot (though *Klein Zaches* reverts to the motif).[4]

In *Prinzessin Brambilla* (1820) Hoffmann makes an explicit allegorical defence of humour as a reconciling force, summing up the dramatic context of the 'capriccio', as the work is called. Looking into the crystal prism (symbolic of the purity of nature) that is the Urdar lake—as one might look at a stage comedy—the characters in an interpolated Märchen see the antics of their own mirror-image, recognize the nonsense of all existence here below, and are amused. Reversing the order of things is a releasing experience; when the self is exteriorized at the same time as the rest of the world a degree of harmony is achieved (*PW* V, 660–2), and one finds autobiographical confirmation of this in a diary entry about the Julia Mark agonizing: 'found, that it is possible to abstract oneself from Kth [the code for Julia]', 8 January 1812 (*Tagebücher*, p. 132).

The mythic elements in the Märchen are reminiscent of Novalis, whom Hoffmann greatly admired; but the unusual feature is that the

[3] But see John Reddick, 'E. T. A. Hoffmann's *Der goldne Topf* and its "durchgehaltene Ironie"', *MLR*, lxxi (1976), 577–94: the 'systematic irony in the story is of the most radical kind, without any equivalent in German prose until Kafka. For it is an irony that undermines every possibility of wholeness, solidity, continuity.'

[4] The previously mentioned letter to Kunz (*Briefwechsel* I, 408) goes into detail: 'der Jüngling ... bekommt zur Mitgift einen goldnen Nachttopf mit Juwelen bestzt—als er das erstemal hineinpißt verwandelt er sich in einen Meerkater u.s.w.—Sie bemerken Freund! daß Gozzi und Faffner [Schnapp surmises Fouqué's version of the dragon in his drama *Sigurd der Schlangentödter*, 1808] spuken!—'

mythic is now itself viewed ironically. Both in *Der goldne Topf* and *Prinzessin Brambilla* the interpolated or interwoven Märchen derive from G. H. von Schubert, and present the disruption of a golden age (a paradisal garden) by the intrusion of reflective consciousness. Themes from astrology, Indian and Nordic mythology, folk magic, demonology, mesmerism and contemporary psychiatry fill out the mythic structure. Anselmus, in *Der goldne Topf*, escapes from the world of philistinism to the aesthetic realm of Atlantis where love reveals the harmony of all things; he has become a poet.

The visionary content is, however, dampened down by the fictional framework, within which Archivarius Lindhorst has had to show the narrator how to finish and interpret his story. The narrator (and we are to think of the artist's position in the real world) bemoans his fate in having to return to his garret and the uncertainties of life, when Lindhorst taps him on the shoulder and reminds him that he has at least 'an agreeable tenant-farm as a poetic possession in Atlantis' (*PW* I, 374). The poetic imagination, the inner world of dreams, provides a link between reality and the supersensual world, even if only a tentative and discontinuous one.

Klein Zaches, gennant Zinnober. Ein Märchen (1818) can be said to continue the contrast between the bourgeois world and that of the imagination, but in less exalted terms and with much bizarre complication. The philistine, rationalistic world, in which much contemporary thought and many aspects of society are satirized, shows itself to be a world of appearance; reality is found only in the aesthetic experience. In the context of the fiction this resides in the humour, the dominating experience in this Märchen. Later, indeed, Hoffmann expressly insists that its chief purpose is fun and resists allegorical interpretations (preface to *Prinzessin Brambilla*, *PW* V, 601).

Hoffmann's last work, *Meister Floh. Ein Märchen in sieben Abenteuern zweier Freunde*, written between August 1821 and February 1822, resulted in his being charged with defaming senior civil servants. As a member of a commission investigating alleged crimes against the state, mainly by liberal and revolutionary students, he had very honourably stood out against illegalities committed by the powerful chief of police, von Kamptz, whom he now caricatured in the so-called Knarrpanti episodes of *Meister Floh*. The result was that the Märchen appeared in censored form little more than a month before Hoffmann's death on 25 June 1822, and it was not published in its entirety until 1908. In the course of the proceedings against him Hoffmann prepared a defence that has recently been interpreted as an important affirmation of his artistic purposes.[5]

[5] See Wulf Segebrecht, 'E. T. A. Hoffmanns Auffassung von Richteramt und vom Dichterberuf', *JDSG*, xi (1967), 62–138.

This is perhaps pitching it a little high. As a poetological statement it amounts to not very much more than a defence of heterogeneity, of the interrelationship of all the parts (in itself a disingenuous defence of the Knarrpanti episodes, which have a very proper function but were also, in all probability, an afterthought). Nevertheless it does show Hoffmann again expounding a theory of aesthetics, this time resting on the base of Carl Friedrich Flögel's *Geschichte der komischen Literatur* (4 vols, Liegnitz and Leipzig, 1784–7), which allows the bringing together of the most disparate elements.

Meister Floh is, if anything, even more marked by grotesque inventiveness than its predecessors, though there is at times an air of contrivance or of downright muddle. Those critics, particularly Hans-Georg Werner, who are concerned to stress the realist in Hoffmann, see in it a fading of commitment to the suprasensual world, and link this to his return to public life and to the political climate of the post-Napoleonic period. A juster appreciation, at least of the content of the Märchen, may however be provided by the satire on the exact sciences, especially in the persons of Leuwenhöck (Leeuwenhoeck) and Swammerdamm, the seventeenth-century Dutch scientists still apparently alive in Frankfurt in the 1820s; Leuwenhöck indeed calls attention to this mythic abolition of time and space when he says to Pepusch, 'you are the only one in Frankfurt who knows that I have been lying in my grave in the old church at Delft since the year 1725' (Reclam, *Floh*, pp. 37–8; *PW* VI, 40). The two are 'crazy retail dealers of nature' (p. 176 and VI, 179) and are condemned because they seek to examine nature's secrets microscopically and competitively instead of lovingly, reverently. Inner, organic, unifying growth, allegorized here in plant life, passes them by. And it is unity with the organic whole that Peregrinus finds at the end of the Märchen through fidelity and love.

The richness of Hoffmann's themes, from spookery to gnosis, from opera buffa to high tragedy, from alchemy to Naturphilosophie, from folk demonology to exploitation of the subconscious, is to be found not only in his Märchen but also in his Novellen. These, after all, are the Tales of Hoffmann on which much of his reputation was founded, and it should be remembered that he was, for the whole of the nineteenth century, must the best known of the German Romantics, read by Pushkin, Turgenev, Gogol, Dostoevsky,[6] Gorki, Herzen and many others in Russia, by Balzac, Musset, Huysmans and Baudelaire in France, by Irv-

---

[6] The twenty-year-old Dostoevsky, writing to his brother on 9 August 1838, claimed to have read everything of Hoffmann's either in Russian or German. One may note, too, the formation of a group of Russian Serapion brethren after the October Revolution. Some of his later influence was due to his assumed movement from Romanticism to Realism. See Charles E. Passage, *The Russian Hoffmannists*, The Hague, Mouton, 1963, 262 pp.

ing, Hawthorne and Poe in America, and by Heine, Immermann, Raabe, Kafka and Thomas Mann in Germany.

The related themes of Doppelgänger and automata are to be seen in *Die Automate* (1814) and *Der Sandmann* (1815). Hoffmann's fascination with automata and mechanical marvels was, no doubt, fed by viewing mechanical musicians constructed by the Kaufmanns of Dresden or by reading Johann Christian Wiegleb's *Die natürliche Magie*, particularly the second volume published in 1786. Their fictional impact, however, goes far beyond trickery; they raise questions about the nature of personality and of knowledge, about the relationship between the inner creative core in man and the dead mechanical construct without; gravest of all they question the necessity of the self. It is not, as some critics claim, that these automata are meant to induce feelings of mystery and horror in us; for the modern reader their implausibility would prevent this. What Olimpia in *Der Sandmann* does to us she does through Nathanael, for in him we see a descent into madness that a shifting narrative perspective enables us to accept as purely pathological or as accompanied by incursions from some fatal magic realm, some dark creative unconscious. The motif of the eye and the fear of losing one's eyes, which Freud equated in this story with the fear of castration, suggests more strongly the loss of identity, the destruction of the mediator between self and world. The feeling of alienation, of metaphysical abandonment is strong.

An allied theme is the dualism in human personality. *Die Bergwerke zu Falun* (1818) is based on Schubert's account in *Die Nachtseite* of the recovery of a miner's body totally preserved after fifty years, a story used by Hebel, by Arnim in a ballad in *Gräfin Dolores* and, based on Hoffmann's account, by Hugo von Hofmannsthal and by Trakl (in the 'Elis' poems). The stress in Hoffmann is on the rift in Elis Fröbom's nature and his withdrawal into the dangerous regions of the subconscious mind and into the mythic, undifferentiated realm of nature. Elis has fled from love, in his search for unattainable knowledge and perfection; he is, literally, petrified (as in his dream of 'his very being melting into the gleaming rock', *PW* III, 225), and finally crumbles into dust.

Das Fräulein von Scuderi (1818) pursues the theme of the split personality, but here it is apparently associated with the problem of artistic creativity. Cardillac, who murders to regain the jewelry he has wrought, seems behind his bourgeois façade to show a wild possessiveness, a projection of himself into his own creation, that allows of no limits. Ellis (1969) has convincingly shown that sexual neurosis must be added to this; Cardillac has an unconscious desire to protect his mother's virtue and to punish her lover. The overt explanation that his ungovernable lust for jewelry arises from pre-natal influences is so far distanced by narrative point of view that we are to understand it as unconscious camouflage.

The moral authority of Fräulein von Scuderi herself, the detailed descriptions, of Paris as of Falun, the criminological interest (we are here dealing with one of the earliest detective stories) all serve to anchor the story in everyday life. This is characteristic of Hoffmann; whatever the excesses of the imagination, the real world remains vividly at hand.

Recent criticism has also tended to emphasize, and perhaps to overemphasize, Hoffmann's conscious manipulation of narrative structure in his two published novels. The first of these, *Die Elixiere des Teufels*, was written between March 1814 and the end of 1815, with about a year's break between the writing of the first and second parts. There is no need to underplay the influence on it of the Gothic horror novel tradition, notably that of Matthew Gregory Lewis's *The Monk* (1795) and Karl Grosse's *Der Genius* (1790–4); but Hoffmann is both psychologically more subtle and fictively more complex. 'Monk' Lewis proceeds in a series of improvisations, piling horror upon horror as invention allows. Hoffmann, too, provides a rich and improbable variety of action, with apparently inextricable confusion (resolved by an operetta-type denouement) and the most complex family relationships—including the motifs of incest and family guilt that also underlie Brentano's *Romanzen*, and that no doubt have some basis in contemporary biological speculations on heredity.

The alleged editor's preface, not just the usual perfunctory distancing device, sets a calm but open base with the eye travelling from shrub to flower to the distant blue mountains, and the imagination is led to the secret thread running through all life and the dark power brooding over it—unifying themes that we are to seek in the papers that follow, the life of the monk Medardus. As we read we know only that Medardus must have lived to write his own story; only towards the end do we know that writing it was the penance for his dissipation and his crimes, forcing him to relive the latter in his imagination. We travel with him the road to self-knowledge, though his later narrative self sometimes breaks through to forewarn, and the fragmentary and enigmatic nature of personal identity reveals itself in the hallucinatory exteriorization of the self that reaches its climax in the figure of the Doppelgänger (or Doppeltgänger in Romantic usage). The double is indeed a physical one, Medardus's half-brother Viktorin; but the effect is almost wholly psychological, a projection of the evil impulses in a part of his nature. The reader, certainly, cannot tell whether the double is really there or not. The breakup of personality also takes the form of madness, which like dreams and visions, somnambulism, mesmerism and other borderline states stands guard at the portals of mystery. Madness transforms the world, rearranges the combinations within it; so that in Medardus's grotesque vision there are Bosch-like ravens with human faces, a skeleton horse whose rider has a luminous owl's head, ants with dancing human feet, heads creeping about on crickets' legs growing at their ears (Reclam, *Elixiere*, pp. 246–7; *PW* II, 280). It may also be an idyllic release from the pressure of life; that is what gives Belcampo's eccentricity its comic edge, as he 'often doubts the existence of the present' (Reclam, p. 108; *PW* II, 125).

Contemporary psychiatric and medical theory here combines with philosophy.[7] Hoffmann had just been reading Schelling's *Weltseele* and, with great enthusiasm, Schubert's *Die Symbolik des Traumes* (1814), and it would be reasonable to construct an equation consisting of Ego (its crisis of identity and its creation of its own world, even of its own Aurelie), of Schubert's duality of matter and spirit in man (combining in dream or somnambulistic state), of access in these subconscious states to higher forms of appreciation and harmony, and of Schelling's struggle to hold the principle of polarity within the living unity of nature (the 'secret thread' of the preface, sustaining us on the edge of chaos: Reclam, p. 6; *PW* II, 9). Exactness in tracing the various elements would be misconceived and we should equally not take too seriously Hoffmann's description through the mouth of Ottmar, one of the Serapion brethren, of the book as 'based on the most profound Catholic mysticism' (*PW* III, 37). At most, one might acknowledge that it is an attempt to integrate dark powers into a traditional Christian framework. Hoffmann is, above all, creating an atmosphere, exploiting the trappings of the horror novel to create fear and tension. For the rest, how much does Hoffmann believe? What significance is there for him in fate, in family curses, unexplained supernatural intervention, the resolute power of evil, the redemptive power of the Catholic Church? Perhaps not all that much; and yet what makes it different from the ordinary Gothic novel is that Hoffmann's feet, too, have dangled over the pit of self-loss; Narcissus with a stone to crack the mirror. Mystery and terror lie not just in the events but in the whole nature of things.

Hoffmann's greatest achievement is, without much doubt, the novel *Lebensansichten des Katers Murr nebst fragmentarischer Biographie des Kapellmeisters Johannes Kreisler in zufälligen Makulaturblättern*, written between May 1819 and December 1821. That there is much of his autobiography in the figure of Kreisler cannot be doubted, but the work is distanced from Hoffmann the narrator by a number of ingenious devices, mainly bearing the stamp of Sterne or Jean Paul. Hoffmann is the editor to

---

[7] Hoffmann's views on mental illness rest heavily on the theories and observations of Johann Christian Reil, one of the earliest advocates of psychiatric treatment in Germany. See Maria M. Tatar, 'Mesmerism, Madness and Death in E. T. A. Hoffmann's *Der goldne Topf*', *SiR*, xiv (1975), 365–89, and her parallel study 'Psychology and Poetics: J. C. Reil and Kleist's *Prinz Friedrich von Homburg*', *GR*, xlviii (1973), 21–34.

whom a friend has given for publication the manuscript of an autobiography by a tomcat. He passed the manuscript to the publishers but, to his horror, when the galleys arrived he found that the cat's life was interspersed with pages from a biography of his master Kreisler. What the tomcat had done was to use pages from an unpublished book as a pad or as blotting paper and these, mixed up with his own manuscript, had been printed. The editor asks for pardon and hopes that the fragments of Kreisler's biography, available through this 'literary vandalism', will be of interest. At the end of the second volume the editor announces the cat's death and for the third volume, which never appeared, promises the rest of the Kreisler biography, this time interspersed with some further reflections of Murr's. Thus the editor is to accept responsibility for the device of interpolation, and the situation of the musician's life being a mere appendage to the cat's is to be reversed. Yet the announcement of the third volume may be just as much part of the fiction as was the preface, in spite of Hoffmann's claims to the publisher that he had already begun it.

Hans von Müller inexplicably published the two strands of the novel as separate pieces in 1946, carefully unpicking the stitches sewn by Hoffmann. Yet the narrative structure, the parallels and contrasts between the Murr and Kreisler episodes are, in fact, the meaning of the novel. Murr's story, as many critics have pointed out, is a parody of the Bildungsroman or, more pointedly, of contemporary society's inadequate concept of education and culture (Bildung), and this is emphasized by the chapter headings: 'The Youth's Experiences of Life. I too was in Arcady' or 'The Months of Apprenticeship [cats' lives are reckoned in months rather than in Wilhelm Meister's years]. The Capricious Play of Fortune'.

Murr is a pretentious, self-satisfied philistine, who has absorbed enough contemporary philosophical and literary jargon to dress up his selfish instincts as high-flown principles, and to give superficial justification to his claim as a writer. Through him, and he is after all a cat and earns our good-humoured if patronizing smile, Hoffmann satirizes contemporary bourgeois society and literary fashions. Kreisler had already featured in *Kreisleriana*, thirteen essays and sketches written between 1809 and 1815, and there he had been daemonic, fevered to the point of madness, awash with music 'the most romantic of all arts' (*PW* I, 96 and 99).[8] In *Kater Murr* Kreisler is, as he himself points out, a 'circler' (Reclam, *Murr*, p. 71; *PW* V, 203). He *turns* helplessly in a dual attempt

---

[8] For a very useful general article on music in Hoffmann, with much reference to Kreisler, see Dorothee Sölle and Wolfgang Seifert, 'In Dresden und in Atlantis. E. T. A. Hoffmann und die Musik', *Neue Zeitschrift für Musik*, cxxiv (1963), 260–73, reprinted in *E. T. A. Hoffmann*, ed. Helmut Prang, 1976, pp. 237–69.

to relate to society, a vain task for an artist in a world full of limitations (not least the intrigues and pretensions of petty aristocracy), and to achieve a vaguely apprehended paradisal state theoretically, though not actually, attainable through love (tainted by sensuality) or art (which has still to be translated into the signatures of the everyday). A commonplace of older criticism was that this dichotomy, this inability to attain harmony, was biographical; a third section could not have produced a resolution, other than the collapse inherent in Kreisler going mad. The novel is, however, an organized fiction, all appearances notwithstanding. There are cross-illuminations between the Murr and Kreisler episodes, with a detached, ironic narrator holding in balance the alleged autobiography of Murr, who is not without traits from Hoffmann himself, and the narrated life of Kreisler, with the imperfectly informed biographer supplemented by information from Murr and Meister Abraham. These narrative devices are themselves statements about the contingency of an artist's life, and of human life; and the whole is a paradigm of the fragmentary nature of reality and our imperfect hold on it. The fierce comedy of *Kater Murr* lies on a road from Sterne to Joyce. The disenchanted eye makes use of all the resources of fictional technique.

There is a good deal to criticize in Hoffmann: an often cliché-ridden and overblown style, an over-ready commitment to the modish tricks of his day's best sellers, an uncritical dabbling in fashionable ideas, a willingness to let theatrical props invade his fiction. Yet the exploitation of the subconscious, the examination of the alienated self, the attempt to show creatures of the imagination placed in the real world and, above all, the holding of these in balance by irony, by narrative point of view, by the resources of art, are a major contribution to modern literature. The very structure of the literary work itself is to serve to create harmony between reason and imagination, by sharing the artist's dominance over both.

Werner

Hoffmann was both influenced by the work, and highly critical of the character, of Zacharias Werner (1768–1823), with whom he became acquainted when both were in the Prussian civil service in Warsaw in 1805–6. The traditional 'romantic' dichotomous personality is seen at its most crass in Werner, much of whose writing is an unconscious attempt to reconcile his own priapism and religiosity. He is undoubtedly the most gifted dramatist of German Romanticism (excluding, as we do, Kleist) and it was his technical virtuosity that particularly fascinated Goethe. Some attempts at a rehabilitation of Werner as more than just an interesting technician and psychological case-study have recently been made; and it is undoubtedly true that much light has been thrown on his development from Enlightenment, through Freemasonry and its symbols coupled with the theosophy of Böhme and Saint-Martin, to priesthood in the Catholic Church and fashionable sermons in Vienna.

En route his discovery of the early Romantics reinforced the esoteric symbolism and the medieval trappings as well as the mystical identity of religion, art and love, and the concept of the artist as mediator, as the modern high priest. The dramas tend to be heavily symbolical (and to have their symbols reinterpreted after his conversion), and both action and characters sometimes suffer from this; but Werner does achieve strong theatrical effects with well-managed tensions and climaxes, show-piece scenes and evocative tableaux.

The accident of literary history makes him appear to be the founder of that most dubious genre, the tragedy of fate (Schicksalstragödie), with his one-act *Der vierundzwanzigste Februar*, written in 1809 but not published until 1815, with only partially identifiable additions and changes. The apparatus of family curse, fatal knife, ominous date, are here the background to a classically taut play in which guilt and forgiveness play a larger part than fatalism (though to call it a play of redemption, as Krogoll does, is pitching it rather high). In other hands the Schicksalstragödie will decline even further from the earnest consideration of the role of fate in drama that we find in Schiller and the Schlegels, Adam Müller or Solger. Yet even in Werner it is difficult not to believe that the intention is often just to make the blood curdle; and throughout his work, behind the eclecticism and sentimentality, the elevated religio-erotic system and the high claims of art, there seeps through a sad sense of contrivance, a whiff of the bogus, that sets him below the major figures of Romanticism, even when, as in *Die Elixiere des Teufels*, their stage properties are equally second-hand and second-rate. Carlyle, in spite of severe criticisms, arrives at a more generous final verdict and may have the last word: 'Werner [had] a richly gifted nature; but never wisely guided or resolutely applied; ... a gorgeous, deep and bold imagination; ... the main elements of no common poet; save only that one was still wanting,—the force to cultivate them, and mould them into pure union.'[9]

---

[9] Thomas Carlyle, 'Life and Writings of Werner', first published in the *Foreign Review*, vol. 1 (1828), with substantial translations from *Die Söhne des Tals*. His splendid invective against Werner's prose deserves to be quoted: 'His prose, again, is among the worst known to us: degraded with silliness; diffuse, nay tautological, yet obscure and vague; contorted into endless involutions; a misshapen, lumbering, complected coil, well-nigh inexplicable in its entanglements, and seldom worth the trouble of unravelling.'

8

Coda:
The Swabians

If we ask, 'What happened to Romanticism? When did it die?' we involve ourselves somewhat unprofitably with definition and classification and the associated danger of attaching more importance to literary history than to literature. Yet they are fair questions, though they cannot be answered in any strictly chronological way. Certainly many of the chief Romantic writers were still active after 1815, but, as we have seen, the pressures of the Restoration period were very different from those of the French Revolution or the Wars of Liberation. The immediate effects of industrialization were beginning, though very gradually, to show themselves in local societies that were still largely agrarian. In 1811 Krupp opened in Essen his first cast-steel plant, and at the end of that year the town of Freiberg in Saxony (the home of the mining academy) began to be lit by gas; and one could multiply such examples. A climate of, by present standards, mild repression in many German states coincided with rather faint liberal movements towards constitutionalism in others. Revolutionary fervour was again to show itself, but, in the immediate aftermath of the Napoleonic period, the majority tendency was to seek change in a very tentative way and by constant and somewhat jingoistic reference to the Germanic past. The legacy of the French Revolution went underground, the cosmopolitan dream receded. There was something of a fear that change, when it came, might be a rough beast, out of control.

Now all this is very generalized, and socio-economic explanations are as partial as any others; but some shift of mood towards what we now recognize as Biedermeier certainly took place.

Müller

Even a poet as derivative as Wilhelm Müller (1794–1827), now mainly remembered for the Schubert settings of his song-cycles, is more complex than he seems and perhaps more responsive to the shift of the times. The influence of the *Wunderhorn* is admittedly very evident in the motifs and limpid verbal structures of 'Die schöne Müllerin' (written 1817–20) and the sentimentalities of late Romanticism pervade 'Die Winterreise' (1823). Yet alongside the simplified view of a limited world there is a wryness, a sense of observing his own naiveté, that reminds us of the Heine of *Buch der Lieder*, who spoke warmly of his debt to Müller.

The Swabians

A good deal of fruitless energy has gone into argument as to whether the Swabian school, also called the 'Tübinger Romantik', are to be assigned to Romanticism or Biedermeier.[1] What one can say with some confidence is that, at least in their early years, they thought of themselves as Romantics in, for instance, the confrontations with Voß and Baggesen.[2]

Kerner. Justinus Kerner (1786–1862) does, indeed, have some very obvious Romantic traits, from infatuation with the *Wunderhorn* to an obsession with death and with quasi-supernatural investigations. He lies uneasily between literature, Naturphilosophie and naive credulity, as in his account of the mediumistic experiences of the somnambulistic neurasthenic *Die Seherin von Prevorst* (1829). Yet he was personally convinced of the empirical nature of his observations; Heine, incidentally, did not fail to note (in *Der Schwabenspiegel*) that among his publications was an essay on poisoning by eating black pudding—less picturesquely, on the effect of fatty acids on the animal organism. Kerner's complicated and gregarious personality deserves more consideration than it has hitherto had—and perhaps more than his works.

[1] Heinz Otto Burger, *Schwäbische Romantik. Studie zur Charakteristik des Uhlandkreises*, Stuttgart, Kohlhammer, 1928, 181 pp., is for Romanticism; Otto Ackermann, *Schwabentum und Romantik. Geistesgeschichtliche Untersuchungen über Justinus Kerner und Ludwig Uhland*, Breslau, Priebatsch, 1939, vii, 131 pp., is for Biedermeier; Gerhard Storz, *Schwäbische Romantik. Dichter und Dichterkreise im alten Württemberg*, Stuttgart, Kohlhammer, 1967, 164 pp., distinguishes between two Swabian groups. There is useful detail on Kerner, Uhland and Hauff in *Dichter aus Schwaben. Ein Führer durch das Schiller-Nationalmuseum*, ed. Bernhard Zeller, Marbach, 1964, 199 pp. See also Hartmut Fröschle, *Justinus Kerner und Ludwig Uhland: Geschichte einer Dichterfreundschaft*, Göppingen, Kümmerle, 1972, 159 pp.

[2] See Richard Ullmann and Helene Gotthard, *Geschichte des Begriffes 'Romantisch'*, 1927, pp. 319–23. Kerner and Uhland produced, from 11 January to 1 March 1807, a handwritten periodical *Sonntagsblatt für gebildete Stände* (the 8 February number alone being 'für Ungebildete') in conscious opposition to Cotta's rationalist *Morgenblatt für gebildete Stände*. The periodical was reproduced in 1961 with a substantial introduction by Bernhard Zeller, Marbach, Schiller-Nationalmuseum, 180 pp.

Uhland. Ludwig Uhland (1787–1862) wrote an enthusiastic essay 'Über das Romantische' in 1807, and one may take from it two pointers to a changed attitude. He gives a list of characters who are essentially 'romantic': monks, nuns, crusaders, knights of the Grail and all 'poetic knights and ladies of the Middle Ages'. Nature, too, has its romantic motifs: flowers, rainbows, sunrise and sunset, cloud formations, moonlit nights, mountains, streams and chasms, places where spirits wander. Nothing could be more evocative of the themes of his own early poetry, with the ballads also drawing on the syntax and vocabulary of the folk tradition or, at any rate, of the *Wunderhorn*. Yet the very compilation of such a list of motifs carries in itself some suggestion of artificiality, some overreliance on convention.

The essay also attempts to define the relationship of the romantic to the infinite. Weary of longing for the unattainable, man comes to seek the infinite in the world of objects. It is true that the mystical and symbolic is still thought of as shining through phenomena, but there can be no doubt that the emphasis has moved from speculative flights and exalted experience to a far more prosaic and circumspect field, markedly objective in character, presenting a community and its idealized past to itself. No longer progressive, universal poetry, but a local, enthusiastically German one, feeding on the trivialization of motifs. Gutzkow, in 'Goethe, Uhland und Prometheus' (1835), was unkind, but not wildly inaccurate: 'The lyrics are so restricted to their little hills and valleys, so domestic, peaceful and happy, that they know of no sorrow in the world except that of coming back from a walk without having picked up a new simile.'

Uhland's lyrics and ballads were well made and undemanding, and were impressed into the consciousness of generations of German schoolchildren. In, for instance, the revised twenty-first (1894) edition of Wolff's enormously popular school-anthology *Mustersammlung deutscher Gedichte* Uhland is represented by twenty-three poems, surpassed only by Schiller with twenty-five. Among other scores: Goethe fifteen, Eichendorff five, Brentano none.

It would, however, be unfair and misleading to leave Uhland there. What he eventually became—apart from a rather ineffectual politician—was a literary historian and folklorist of distinction. The Romantic afflatus subsides, but the whole movement's latent commitment to the past takes over.

Hauff. Indeed in *Lichtenstein* by Wilhelm Hauff (1802–27) the Swabian school, which only acknowledged such a best-selling prose writer rather reluctantly, produced in 1826 a prototype of the regional historical novel which was also being developed by Alexis, both heavily influenced by Walter Scott.

Hauff still draws many of his motifs from Romanticism; *Lichtenstein* is subtitled 'eine romantische Sage', and the historical background, authenticated by explanatory notes, provides a décor for them. What it does not do is to tap the resources of the Romantic historical imagination and adapt them for the present in the way Arnim's novels do.[3] His Märchen (1826-8) are a good deal more significant, not just because of their overwhelming popularity for a hundred and fifty years, but because of their narrative verve, their total dedication to the story. They have none of the Romantic Märchen's tortuous allegory; they may incorporate Hoffmannesque themes, but the fantastic becomes the narratively sensational and reality is no longer unnervingly undermined. The belletristic tradition is here reaching back to the eighteenth century; but Hauff, who in his short life pre-eminently learned to give the public what it wanted, equally moved towards a realistic portrayal of society (like the later Tieck) even if the appurtenances were sometimes those of the trivial inheritors of Romantic themes. He was an entertainer of a high order, an eclectic who would pillage anywhere in the interests of narrative; and what ultimately separates him from the Romantics is a lack of belief in the regenerative function of language.

---

[3] Hauff himself, in a letter to Hofrat Winkler (the writer Theodor Hell) on 17 April 1827, acknowledges that he may not be able to avoid formal influences from his contemporaries 'doch soll mir der Geist ungegöthet, ungetieckt, ungeschlegelt und ungemeistert bleiben'.

Abbreviations

I: General

ann., annotated (by)
art., article
bibl., bibliography, etc.
c., century
ca, circa
comm., commentary (by)
coll., collection
crit., critical, criticism
diss., dissertation
ed., editor, edited by, edition
Fest., Festschrift
incl., including, includes
introd., introduction, introduced by
Jb., Jahrbuch
Jg, Jahrgang
Jh., Jahrhundert
lit., literature, Literatur, littérature
n.d., no date
n.ser., new series
no., number
publ., publication, published (by)
R., Romantic, Romantik, etc. (e.g. r.e=romantische)
repr., reprint(ed)
revd, revised
supp., supplement(ed)
transl., translated (by), translation
U.P., University Press
vol., volume

II. Periodicals, Series, Publishers

AKML, Abhandlungen zur Kunst-, Musik- und Literaturwissenschaft
CG, Colloquia Germanica
CL, Comparative Literature
DDRW, Deutsche Dichter der Romantik, ed. B. v. Wiese, 1971 (see Bibliog. Guide I. 6a)
DL, Deutsche Literatur in Entwicklungsreihen
DU, Der Deutschunterricht (Stuttgart)
DVLH, Deutsche Vierteljahrsschrift für Literaturwissenschaft und Geistesgeschichte
EG, Études Germaniques
Euph, Euphorion
GLL, German Life and Letters
GQ, German Quarterly
GR, Germanic Review
GRM, Germanisch-Romanische Monatsschrift
JAAC, Journal of Aesthetics and Art Criticism
JDSG, Jahrbuch der deutschen Schiller-Gesellschaft
JEGP, Journal of English and Germanic Philology
JFDH, Jahrbuch des Freien Deutschen Hochstifts
JiG, Jahrbuch für Internationale Germanistik
JWGV, Jahrbuch des Wiener Goethe-Vereins
LJb, Literaturwissenschaftliches Jahrbuch der Görres-Gesellschaft
MLN, Modern Language Notes
MLQ, Modern Language Quarterly
MLR, Modern Language Review
NRu, Die Neue Rundschau
OGS, Oxford German Studies
OL, Orbis Litterarum
PEGS, Publications of the English Goethe Society
RG, Recherches Germaniques
Ro, Romantisme
SiR, Studies in Romanticism
SM, Sammlung Metzler
UB, Universal-Bibliothek, Reclam
UNCSGLL, University of North Carolina Studies in the Germanic Languages and Literatures
WB, Weimarer Beiträge
Wiss BG, Wissenschaftliches Buchgesellschaft, Darmstadt
WW, Wirkendes Wort
ZBLG, Zürcher Beiträge zur deutschen Literatur- und Geistesgeschichte
ZDP, Zeitschrift für deutsche Philologie

Bibliographical Guide

Except for works of considerable, sometimes historical importance this guide limits itself, though not slavishly, to publications of the last fifteen years or so. Other works, notably Osborne, provide comprehensive listings of earlier studies. 'Romantic', 'Romantik', etc., are throughout abbreviated to 'R.', and their derivatives appropriately. Over-elaborate subtitles and unhelpful series indications have been silently omitted, and the titles of *Festschriften* are often drastically curtailed, with only the first editor named. Other abbreviations are either self-explanatory or are in the List of Abbreviations. Square brackets enclose references to the section of this guide containing fuller details of works cited in abbreviated form.

I

1a **Bibliography.** John Osborne, *R.*, Bern and Munich, Francke, 1971, 166 pp.; very full, up to 1968. For annual listings with crit. comments, too often in a Germanic English, see *The R. Movement: A Selective and Crit. Bibl.*, publ. each autumn as a supplement to *English Language Notes*; also, of course, the relevant sections in *Germanistik* and in *The Year's Work in Modern Language Studies*. In spite of its title the annual Weimar *Internationale Bibl. zur deutschen Klassik 1750–1850* incls all the R. writers.

1b **Research.** Joachim Müller, 'R. forschung', I in *DU*, xv (1963), II in xvii (1965), III in xx (1968), IV in xxiv (1974); Heide Eilert, 'R. (Forschungsbericht)'. *WW*, xxvii (1977), 132–42, to be continued.

1c **Periodicals and almanacs.** To Houben and Walzel (1904), Pissin (1910), Bobeth (1911) and Lanckoronska and Rümann (1954), add Sibylle Obenaus, *Die deutschen allgemeinen kritischen Zeitschriften in der ersten Hälfte des 19. Jhs*, Frankfurt, Buchhändler-Vereinigung, 122 columns (from *Archiv für Geschichte des Buchwesens*, xiv (1973)); and Paul Hocks and Peter Schmidt, *Literarische und politische Zeitschriften 1789–1805*, Stuttgart, Metzler, 1975, vi, 141 pp. (=SM, 121).

It is worth noting, too, that the periodicals of the period, over twenty of them between the years 1796–1830, have been repr. by Kraus, Nendeln, Liechtenstein.

2a **Anthologies.** The twenty-three vols of the R. series (1931–50) in *Deutsche Lit. in Entwicklungsreihen* [DL], Leipzig, Reclam, remain indispensable; repr. Darmstadt, Wiss BG, 1964–71. The best anthology for general use is *Die deutschen R. er*, 2 vols, ed. Gerhard Stenzel, Salzburg and Stuttgart, Bergland-Buch, [*ca* 1964], 1133, 1104 pp. *R.*, 2 vols, ed. Hans-Jürgen Schmitt, Stuttgart, Reclam, 1974, 318, 304 pp. (= Die deutsche Lit. in Text und Darstellung, UB, 9629–36), is also useful. Ronald Taylor's *The R. Tradition in Germany*, London, Methuen, 1970, xii, 272 pp., confines itself to theoretical writings and extends the definition to include Herder, Schopenhauer and Wagner; excellent introds to each selection.

2b *Der Poesiebegriff der deutschen R.*, ed. Karl Konrad Polheim, Paderborn, Schöningh, 1972, 500 pp., is a wide-ranging compilation of the R's' own statements. Contemporary reviews are extensively ann. Oscar Fambach in his *Ein Jh. deutscher Lit. kritik (1750–1850)*, Berlin, Akademie, particularly vols IV, *Das große Jahrzehnt*, 1958, xix, 684 pp., and V. *Der r.e. Rückfall*, 1963, xxxiii, 797 pp. *Die andere R.*, ed. Helmut Schanze, Frankfurt, Insel, 1967, 216 pp., is a modest coll. of pieces, mainly by Fr. Schlegel, designed to show the public that R. was not just dreamy and Germanic.

2c The great quarry for R. letters is Josef Körner's *Krisenjahre der Frühr.: Briefe aus dem Schlegelkreis*, 3 vols, Bern and Munich, Francke, vols I and II as a 2nd, unchanged version, 1968, xxiv, 669, 548 pp., of the original Brünn, 1936–7 ed., and vol. III, *Kommentarband*, 1958, 726 pp.

2d A flavour of the popular lit. of the period is given in *Lieblings-Bücher von dazumal. Eine Blütenlese aus den erfolgreichsten Büchern von 1750–1860*, selected by Ernst Heimeran with an introd. by Horst Kunze, first publ. in 1938 and repr. 1965, Munich, Heimeran, 439 pp. Kunze later made his own selection with a revd introd. and omitting non-fiction: *Gelesen und geliebt. Aus erfolgreichen Büchern 1750–1850*, Berlin, Rütten & Loening, 1959, 387 pp.

3 **The term.** The most comprehensive treatment is now '*R.*' *and its Cognates. The European History of a Word*, ed. Hans Eichner, Manchester U.P. and Toronto U.P., 1972, 536 pp. Raymond Immerwahr contributes, but see also his *R.isch. Genese und Tradition einer Denkform*, Frankfurt, Athenäum, 1972, 211 pp. For many details one still needs to refer to Richard Ullmann and Helene Gotthart, *Geschichte des Begriffes 'R.isch' in Deutschland*, Berlin, Ebering, 1927, xiii, 378 pp.

4 **History of scholarship.** Attitudes to R. are traced by Karl Tober in a chapter on 'Das Epochenproblem' in his *Urteile und Vorurteile über Lit.*, Stuttgart, Kohlhammer, 1970, pp. 18–28; and by Hans Meyer, 'Fragen der R.forschung', in his *Zur deutschen Klassik und R.*, Pfullingen, Neske, 1963, pp. 263–305. Henry H. H. Remak has a number of excellent arts with full bibl.: see especially his chapter 'Trends of Recent Research on West Euro-

pean R.', in 'R.' and its Cognates, pp. 475–500, and 'West European R.: Definition and Scope', in *Comparative Lit.*, ed. Newton P. Stallkecht, Carbondale, Southern Illinois U.P., 1961, pp. 223–59. See also Günter Hartung, 'Zum Bild der deutschen R. in der Lit.wissenschaft der DDR', *WB*, xxii (1976), 167–76.

5 **Origins.** The most extensive survey is Roger Ayrault, *La Genèse du r. allemand*, 4 vols, Paris, Aubier, 1961–76, 382, 400, 572, 576 pp., though the later vols are about the Rs themselves rather than their predecessors. Van Tieghem's various works on preromanticism are still of value. See also Ernst Benz, *Les Sources mystiques de la philosophie r. allemande*, Paris, Vrin, 1968, 153 pp.; and Hans Graßl, *Aufbruch zur R.: Bayerns Beitrag zur deutschen Geistesgeschichte 1765–1785*, Munich, Beck, 1968, xiv, 494 pp.

Klaus Weimar, *Versuch über Voraussetzung und Entstehung der R.*, Tübingen, Niemeyer, 1968, 90 pp., is a not altogether successful attempt to trace its origins in attitudes to music and the visual arts.

Ulrich Hubert, *Karl Philipp Moritz und die Anfänge der R.: Tieck — Wackenroder — Jean Paul — Fr. und A. W. Schlegel*, Frankfurt, Athenäum, 1971, xxiii, 229 pp.

6a **General surveys.** Works by the following are still of crit. as well as historical interest, but bibl. details may be found in Osborne's *R.*: Benz, Gundolf, Haym, Heine (there is a new crit. ed. of *Die r.e. Schule*, ed. Helga Weidmann, Stuttgart, Reclam, 1976, 451 pp. = UB, 9831(5)), Huch, Kluckhohn, Körner, Korff, Linden, Nadler, Petersen, Strich, Walzel. Selections from many of them, and from others, are to be found in *Begriffsbestimmung der R.*, ed. Helmut Prang, Darmstadt, Wiss BG, 1968, 441 pp., and in *The R. Movement* by Anthony Thorlby, London, Longmans, 1966, xv, 176 pp., with extensive comm. and also short selections from the R. writers themselves. Neither of these is limited to German lit., as are the following: *Deutsche Dichter der R.: Ihr Leben und Werk* [*DDRW*], ed. Benno von Wiese, Berlin, Erich Schmidt, 1971, 530 pp., fiercely reviewed by Oskar Seidlin, *JEGP*, lxxii (1973), 594–8, but with some excellent pieces; *Die deutsche R.: Poetik, Formen und Motive*, ed. Hans Steffen, Göttingen, Vandenhoeck & Ruprecht, 1967, 288 pp.; and *The R. Period in Germany: Essays*, ed. Siegbert Prawer, London, Weidenfeld & Nicolson, 1970, 343 pp. In the series 'Erläuterungen' the vol. *R.*, ed. Johannes Mittenzwei, Berlin, Volk und Wissen, 1967, 668 pp., is also a collective work, though in this case a systematic history, much of it good, some crudely propagandist. The best introd. to all the various aspects of the period is still *R.: Ein Zyklus Tübinger Vorlesungen*, ed. Theodor Steinbüchel, Tübingen and Stuttgart, Wunderlich, 1948, 271 pp. A useful essay is that by Clemens Heselhaus, 'Die r.e. Gruppe', in *Die europäische R.*, by Ernst Behler and others, Frankfurt, Athenäum, 1972, pp. 44–162. *Dichter der deutschen R.*, ed. Detlev Luders, 117 pp., is the catalogue of a 1976 exhibition by the Freies Deutsches Hochstift. The 1978 *DVLG* supp. vol. *R. in Deutschland* is a major coll. of contributions to a symposium on R.

6b Two attempts at characterization of the R. movement stand out: Wilhelm Emrich, 'R. und modernes Bewußtsein', in his *Geist und Widergeist*, Frankfurt, Athenäum, 1965, pp. 236–57, also as *Der Universalismus der deutschen R.*, in *Abhandlungen der... Mainzer Akademie*, Jg. 1964, 1; and Arthur Henkel, 'Was ist eigenlitch r.isch?', in *Fest. Alewyn*, ed. Herbert Singer, Cologne and Graz, Böhlau, 1967, pp. 292–308.

6c German R. has its proper place in H. G. Schenk's *The Mind of the European Rs*, London, Constable, 1968, xxiv, 303 pp., and Lilian R. Furst, *R. in Perspective. A Comparative Study of Aspects of the R. Movements in England, France and Germany*, London, Macmillan, 1969, 366 pp., though neither does full justice to its complexity.

The main study in English is still Ralph Tymms, *German R.*, London, Methuen, 1955, vii, 406 pp., full of insights and strong opinions. *German Lit. of the 18th and 19th cs*, by E. L. Stahl and W. E. Yuill, London, Cresset, 1970 (= Introds to German Lit., 3), disposes of R. very briskly in pp. 112–43; there is a very full bibl. section. L. A. Willoughby, *The R. Movement in Germany*, Oxford U.P., 1930, vi, 192 pp., was a fine conspectus in its day, but reprinting it in 1966 (New York, Russell) was no service. Roger Cardinal's *German Rs in Context*, London, Studio Vista, 1975, 160 pp., should not be written off as a small book with many pictures; it gives the right feel of the movement of ideas in the various arts. Marcel Brion, *L'Allemagne r.*, Paris, Albin Michel, vol. 1, 1962, 356 pp.; II, 1963, 383 pp.; III/1, 1977, 288 pp., is generalized and mainly biographical in approach.

The only major German surveys of recent years are Werner Kohlschmidt's first-rate *Geschichte der deutschen Lit.*, vol. III, *Von der R. bis zum späten Goethe*, Stuttgart, Reclam, 1974, 764 pp.; and Gerhard Storz, *Klassik und R.*, Mannheim, Bibliographisches Institut, 1972, 247 pp., straightforward but dated. Attention should also be drawn to the many retrospective references to R. in Friedrich Sengle's monumental *Biedermeierzeit*, 2 vols, Stuttgart, Metzler, 1971–2, xx, 727, xvi, 1152 pp. Colls of essays by individuals are Gerhard Schneider, *Studien zur deutschen R.*, Leipzig, Koehler & Amelang, 1962, 269 pp., forcing too much into an ideological framework; and Klaus J. Heinisch, *Deutsche R. — Interpretationen*, Paderborn, Schöningh, 1966, 220 pp., sensible.

There is much elegant and illuminating comment on German lit. and thought in a work primarily on English R.: M. H. Abrams, *Natural Supernaturalism. Tradition and Revolution in R. Lit.*, London, Oxford U.P., 1971, 550 pp. Two highly intelligent comparative studies are Eudo C. Mason, *Deutsche und englische R.: Eine Gegenüberstellung*, Göttingen, Vandenhoeck & Ruprecht, 1959, 2nd enlarged ed. 1966, 140 pp.; and René Wellek, 'German and English R.: A Confrontation', in his *Confrontations*, Princeton, U.P., 1965, pp. 3–33. See also Horst Oppel, *Englisch-deutsche Lit. beziehungen*, 2 vols, Berlin, Erich Schmidt, 1971, 142, 160 pp., with excellent bibls. A regional study by Arno Lubos is announced: *Schlesisches Schrifttum der R. und Populärr.*, Munich, Fink.

II Contemporary background

1 **Art.** Major new works are: Helmut Börsch-Supan and Karl Wilhelm Jähnig, *Caspar David Friedrich*, Munich, Prestel, 1973, 512 pp. (also Bösch-

Supan's *C.D.F.*, London, Thames & Hudson, and New York, Braziller, 184 pp.); and Jörg Traeger, *Philipp Otto Runge und sein Werk*, Munich. Prestel, 1975, 556 pp. Both works have exhaustive bibls, and Kurt Speth also reviews recent lit. on Friedrich in *Aurora*, xxxvi (1976), 75–106. See also Rudolph M. Bisanz, *German R. and Ph. O. Runge: A Study in 19th c. Art Theory and Iconography*, Dekalb, Northern Illinois U.P., xi, 144 pp., though with reservations; Gerhard S. Kallienke, *Das Verhältnis von Goethe und Runge im Zusammenhang mit Goethes Auseinandersetzung mit der Frühr.*, Hamburg, Buske, 1973, 158 pp.; Ulrich Finke, *German Painting from R. to Expressionism*, 1974, 256 pp., and the sparkling Robert Rosenblum, *Modern Painting and the Northern R. Tradition: Friedrich to Rothko*, 1975, 240 pp., both London, Thames & Hudson; Christa Franke, *Ph. O. Runge und die Kunstansichten Wackenroders und Tiecks*, Marburg, Elwert, 1974, x, 130 pp., a careful study; and *Ph. O. Runge. Leben und Werk in Daten und Bildern*, ed. Stella Wega Mathieu, Frankfurt, Insel, 1977. *Bildende Kunst und Lit.: Beiträge zum Problem ihrer Wechselbeziehungen im 19. Jh.*, ed. Wolfdietrich Rasch, Frankfurt, Klostermann, 1970, 192 pp., incls Fr. Schlegel, Tieck, Brentano, Runge, Görres, Hoffmann.

2 **Music.** Works on Lieder are listed later, as are studies of music in individual cases, e.g. Hoffmann and Wackenroder. Many parallels between lit. and music are drawn in Georg Knepler, *Musikgeschichte des 19. Jhs.* 2 vols, Berlin, Henschel, 1961, 1038 pp., a Marxist interpretation.

3 **History and social background.** Golo Mann, *The History of Germany since 1789*, London, Chatto & Windus, 1968, xii, 547 pp., is perhaps the best starting point. On the French Revolution and its aftermath see Jacques Droz, *L'Allemagne et la révolution française*, Paris, P.U.F., 1949, vii, 500 pp., and *Le r. allemand et l'état. Résistance et collaboration dans l'Allemagne napoléonienne*, Paris, Payot, 1966, 310 pp.; *Deutsche Lit. und Französische Revolution. Sieben Studien*, Göttingen, Vandenhoeck & Ruprecht, 1974, 191 pp.; Ernst Behler, 'Die Auffassung der Revolution in der deutschen Frühr.', in *Essays on European Lit.: Fest.* Dieckmann, ed. Peter Uwe Hohendahl, St Louis, Washington U.P., 1972, pp. 191–215. See also the excellent anthology by Claus Träger, *Die französische Revolution im Spiegel der deutschen Lit.*, Leipzig, Reclam, 1975, 1134 pp. (UB, 597).

Geneviève Bianquis, *La Vie quotidienne en Allemagne à l'époque r. (1795–1830)*, Paris, Hachette, 1958, 264 pp., is useful; Inge Stephan, *Literarischer Jakobinismus in Deutschland (1789–1806)*, Stuttgart, Metzler, 1976, vii, 202 pp. (=SM, 150), has excellent general documentation of the period.

4a **Philosophy.** Entries for Baader, Fichte, Schelling and Schleiermacher follow in VI.

In spite of its age the best general introd. is still Nicolai Hartmann, *Die Philosophie des deutschen Idealismus*, in 2 vols 1923–9, repr. 1960 in 1 vol., Berlin, de Gruyter, 575 pp. For concepts see the entirely new ed. of Rudolf Eisler's *Wörterbuch der philosophischen Begriffe*, now called *Historisches Wörterbuch der Philosophie*, ed. Joachim Ritter and Karlfried Gründer, Basel, Schwabe, 1971 ff., to be completed in 9 or 10 vols.

4b **Religion.** For the religious history see Karl Barth, *Die protestantische Theologie im 19. Jh.*, Zollikon/Zürich, Evangelischer Verlag, 1947, vii, 611 pp., and in a number of subsequent eds; Claude Welch, *Protestant Thought in the 19th c.*, vol. 1, *1799–1870*, New Haven and London, Yale U.P., 1972, x, 325 pp., with a discussion of other histories; *Katholizismus*, ed. Langer, see under VI, Adam Müller.

4c **Philosophy of history.** *Deutsche Geschichtsphilosophie von Lessing bis Jaspers*, Bremen, Schünemann, 1959, ic, 468 pp., a selection of extracts, has a long and lucid introd. by Kurt Rossmann. See also: George G. Iggers, *The German Conception of History ... from Herder to the Present*, Middletown (Conn.), Wesleyan U.P., 1968, xii, 363 pp.; Gerda Heinrich, *Geschichtsphilosophische Positionen der deutschen Frühr. (Fr. Schlegel und Novalis)*, Berlin, Akademie, 1976, 261 pp.

4d **Naturphilosophie.** There is still no substitute for the ann. anthology *R.e Naturphilosophie*, ed. Christoph Bernoulli and Hans Kern, Jena, Diederichs, 1926, xix, 431 pp., but consult also: the lengthy arts with detailed bibls in the *Dictionary of Scientific Biography*, New York, Scribner, 1970 ff., to be completed in some 20 vols; M. J. Petry's introd. to his ed. and transl. of *Hegel's Philosophy of Nature*, 3 vols, London, Allen and Unwin, 1970, very detailed; Barry Gower, 'Speculation in Physics: The History and Practice of "Naturphilosophie"', *Studies in the History and Philosophy of Science*, iii (1973), 301–56; H. A. M. Snelders, 'R. and Naturphilosophie and the Inorganic Natural Sciences 1797–1840', *SiR*, ix (1970), 193–215; Walter D. Wetzels, 'Aspects of Natural Science in German R.', *SiR*, x (1971), 44–59; Elinor Shaffer, 'Das "Bild der Natur" in der r.en Naturphilosophie', in *Akten des V. Internationalen Germanisten-Kongresses, Cambridge 1975*, ed. Leonard Forster, Bern and Frankfurt, Lang, 1976, III, 156–61.

III Genres

1 **Lyric.** There is no adequate modern study of the R. lyric. Of the general surveys Rudolf Haller, *Geschichte der deutschen Lyrik... bis zu Goethes Tod*, Bern and Munich, Francke, 1967, 486 pp. (=Sammlung Dalp, 101), is competent; Johannes Klein's voluminous *Geschichte der deutschen Lyrik*, Wiesbaden, Steiner, 1957, xiv, 876 pp., cannot be recommended.

Hans-Henrick Krummacher, *Das 'als ob' in der Lyrik*, Cologne and Graz, Böhlau, 1965, 227 pp., has some 70 interesting pages on the Rs. Gaudenz Ruf, *Wege der Spätr.: Dichterische Verhaltensweisen in der Krise des Lyrischen*, Bonn, Bouvier, 1969, 248 pp. (=AKML, 83), is, in fact, less concerned with the genre than with the subjective attitude.

2a **Narrative.** Walter Bausch, *Theorie des epischen Erzählens in der deutschen Frühr.*, Bonn, Bouvier, 1964, 179 pp., mainly Fr. Schlegel; Hans Hiebel, *Individualität und Totalität. Zur Geschichte und Kritik des bürgerlichen Poesiebegriffs von Gottsched bis Hegel anhand der Theorien über Epos und Roman*, Bonn, Bouvier, 1974, 295 pp. (=AKML, 148); Hans-Georg Werner, 'Die Erzählkunst im Umkreis der R. (1806–15)', *WB*, xvii (1971), 11–38 and 82–111.

2b **Novel.** Hildegard Emmel writes sensibly about the Rs in vol. 1 of her *Geschichte des deutschen Romans*, Bern and Munich, 1972, 372 pp. (=Sammlung Dalp, 103), as does Hans Eichner in *The R. Period*, ed. Prawer [I.6a], pp. 64–96. Four important works on the theory of the novel are relevant: Bruno Hillebrand, *Theorie des Romans*, 2 vols, Munich, Winkler, 1972, 234, 296 pp. ('Goethezeit und R.', I, 125–94); *Romantheorie. Dokumentation ihrer Geschichte in Deutschland 1620–1880*, ed. Eberhard Lämmert, Cologne, Kiepenheuer & Witsch, 1971, xxiv, 407 pp.; *Theorie und Technik des Romans im 17. und 18. Jh.*, vol. II, *Spätaufklärung, Klassik und Frühr.*, ed. Dieter Kimpel and Conrad Wiedemann, Tübingen, Niemeyer, 1970, 159 pp.; and *Deutsche Romantheorien*, ed. Reinhold Grimm, Frankfurt, Athenäum, 1968, 420 pp. See also Diana Behler, *The Theory of the Novel in Early German R.*, Bern, Lang, 1977, 150 pp.

Gerhard Schmidt-Henkel's 'Anfang und Wiederkehr. Romananfänge und Romanschlüsse der deutschen R.', in *Romananfänge*, ed. Norbert Miller, Berlin, Literarisches Colloquium, 1965, pp. 92–134 (also pp. 135–48, Christa Hunscha on *Godwi*), is now paralleled by Marianne Schuller, *Romanschlüsse der R.: Zum frühr.en Problem von Universalität und Fragment*, Munich, Fink, 1974, 198 pp., dealing with Fr. Schlegel, Novalis, Brentano and Eichendorff.

Werner Hahl, *Reflexion und Erzählung. Ein Problem der Romantheorie von der Spätaufklärung bis zum programmatischen Realismus*, Stuttgart, Kohlhammer, 1971, 256 pp., convincingly relates changes in narrative technique to changes in society. Erika Voerster, *Märchen und Novellen im klassisch-r.en Roman*, Bonn, Bouvier, 1964, 412 pp. (=AKML, 23), is comprehensive and imaginative. See also Esther Hudgins, *Nicht-epische Strukturen des r.en Romans*, The Hague, Mouton, 1975, 189 pp.

Horst Meixner, *R.er Figuralismus. Kritische Studien zu Romanen von Arnim, Eichendorff und Hoffmann*, Frankfurt, Athenäum, 1971, 266 pp., is a major discussion of the allegorical nature of the novels. For novels by Arnim, Eichendorff and Tieck see also Joachim Worthmann, *Probleme des Zeitromans. Studien zur Geschichte des deutschen Romans in 19. Jh.*, Heidelberg, Winter, 1974, 179 pp. The essays in *Interpretationen 3: Deutsche Romane*, ed. Jost Schillemeit, Frankfurt and Hamburg, Fischer, 1966, 320 pp., are listed under the novels concerned.

Influences in the sphere of the novel are discussed in Clemens Heselhaus, 'Die Wilhelm Meister-Kritik der R.er und die r.e Romantheorie', in *Nachahmung und Illusion*, ed. H. R. Jauß, Munich, Eidos, 1964, pp. 113–27; Jürgen Jacobs, *Wilhelm Meister und seine Brüder: Untersuchungen zum deutschen Bildungsroman*, Munich, Fink, 1972, 332 pp., lucid; Jürgen Kolbe, *Goethes 'Wahlverwandtschaften' und der Roman des 19. Jhs*, Stuttgart, Kohlhammer, 1968, 227 pp., particularly on *Gräfin Dolores*; Roland Heine, *Transzendentalpoesie. Studien zu Fr. Schlegel, Novalis und E. T. A. Hoffmann*, Bonn, Bouvier, 1974, 209 pp. (=AKML, 144), relates attitudes to *Wilhelm Meister* to theory and then to *Ofterdingen* and *Der goldne Topf* in an illuminating way. There is a comprehensive survey of work on the 'Entwicklungs- und Bildungsroman' by Lothar Köhn in *DVLG*, xlii (1968), 427–73 and 590–624.

2c **Novelle.** There is a brief history of the R. Novelle, with a bibl., in Benno von Wiese, *Novelle*, Stuttgart, Metzler, 1963, vi, 89 pp. (=SM, 27), and an extensive survey *Novellentheorie und Novellenforschung... 1945–64*, by Karl Konrad Polheim, Stuttgart, Metzler, 1965, vi, 122 pp. (from *DVLG*, xxxviii (1964), special no.). Many isolated references to R. Novellen occur in Hans Herman Malmede's *Wege zur Novelle*, Stuttgart, Kohlhammer, 1966, 204 pp. Rolf Schröder, *Novelle und Novellentheorie in der frühen Biedermeierzeit*, Tübingen, Niemeyer, 1970, 243 pp., is relevant particularly for Tieck.

Extracts from the R. writers themselves are among the many basic texts in *Novelle*, ed. Josef Kunz, Darmstadt, Wiss BG, 1968, viii, 505 pp., also with a bibl. of the theory. Kunz's own *Die deutsche Novelle zwischen Klassik und R.*, Berlin, Erich Schmidt, 1966, 164 pp., incls half-a-dozen R. writers. Benno von Wiese's two vols, *Die deutsche Novelle von Goethe bis Kafka*, Düsseldorf, Bagel, 1956–62, 352, 355 pp., and *Interpretationen 4: Deutsche Erzählungen*, ed. Jost Schillemeit, Frankfurt and Hamburg, Fischer, 1966, 341 pp. In English see E. K. Bennett, *A History of the German Novelle*, Cambridge U.P., 1934, xiii, 296 pp., 2nd ed. revd. H. M. Waidson, 1961, xiv, 315 pp., in its day a pioneering work; and Brian Rowley, 'The Novelle', in *The R. Period*, ed. Prawer [I. 6a], pp. 121–46.

2d **Märchen.** Marianne Thalmann, *Das Märchen und die Moderne. Zum Begriff der Surrealität im Märchen der R.*, Stuttgart, Kohlhammer, 1961, 112 pp., has been transl. as *The R. Fairy Tale*, Ann Arbor, U. of Michigan P., 1964, vii, 133 pp.; eccentric interpretations but very readable. Ingrid Merkel, 'Wirklichkeit im r.en Märchen', *CG*, ii (1969), 162–83; Jack D. Zipes, 'Breaking the Magic Spell; Politics and the Fairy Tale', *New German Crit.* (1975), pp. 116–35, and 'The Revolutionary Rise of the R. Fairy Tale in Germany', *SiR*, xvi (1977), 409–50; James Trainer in *The R. Period*, ed. Prawer [I.6a], pp. 97–120. See also under V. l. The Marvellous and VI: Grimm.

Jens Tismar, *Kunstmärchen*, Stuttgart, Metzler, 1977, vi, 80 pp. (=SM, 155), covers the Rs on pp. 31–54. Hans Schumacher, *Narziß an der Quelle. Das r.e Kunstmärchen*, Wiesbaden, Athenaion, 1977, vi, 202 pp., has some new insights; good bibl. and detailed interpretations.

2e **Autobiography.** Klaus-Detlef Müller, *Autobiographie und Roman. Studien zur literarischen Autobiographie der Goethezeit*, Tübingen, Niemeyer, 1976, viii, 392 pp.

2f **Drama.** Peter Schmidt, 'R.es Drama. Zur Theorie eines Paradoxons', in *Deutsche Dramentheorien*, ed. Reinhold Grimm, Frankfurt, Athenäum, 1971, vol. I, 245–69; Roger Paulin in *The R. Period*, ed. Prawer [I.6a], pp. 173–203.

Comedy in Marianne Thalmann, *Provokation und Demonstration in der Komödie der R.*, incl. Tieck, Brentano, Schlegel, Berlin, Erich Schmidt, 1974, 119 pp.; Gerhard Kluge, 'Das Lustspiel der deutschen R.', in *Das deutsche Lustspiel*, ed. Hans Steffen, Göttingen, Vandenhoeck & Ruprecht, vol. I, 1968, 181–203; Helmut Arntzen, *Die ernste Komödie*, Munich, Nymphenburger, 1968, 304 pp., incls Tieck and Brentano.

For the theatre see Heinz Kindermann, *Theatergeschichte Europas*, vol. VI, *R.*, Salzburg, Otto Müller, 1964, 464 pp.

2g **Criticism.** René Wellek, *The R. Age*, vol. II of *A History of Modern Crit.: 1750–1950*, London, Cape, 1955, 459 pp., is an incomparable and indispensable survey, with much emphasis on the Germans. Anni Carlsson, *Die deutsche Buchkritik*, Bern and Munich, Francke, 1969, 421 pp., assembles much detail.

Eugen Klin deals with a minor early figure in *August Ferdinand Bernhardi als Kritiker und Lit. theoretiker*, Bonn, Bouvier, 1966, 162 pp.

IV

a **Poetic theory.** Bruno Markwardt, *Geschichte der deutschen Poetik*, vol. III, Klassik und R., Berlin, de Gruyter, 1958, vii, 730 pp., is an unsatisfactory but necessary work, with a comprehensive index to concepts. A valuable corrective is Armand Nivelle, *Frühr.e Dichtungstheorie*, Berlin, de Gruyter, 1970, vii, 225 pp. See also Paul Böckmann, 'Zum Poesie-Begriff der R.', in *Wissen aus Erfahrungen. Fest.* Hermann Meyer, ed. Alexander von Bormann, Tübingen, Niemeyer, 1976, pp. 371–83. Marianne Thalmann, *R.er als Poetologen*, Heidelberg, Stiehm, 1970, 122 pp., is highly idiosyncratic. Heinz-Dieter Weber, *Über eine Theorie der Lit.kritik: Die falsche und die berechtigte Aktualität der Frühr.*, Munich, Fink, 1971, 70 pp., attempts to apply Fr. Schlegel's principles to our contemporary crit. confusion.

John Neubauer, 'Intellektuelle, intellektuale und ästhetische Anschauung: Zur Entstehung der r.en Kunstanschauung', *DVLG*, xlvi (1972), 294–319; Christa Karoli, *Ideal und Krise enthusiastischen Künstlertums in der deutschen R.*, Bonn, Bouvier, 1968, 272 pp. (=AKML, 48); Jochen Hörisch, *Die fröhliche Wissenschaft der Poesie. Der Universitalitätsanspruch von Dichtung in der frühr.e Poetologie*, Frankfurt, Suhrkamp, 1976, 234 pp.; Ruediger von Tiedemann, *Fabels Reich. Zur Tradition und zum Programm r.er Dichtungstheorie*, Berlin, de Gruyter, 1978, 253 pp.; good comparison with English R.

An interesting work is Peter Kapitza, *Die frühr.e Theorie der Mischung. Uber den Zusammenhang von r.er Dichtungstheorie und zeitgenösischer Chemie*, Munich, Hueber, 1968, 204 pp., also his '"Physik" der Poesie', *LJb*, xii (1971), 97–112.

b **Poetic practice.** Peter Buchka, *Die Schreibweise des Schweigens. Ein Strukturvergleich r.er und zeitgenössischer Lit.*, Munich, Hanser, 1974, 183 pp., in the Adorno tradition and impressively argued. Marianne Thalmann, *Zeichensprache der R.*, Heidelberg, Stiehm, 1967, 115 pp., transl. as *The Literary Sign Language of German R.*, Detroit, Wayne State U.P., 1972, x, 152 pp., a structural examination, mainly of Märchen, with many isolated illuminations. Helmut Schanze, 'R. und Rhetorik', in *Rhetorik. Beiträge zu ihrer Geschichte in Deutschland*, ed. by him, Frankfurt, Athenäum Fischer Taschenbuch Verlag, 1974, pp. 126–44.

V Single aspects and themes

a **Bible.** Abraham Albert Avni, *The Bible and R.: The Old Testament in German* *and French R. Poetry*, The Hague, Mouton, 1969, 299 pp., incls Novalis, Brentano and Eichendorff.

b **City.** Marianne Thalmann, *R.er entdecken die Stadt*, Munich, Nymphenburger, 1965, 146 pp., with a wealth of ideas; Karl Riha, *Die Beschreibung der 'Großen Stadt'... in der deutschen Lit. (ca. 1750–ca. 1850)*, Bad Homburg, Gehlen, 1970, 182 pp.

c **Dreams.** Albert Béguin's major work is still relevant; first publ. in 1937 in 2 vols as *L'âme r. et le rêve: essai sur le r. allemand et la poésie française*, Marseilles, Cahiers du Sud, 1937, and then reissued in 1 vol. without the crit. apparatus, Paris, Corti, 1939, xvii, 416 pp.; now in German, *Traumwelt und R.*, ed. Peter Grotzer, Bern and Munich, Francke, 1972, 558 pp. Jacques Bousquet, *Les Thèmes du rêve dans la litt. r.*, Paris, Didier, 1964, 656 pp., is magnificent as a catalogue, but less strong on German R. than on English and French.

d **Gothic.** W. D. Robson-Scott, *The Literary Background of the Gothic Revival in Germany*, Oxford, Clarendon, 1965, xii, 334 pp., is an admirable work, far more comprehensive than the German sections of Paul Frankl, *The Gothic. Literary Sources and Interpretations*, Princeton U.P., 1960, x, 916 pp.

e **Hero.** Jack D. Zipes, *The Great Refusal. Studies of the r. hero in German and Austrian lit.*, Bad Homburg, Athenäum, 1970, 158 pp., incls *Der goldne Topf*, *Ahnung und Gegenwart* and *Florentin*.

f **Imagery.** Heinz Hillmann, *Bildlichkeit der deutschen R.*, Frankfurt, Athenäum, 1971, 340 pp., is an attempt at classification, with a useful reference list to images in R. writers.

g **Influences.** See I.6c and add: for Spain, 2 exhaustive vols by Werner Brüggemann in Ser. 2 of the 'Spanische Forschungen der Görresgesellschaft', Münster, Aschendorff; *Cervantes... in Kunstanschauung und Dichtung der deutschen R.*, 380 pp., vol. VII, 1958, and *Spanisches Theater und deutsche R. I*, 275 pp., vol. VIII, 1964. Also Swana L. Hardy, *Goethe, Calderón und die r.e Theorie des Dramas*, Heidelberg, Winter, 1965, 200 pp.

For Italy see 2 vols in the 'Studi Italiani' series of Böhlau, Cologne and Vienna: H. Feldmann, *Die Fiabe Carlo Gozzis. Die Entstehung einer Gattung und ihre Transposition in das System der deutschen R.*, 1971, 164 pp. (=no. 11), and Herbert Frenzel, *Ariost und die r.e. Dichtung*, 1962, 72 pp. (=no. 7); an Italian transl. of the latter is appended to Maria Teresa Dal Monte, *Ariosto in Germania*, Imola, Galeati, 1971, 231 pp.

For Denmark see the full study by Victor A. Schmitz, *Dänische Dichter in ihrer Begegnung mit deutscher Klassik und R.*, Frankfurt, Klostermann, 1974, 259 pp.; incls Baggesen and Steffens.

h **Irony.** There are two excellent short surveys, both publ. 1972 by the Wiss BG, Darmstadt: Helmut Prang, *Die r.e. Ironie*, viii, 118 pp., a lucid portrayal of the Rs' own views and of subsequent crit.; and Ernst Behler, *Klassische Ironie — R.e Ironie — Tragische Ironie. Zum Ursprung dieser Begriffe*, 170 pp., incorporating earlier arts. The study to be argued with is still, however, Ingrid Strohschneider-Kohrs, *Die r.e. Ironie in Theorie und Gestaltung*, Tübingen, Niemeyer, 1960, 446 pp. (=Hermaea, n.ser., 6), now in a 2nd ed., 1977, 471 pp. See also Beda Allemann, *Ironie und Dichtung*, Pfullingen, Neske, 2nd ed. 1969, 249 pp. (first publ. 1957), and D. C. Muecke, *The Compass of Irony*, London, Methuen, 1969, xi, 276 pp., usefully setting German R. in a wider context.

i **Landscape.** It is still important to turn back to three works: Helmut Rehder, *Die Philosophie der unendlichen Landschaft*, Halle/Saale, Niemeyer, 1932, viii, 228 pp. (=*DVLG* Buchreihe, 19); Andreas Müller, *Landschaftserlebnis und Landschaftsbild*, Stuttgart, Kohlhammer, 1955, 247 pp.; and Willi Wolfradt, *C. D. Friedrich und die Landschaft der R.*, Berlin, Mauritius, 1924, 224 pp.

j **Lied.** Jack M. Stein, *Poem and Music in the German Lied from Gluck to Hugo Wolf*, Cambridge (Mass.), Harvard U.P., 1971, 238 pp., is a more scholarly work than Elaine Brody and Robert A. Fowkes, *The German Lied and its Poetry*, New York U.P., 1971, viii, 316 pp. See also Eichendorff chapter above, notes 9 and 10.

k **Mannerism.** Marianne Thalmann, *R. und Manierismus*, Stuttgart, Kohlhammer, 1963, 213 pp.

l **The Marvellous.** Heinrich Bosse, 'The Marvellous and R. Semiotics', *SiR*, xiv (1975), 211–34, and Gonthier-Louis Fink, *Naissance et apogée du conte merveilleux en Allemagne 1740–1800*, Paris, Les Belles Lettres, 1966, 766 pp.

m **Medicine.** A good introd. is Peter Schmidt, 'Gesundheit und Krankheit in r.er Medizin und Erzählkunst', *JFDH*, 1966, pp. 197–228. Werner Leibbrand's *Die spekulative Medizin der R.*, Hamburg, Claassen, 1956, 323 pp., recasts his *R.e Medizin*, Hamburg and Leipzig, Goverts, 1937, 210 pp., and largely supplants it. See also note 14 to Chapter 1 above on John Brown.

n **Middle Ages.** It is still necessary to consult Josef Körner, *Nibelungenforschung der deutschen R*, Leipzig, 1911, repr. Wiss BG, Darmstadt, 1968, x, 273 pp., and Gottfried Salomon, *Das Mittelalter als Ideal in der R.*, Munich, Drei Masken, 1922, 127 pp. See also V.d. Gothic and *Mittelalterrezeption. Texte zur Aufnahme altdeutscher Lit. in der R.*, ed. Gerhard Kozielek, Tübingen, Niemeyer, 1977, 200 pp.

o **Music.** Steven Paul Sher, *Verbal Music in German Lit.*, New Haven and London, Yale U.P., 1968, viii, 181 pp., analyses descriptions of pieces of music in Wackenroder, Tieck and Hoffmann.

p **Myth.** Karl S. Guthke, *Die Mythologie der entgötterten Welt: Ein literarisches Thema von der Aufklärung biz zur Gegenwart*, Göttingen, Vandenhoeck & Ruprecht, 1971, 372 pp., has a chapter on R. There is an important art. on 'Mythos und Dichtung' by Klaus Ziegler in the 2nd ed. of the Merker-Stammler *Reallexikon*, II, 569–84. Dieter Schrey, *Mythos und Geschichte bei Johann Arnold Kanne und in der r.en Mythologie*, Tübingen, Niemeyer, 1969, ix, 264 pp.

q **Night.** Hannes Leopoldseder, *Groteske Welt: Ein Beitrag zur Entwicklungsgeschichte des Nachtstücks in der R.*, Bonn, Bouvier, 1973, 208 pp. (=AKML, 127).

r **Nihilism.** Dieter Arendt, *Der 'poetische Nihilismus' in der R.: Studien zum Verhältnis von Dichtung und Wirklichkeit in der Frühr.*, 2 vols, Tübingen, Niemeyer, 1972, 259, 328 pp.; vol. II on Wackenroder, Tieck, *Godwi* and the *Nachtwachen.* Arendt also eds selections in *Nihilismus. Die Anfänge von Jacobi bis Nietzsche*, Cologne, Hegner, 1970, 393 pp.

s **Orient.** René Gérard, *L'Orient et la pensée r. allemande*, Paris, Didier, 1963, 278 pp., and A. Leslie Willson, *A Mythical Image: The ideal of India in German R.*, Durham (N.C.), Duke U.P., 1964, xiv, 261 pp., are both important studies. Susanne Sommerfeld, *Indienschau und Indiendeutung r.er Philosophen*, Zürich, Rascher, 1943, 108 pp., remains valuable for Schelling. See also note 15 to the Schlegel chapter above.

t **Politics.** The introd. by Hans Reiss to his anthology, *The Political Thought of the German Rs (1793-1815)*, Oxford, Blackwell, 1955, 211 pp., is the basis for his expanded *Politisches Denken in der deutschen R.*, Bern and Munich, Francke, 96 pp. There is also a useful introd. by Jacques Droz to his selection, *Le r. politique en Allemagne*, Paris, Armand Colin, 1963, 210 pp. Peter Stein, *Politisches Bewußtsein und künstlerischer Gestaltungswille in der politischen Lyrik 1780-1848*, Hamburg, Lüdke, 1971, iii, 262 pp.

u **Popular literature.** See the anthologies in 1.2d and Marianne Thalmann, *Die R. des Trivialen: Von Grosses 'Genius' bis Tiecks 'William Lovell'*, Munich, List, 1970, 138 pp.

v **Religion and clergy.** Klaus Lindemann, *Geistlicher Stand und religiöses Mittlertum. Ein Beitrag zur Religionsauffassung der Früh. in Dichtung und Philosophie*, Frankfurt, Athenäum, 1971, 307 pp., is stronger on the theory of the mediator in Schlegel and Novalis than on the fictional depiction of the clergy.

w **Sociology.** Leo Löwenthal, *Erzählkunst und Gesellschaft. Die Gesellschaftsproblematik in der deutschen Lit. des 19. Jhs*, Neuwied, Luchterhand, 1971, 250 pp., deals in the 3rd chapter with R. as suppressed revolution. Hans Kals, *Die soziale Frage in der R.*, Cologne and Bonn, Hanstein, 1974, vi, 328 pp.

x **Symbol.** Bengt Algot Sørensen, *Symbol und Symbolismus in den ästhetischen Theorien des 18 Jhs und der deutschen R.*, Copenhagen, Munksgaard, 1963, 332 pp., is detailed and persuasive; he has also ed. a selection, *Allegorie und Symbol. Texte zur Theorie des dichterischen Bildes im 18, und frühen 19 Jh.*, Frankfurt, Athenäum, 1972, 268 pp. Doris Starr, *Über den Begriff des Symbols in der deutschen Klassik und R. unter besonderer Berücksichtigung von Fr. Schlegel*, Reutlingen, Hutzler, 1964, 103 pp., should be treated with reserve. Michael Titzmann, *Transformation der philosophischen Ästhetik zwischen Goethezeit und 19. Jh. Der Symbolbegriff als Paradigma*, Stuttgart, Kohlhammer, 1976, 160 pp.

y **Time.** Manfred Frank, *Das Problem 'Zeit' in der deutschen R.*, Munich, Winkler, 1972, 486 pp., is mainly on Tieck, but also considers Fr. Schlegel, Solger and Novalis.

z **Translation.** Andreas Huyssen, *Die frühr.e Konzeption von Übersetzung und Aneignung*, Zürich, Atlantis, 1969, 199 pp. (=ZBLG, 33), scarcely discusses practice but is interesting on the theory. Many references in Ralph-Rainer Wuthenow, *Das fremde Kunstwerk. Aspekte der literarischen Übersetzung*, Göttingen, Vandenhoeck & Ruprecht, 1969, 187 pp.

VI
Arnim

a Any serious study must now begin with Volker Hoffmann's 'Die A.-Forschung 1945-72', *DVLG*, xlvii (1973)), Sonderheft, 270*-342*, especially as it summarizes the unpubl. diss in which so much good recent work has been done.

b **Texts.** The only satisfactory ed. is *Sämtliche Romane und Erzählungen* [SRE], 3 vols, ed. Walther Migge, Munich, Hanser, 1962-5. The text is based on the original eds, as there were many alterations in the ed. prepared by Bettina after A.'s death. The second part of the final vol. of that ed., assembled by Varnhagen but not publ., has now been issued as *Gedichte. Zweiter Teil* by Herbert R. Liedke and Alfred Anger, Tübingen, Niemeyer, 1975, ix, 290 pp. Several important and previously unpubl. drafts, essays, etc., are now coming to light. For the *Wunderhorn* eds see VI. Brentano.

Isabella was publ. in an important bilingual ed. by René Guignard, Paris, Aubier, 1950, 336 pp.; *Das Loch*, together with Eichendorff's *Das Incognito*, ed., with extensive notes, Gerhard Kluge, Berlin, de Gruyter, 1968, 130 pp. (=Komedia, 13).

For the letters one still refers to R. Steig's 3 vols, 1894-1913, adding the well-presented *Achim und Bettina in ihren Briefen* [1811-31] in 2 vols, ed. Werner Vordtriede, Frankfurt, Suhrkamp, 1961, lxvii, 987 pp., with a long introd. by Rudolf Alexander Schröder. Helene M. Kastinger Riley's biographically important *L. A v. A. S. Jugend-und Reisejahre*, Bonn, Bouvier, 1978 (=AKML, 266) has some unpubl. letters.

c **Translations.** *Der tolle Invalide* has been transl. several times, most recently by M. M. Yuill in *German Narrative Prose I*, ed. E. J. Engel, London, Wolff, 1965, pp. 29-50.

d **General studies.** The only full-length introd. is still René Guignard, *A. v. A.*, Paris, Les Belles Lettres, 1936, 219 pp., repr. 1953; dated but judicious. Werner Vordtriede in *DDRW*, pp. 253-79, is a good summary of a more modern overall view. Gerhard Rudolph, *Studien zur dichterischen Welt A. v. A.s*, Berlin, de Gruyter, 1958, 171 pp., is thorough but over-schematic and has not worn well.

e **Individual topics.** Roland Hoermann, 'The R. Golden Age in A.'s Writings', *Monatshefte*, l (1958), 21-9, and 'Symbolism and Mediation in A.'s View of R. Phantasy', *Monatshefte*, liv (1962), 201-15. Hermann Friedrich Weiss, 'The Use of the Leitmotif "Kirchenordnung" und die religiöse Situation zu Beginn der Restaurationsepoche', *OL*, xxxi (1976), 30-42; Jacques Peyraube, 'La sensibilité d'A. dans sa correspondance avec Bettina', *EG*, xxi (1966), 188–204; Helene M. Riley, '... Faust in the Work of A. v. A.', *Seminar*, xiii (1977), 1–12.

f **Prose.** Much of the best crit. is in recent diss; see the summaries in Volker Hoffmann. Bernd Haustein, *R.er Mythos und R.kritik in Prosadichtungen A. v. A.s*, Göppingen, Kümmerle, 1974, 109 pp., examines his ambivalent attitude to R. Wolfdietrich Rasch, 'A. v. A.s Erzählkunst', *DU*, vii, 2 (1955), 38–55.

For *Gräfin Dolores* see Meixner, *Figuralismus* [III.2b], pp. 13–101; Worthmann, *Zeitroman* [III.2b], pp. 18–24; Kolbe, '*Wahlverwandschaften*' [III.2b], pp. 36–55; and, above all, the diss. by Offermanns, 1959 (see Hoffmann), and Herbert R. Liedke's publ. of preliminary studies for the novel in *JFDH*, 1964, pp. 236–342; 1965, pp. 237–313; and 1966, pp. 229–308. Now also Renate Moering, *Die offene Romanform von A.s 'G.D.'*, Heidelberg, Winter, 1978, 259 pp.

For *Die Kronenwächter* see Werner Vordtriede, *NRu*, lxxiii (1962), 136–45, repr. in *Interpretationen 3* [11.2b], pp. 155–63; R. F. Holt, 'A. v. A. and Sir Walter Scott', *GLL*, xvi (1973), 142–60; and the diss. by Elchlepp.

For *Isabella* see Guignard's ed., Peter Horst Neumann, *JDSG*, xii (1968), 296–314, and Claude David, *Fest.* Alewyn [I.6b], pp. 328–45.

For *Die Majoratsherren* see Heinrich Henel in *Weltbewohner und Weimaraner. Fest.* Beutler, ed. Benno Reifenberg, Zürich and Stuttgart, Artemis, 1960, pp. 73–104, revd in *Interpretationen 4* [III.2c], pp. 151–78; Heinisch, *Deutsche R.* [I.6c], pp. 49–63; H. Günther Nerjes, *Seminar*, iii (1967), 127–37; and Bruce Duncan, *Monatshefte*, lxviii (1976), 51–9.

For *Der tolle Invalide* see Benno von Wiese in his *Die deutsche Novelle* [III.2c], II, 71–86; Walter Silz, *Realism and Reality* Chapel Hill, 1954 (=UNGSGLL, 11), pp. 29–35; Ernst Feise, *JEPG*, liii (1954), 403–9; F. Lösel, *New German Studies* (Hull), v (1977), 75–90; C. Butler, *SiR*, xvii (1978), 149–62.

For *Owen Tudor* see Elizabeth Stopp, *GLL*, xxix (1975), 155–65.

g **Drama.** Gerhard Falkner, *Die Dramen A. v. A.s*, Zürich, Atlantis, 1962, 229 pp. (=ZBLG, 20), and Roger Paulin, *Gryphius' 'Cardenio und Celinde' und As 'Halle und Jerusalem'*, Tübingen, Niemeyer, 1968, ix, 188 pp. are both works of substance.

h **Other writings.** Herbert R. Liedke, *Literary Crit. and R. Theory in the Work of A. v. A.*, New York, Columbia U.P., 1937, xi, 187 pp.; Jürgen Knaack, *A. v. A. — Nicht nur Poet. Die politischen Anschauungen As in ihrer Entwicklung. Mit ungedruckten Texten und einem Verzeichnis sämtlicher Briefe*, Darmstadt, Thesen Verlag Vowinckel, 1976, 197 pp., stresses the complexity of his political views. See also Herman F. Weiss, 'Unveröffentlichte Prosaentwürfe A. v. A.s zur Zeitkritik (um 1810)', *JFDH*, 1977, pp. 251–91.

Baader.

Several selections are available. Hans Graßl has ed. *Über Liebe, Ehe und Kunst*, 1953, 269 pp., and *Gesellschaftslehre*, 1957, 332 pp., both for Kösel, Munich; *Vom Sinn der Gesellschaft. Schriften zur Social-Philosophie*, ed. Hans A. Fischer-Barnicol, Cologne, Hegner, 1966, 334 pp.; *Sätze aus der erotischen Philosophie*, ed. Gerd-Klaus Kaltenbrunner, Frankfurt, Insel, 1966, 204 pp.

David Baumgart's important *F. v. B. und die philosophische R.*, Halle/ Saale, Niemeyer, 1927, 402 pp. (=*DVLG* Buchreihe, 10), has been repr. Hildesheim, Gerstenberg, 1976. Josef Siegl, *F. v. B.*, Munich, Bayerischer Schulbuch-Verlag, 1957, 107 pp., is the most generally useful account. See also Stefan Schmitz, *Sprache, Sozietät und Geschichte bei F. v. B.*, Bern, Lang, 1975, 185 pp.; and Heinz-Jürgen Görtz, *F. v. B.s anthropologischer Standpunkt*, Freiburg, Alber, 1977, 400 pp.

Brentano

a Wolfgang Frühwald's 'Stationen der B.-Forschung 1924–72', *DVLG*, xlvii (1973), Sonderheft, 182*–269*, is an indispensable *tour de force*, listing and discussing much and adding a good deal of his own. Supp. with John Fetzer, 'Old and New Directions in C. B. Research (1931–68)', *LJb*, xi (1970), 87–119 and xii (1971), 113–203, and 'Recent Trends... 1968–70:, xiii (1972), 217–32, also remarkably informative.

b **Texts.** The vast new crit. ed. has been taken over by Kohlhammer, Stuttgart, and the early vols. ed. Heinz Rölleke, are devoted to the *Wunderhorn*; vols VI (1976), VII (1976) and VIII (1977) give the texts and vol. IX, in three parts (1 in 1976), consists of variants and notes. For most purposes use *Werke* [W] in 4 vols, ed. Friedhelm Kemp, W. Frühwald and B. Gajek, Munich, Hanser, 1963–8, with very good notes, comments and bibls, which the 2-vol. distillation (1972) brings up to date.

The two most useful eds of the *Wunderhorn*, though needing revision after Rölleke's findings, are both in 3 vols: Munich, dtv, 1963, with a good postcript by Arthur Henkel; and Berlin, Rütten & Loening, 1966, ed. Hans-Günther Thalheim and Gisela Fritzsche.

The other eds needed to supp. the Hanser ed., apart from its neglect of the later devotional works, are: *Gedichte*, ed. W. Frühwald, Reinbek, Rowohlt, 1968, 250 pp.; *Ponce de Leon*, ed. Siegfried Sudhof, Stuttgart, Reclam, 1968, 175 pp. (=UB, 8542–3); *Die Chronika des fahrenden Schülers: Urfassung*, ed. Elisabeth Stopp, Stuttgart, Reclam, 1971, 136 pp. (=UB, 9912–3); and *Histoire du brave Gaspard et de la belle Annette*, transl. and ed. J. F. A. Ricci, Paris, Aubier-Flammarion, 1971, 177 pp., in their bilingual series.

See also *C. B.: Dichter über ihre Dichtungen*, ed. Werner Vordtriede and Gabriele Bartenschlager, Munich, Heimeran, 1970, 325 pp., now also Munich, 1977, dtv 6089; and Hartwig Schultz, 'Vorarbeiten C. B.s zu einer Sammelausgabe seiner Werke', *JFDH*, 1976, pp. 316–51.

For the letters one still refers to *Das unsterbliche Leben. Unbekannte Briefe von C. B.*, ed. Wilhelm Schellberg and Friedrich Fuchs, Jena, Diederichs, 1939, 561 pp., with its extensive comms; and *Briefe*, 2 vols ed. Friedrich Seebaß, Nuremberg, Carl, 1951, xlviii, 424, 468 pp. There is a good introd. to *C. B.: Briefwechsel mit H. R. Sauerländer*, ed. Anton Krättli, Zürich, Artemis, 1962, 139 pp. For the letters to Runge see Chapter 5, note 7, above. The handiest eds of the *Frühlingskranz*, Bettina's memorial to him, are: Munich, Winkler, 1967, 271 pp,. with a postcript by Wulf Segebrecht, and Leipzig, Reclam, 1974, 386 pp., ed. Heinz Härtl. The letters to Emilie

Linder are ed. Wolfgang Frühwald, Bad Homburg, Gehlen, 1969, 332 pp., with additions in *JFDH*, 1976, pp. 216–315.

c **General studies.** Werner Hoffmann's *C. B..*, Bern and Munich, Francke, 1966, 425 pp., is not satisfactory as crit., and as biography should be supp. and corrected by the admirable exhibition catalogue, *C. B., Freies Deutsches Hochstift 1970*, ed. Jürgen Behrens and others, Bad Homburg, Gehlen, 1970, 167 pp. Of older biographies Wolfgang Pfeiffer-Belli's *C. B., Freiburg*, Herder, 1947, 214 pp., is still of interest. The most dependable account of the Emmerick period is Joseph Adam, *C. B.s Emmerick-Erlebnis*, Freiburg, Herder, 1956, xvii, 359 pp.; but see also Oskar Katann, 'Die Glaubwürdigkeit von C. B.s Emmerick-Berichten', *LJb*, vii (1966), 145–94. New documentation by Jürg Mathes in *JFDH*, 1971, pp. 198–310, and 1972, pp. 228–76.

Bernard Gajek has ed. *C. und Christian B.s Bibliotheken: Die Versteigerungskataloge von 1819 und 1853*, Heidelberg, Winter, 1974, 348 pp., an important reprint. K. Feilchenfeldt, *B.-Chronik*, Munich, Hanser, 1978, 208 pp. is a valuable guide.

Gajek's *Homo Poeta: Zur Kontinuität der Problematik bei C. B.*, Frankfurt, Athenäum, 1971, 629 pp., though dealing with minor poems, is full of fresh comments and new information on the life and works. Frühwald's chapter in *DDRW*, pp. 280–309, is the best general introd., and his *Das Spätwerk C. B.s (1815–42). Romantik im Zeitalter der Metternichschen Restauration*, Tübingen, Niemeyer, 1977, xiv, 415 pp. (= Hermaea, n.ser., 37), bristles with information and confirms his subtle interpretation of the late works. Walther Migge, *C. B.: Leitmotive seiner Existenz*, Pfullingen, Neske, 1968, 54 pp., is a summary of his 1940 Munich diss. Ian Hilton has a judicious introd. in *German Men of Letters V*, ed. Alex Natan, London, Wolff, 1969, pp. 51–74; see also Claude David in *Die deutsche R.*, ed. Steffen [I. 6a], pp. 159–79.

d **Individual topics.** There are several substantial works; Klaus Wille, *Die Signatur der Melancholie im Werk C. B.s*, Bern, Lang, 1970, 197 pp., exaggerating the theme's importance; Hans Peter Neureuter, *Das Spiegelmotiv bei C. B.: Studie zum r.en Ich-Bewußtsein*, Frankfurt, Athenäum, 1972, 259 pp.; Gerhard Schaub, *Le génie enfant. Die Kategorie des Kindlichen bei C. B.*, Berlin, de Gruyter, 1973, 255 pp., important for biography as well as analyses; John F. Fetzer, *R. Orpheus. Profiles of C. B.*, Berkeley, U. of California P., 1974, xi, 313 pp., on his musicality, well documented; Nikolaus Reindl, *Die poetische Funktion des Mittelalters in der Dichtung C. B.s*, 1976, 353 pp. (= Innsbrucker Beiträge, 6); Dieter Dennerle, *Kunst als Kommunikationsprozeß. Zur Kunsttheorie C. B.s*, Bern–Frankfurt, Lang, 1976, 249 pp., deals primarily with his letters and reviews.

e **Poetry.** Hans Magnus Enzensberger's *B.s Poetik*, Munich, Hanser, 1961, 157 pp., reissued as dtv 118, 1973, 125 pp., should, no doubt, have been revd since its 1955 origin as a diss., but it remains an exciting aesthetic interpretation. See also Karl Tober, 'Das "r.e." Gedicht? *Gedanken zu C. B.s Lyrik*', CG, 1968, pp. 137–51; and the excellent Walter Müller-Seidel, 'B's naive und sentimentalische Poesie', *JDSG*, xviii (1974), 441–65, discussing 'Der Jäger an den Hirten' and 'Der Spinnerin Lied'.

On the late lyrics see Luciano Zagari, *'Paradiso' artificiale e 'sguardo elegiaco sui flutti': La lirica religiosa di B.*, Rome, Bulzoni, 1971, 167 pp.; René Guignard's *Chronologie des poésies de C. B.*, Paris, Droz, 1933, 144 pp., is still valuable if used with care.

f **Individual poems.** To the list of interpretations in *SRE* I, 1259–61 add, on 'Der Spinnerin Lied', Joachim Klein, *Sprachkunst*, v (1974), 17–26, Lida Kirchberger, *Monatshefte*, lxvii (1975), 417–24, Hans Joachim Schrimpf, in *Wissen aus Erfahrungen* [IV.a], pp. 384–91, and Frühwald, *Das Spätwerk C. B.s* [c. above], pp. 229–38; on 'Schweig Herz!', Gcri D. Greenway, *Monatshefte*, lxvi (1974), 166–72; on 'O schweig nur Herz!', Siegfried Sudhof, *ZDP*, xcii (1973), 211–31, and in *JFDH*, 1977, Heinrich Henel, pp. 309–49, a first-rate analysis, with discussions of other interpretations, and Hartwig Schultz, pp. 350–63, with his discovery (*JFDH*, 1976) that B., between 1837 and 1840, was preparing an ed. of his works and had supplied a title 'Wiegenlied eines jammernden Herzen' for this poem; on 'Wenn der lahme Weber', Rosemarie Hunter, *GRM*, l (1969), 144–52; on 'Nachklänge Beethovenscher Musik', Gerhard Friesen in *Traditions and Transitions. Fest. Jantz.*, ed. Liselotte E. Kurth, Munich, Delp, 1972, pp. 194–209; on 'Der Jäger an den Hirten', Oskar Seidlin, *Euph.* lxx (1976), 117–28; and Hennig Boetius, *JFDH*, 1970, pp. 258–80, dating 'Die Erde war gestorben', 'Aus Immergrün gewunden' and 'Die Abendwinde wehen' at about 1817.

Prose. *Godwi.* See *SRE* I, 1263, and add: Gerhard Storz, in *Fest Beißner*, ed. Ulrich Gaier, Bebenhausen, Rotsch, 1974, pp. 436–46; Benno von Wiese, in his *Von Lessing bis Grabbe*, Düsseldorf, Bagel, 1968, pp. 191–247; Arendt [V.r. Nihilism]; and Horst Dieter Hayer, *B.s 'Godwi': ein Beispiel des früh .en Subjektivismus*, Bern, Lang, 1977, 160 pp. The indispensable arts are those by Mennemeier, *WW*, xvi (1966), 24–33, and Meixner, *JDSG*, xi (1967), 435–68.

Kasperl und Annerl has had more than its share of interpretations. The two that stand out are by Alewyn, now revd in *Interpretationen 4* [III.2c], pp. 101–50, and Gerhard Kluge, *JFDH*, 1971, pp. 143–97, on the narrative perspective. *SRE* I, 1263–4, lists another eight, to which may be added: Peter Horwarth, *GQ* xliv (1971), 24–34; Peter Paul Schwarz, *Aurora*, xxxii (1972), 69–83; Heinz Rölleke, *JFDH*, 1970, 244–57, on the sources; and Herbert Lehnert, in *Geschichte—Deutung—Kritik: Fest. Kohlschmidt*, ed. Maria Bindschedler, Bern, Francke, 1969, pp. 199–223.

The *Chronika*: in addition to her Reclam ed. Elisabeth Stopp has written devastatingly of the 1818 revision in *Sprache und Bekenntnis: Fest.* Kunisch, ed. Wolfgang Frühwald, Berlin, Duncker & Humblot, 1971, pp. 161–84. Michael Huber, *C. B.: Die Chronika... Eine Analyse der Figurenkonstellation und der kompositorischen Prinzipien der Urfassung*, Bern, Francke, 1976, 326 pp., is an important study. See also Anton Kathan, *LJb*, xiii (1972), 181–215, on the narrative structure.

The Märchen: see *SRE* I, 1264–5. Frühwald, 'Das verlorene Paradies', *LJb*, iii (1962), 113–92, is matched in importance by Oskar Seidlin's 'Wirklich nur eine schöne Kunstfigur? Zu B.s Gockel-Märchen', in *Texte und Kon-*

texte: Fest. Fürst, ed. Manfred Durzak, Bern, Francke, 1973, pp. 235-48. On the *Rheinmärchen* see Karsten Hvidfelt Nielsen, *OL*, xxvii (1972), pp. 77-101; and for the revision of *Fanfarlieschen*, and the light it throws on B.'s methods, see Seidlin, in his *Klassische und moderne Klassiker*, Göggingen, Vandenhoeck & Ruprecht, 1972, pp. 38-60, also in *Probleme des Erzählens; Fest.* Hamburger, ed. Fritz Martini, Stuttgart, Klett, 1971, pp. 101-26. See also Heinz Rölleke, 'B.s "Märchen von der Schulmeister Klopfstock" als literarhistorische Allegorie', *JFDH*, 1977, pp. 292-308.

h **Plays.** See *SRE* I, 1263-4, adding Sudhof's ed. of *Ponce de Leon* and Seidlin's comparison of the Libussa figures of B. and Grillparzer, in *Austriaca. Fest.* Politzer, ed. W. Kudszus, Tübingen, Niemeyer, 1974, pp. 201-29.

Chamisso

a **Texts.** The standard ed. is now *Sämtliche Werke*, ed. Jost Perfahl, 2 vols, Munich, Winkler, 1975, with bibl. and postscript by Volker Hoffmann. There is a reasonable one-vol. selection ed. Peter Wersig, Berlin, Aufbau, 1967.

Peter Schlemihl has been ed. James Boyd, Oxford, Blackwell, 1956, xli, 81 pp. There are many transls, the first in 1824 with plates by Cruikshank, the most recent by Leopold von Loewenstein-Wertheim, London, Calder, 1957, 93 pp., and by Fred Honig in *Three Great Classics*, New York, Arco, 1964.

b **General studies.** René Riegel, *A. de Ch. Sa vie et son œuvre*, 2 vols, Paris, Les Éditions Internationales, 1934, 411 and 421 pp., is still useful, but has generally been overtaken by Werner Feudel, *A. v. Ch. Leben und Werk*, Leipzig, Reclam, 1971, 243 pp. (=UB, 490). See also Peter A. Kroner in *DDRW*, pp. 371-90, and, on Ch.'s resumption of writing political poems, Volker Hoffmann in *JDSG*, xx (1976), 38-86.

c **Peter Schlemihl.** Ulrich Baumgartner, *A. v. Ch.s Peter Schlemihl*, Frauenfeld and Leipzig, Huber, 1944, 128 pp. (=Wege zur Dichtung, 42), also has a good deal of general material about Ch.; Benno von Wiese in his *Die deutsche Novelle* [III.2c], I, 97-116; Ernst Loeb, *GRM*, xlvi (1965), 398-408; Hermann J. Weigand, in *Surveys and Soundings*, ed. A. Leslie Willson, Princeton U.P., 1966, pp. 208-22; Paul Neumarkt, *Lit. and Psychology*, xvii (1967), 120-7; Franz Schulz, *GQ*, xlv (1972), 429-42; Ralph Flores, *GQ*, xlvii (1974), 567-84; Heinisch in his *Deutsche R.* [I.6c], pp. 371-90; and Colin A. Butler, *Monatshefte*, lxix (1977), 5-16.

Eichendorff

a **Bibliography.** One turns first to Ansgar Hillach and Klaus-Dieter Krabiel's *E.-Kommentar*, 2 vols, Munich, Winkler, 1971-2, 230 and 223 pp. The relatively short bibl., II, 211-21, is supp. by crit. comms in the anns to individual works. Krabiel also summarizes arguments briefly in his *J. v. E.: Kommentierte Studienbibl.*, Frankfurt, Athenäum, 1971, 90 pp. See also Karl von E., *Ein Jh, E.-Lit.*, vol. XXII of *HKA*, Regensburg, Habbel, 1927, 160 pp.; Wolfgang Kron, 'E'-Bibl.', in *E. Heute. Stimmen der Forschung*, ed. Paul Stöcklein, Munich, Bayerischer Schulbuch-Verlag, 1960, pp. 280-329

(2nd ed. Darmstadt, Wiss BG, 1966); Wolfram Mauser in supps to *DU*, xiv, 4 (1962), and xx, 3 (1968); and the annual bibl. in *Aurora*, the excellent yearbook of the E.-Gesellschaft.

Arts in *Aurora* and *E. Heute* are generally not listed separately below.

b **Texts.** The crit. ed., *Sämtliche Werke... Historisch-kritische Ausgabe* [*HKA*] has been under way since 1908, but is little more than half finished. Recent important additions to it have been vol. IX, *Geschichte der poetischen Lit. Deutschlands*, and vol. XVIII, in 3 parts, *J. v. E. im Urteil seiner Zeit*, 1975–77 (now publ. Stuttgart, Kohlhammer, not Habbel). Three selected eds are in general use. The best, when completed, will be *Werke* [*W*], Munich, Winkler; 2 vols with the creative works, ed. Jost Perfahl and Ansgar Hillach, appeared in 1970, and vol. III, *Schriften zur Lit.*, ed. Marlies Korfsmeyer and Klaus-Dieter Krabiel, in 1976; 2 other vols are in preparation. There are then the 4-vol. *Neue Gesamtausgabe*, ed. Gerhart Baumann and Siegfried Grosse, Stuttgart, Cotta, 1957–8; and the 3-vol. *Gesammelte Werke*, ed. Manfred Häckel, Berlin, Aufbau, 1962, a useful working ed.

Other noteworthy individual eds are: *Sämtliche Gedichte*, ed. Wolfdietrich Rasch, Munich, dtv, 1975, 524 pp., based on his 1-vol. *Werke*, Munich, Winkler, 4th revd ed., 1971 (he has also produced a 1-vol. ed. for Hanser, Munich and Vienna, 1977); J. M. Ritchie's *Taugenichts*, London, Harrap, 1970, 191 pp., an ann. pedagogic ed. with a first-rate introd.; and the puppet-play *Das Incognito* (see Arnim, b).

c **Translations.** The *Taugenichts* has been transl. by C. G. Leland (1866), Bayard Quincy Morgan, *Memoirs of a Good-for-Nothing*. New York, Ungar, and London, Calder, 1955, and, under the same title and better, by Ronald Taylor, London, Calder and Boyars, 1966.

d **Biography.** There is no adequate life; in default see Hans Brandenburg, *J. v. E.*, Munich, Beck, 1922, xiii, 531 pp.; Paul Stöcklein, *J. v. E. in Selbstzeugnissen und Bilddokumenten*, Reinbek, Rowohlt, 1963, 171 pp.; and, best of all, Wolfgang Frühwald, *E.-Chronik. Daten zu Leben und Werk*, Munich and Vienna, Hanser, 1977, 260 pp.

Willibald Köhler, *J. v. E.*, Augsburg, Oberschlesischer Heimatverlag, 1956, 275 pp., is hagiography. Gerhard Möbus, *E. in Heidelberg*, Düsseldorf, Diederichs, 1954, 128 pp., is a scholarly study of influences. There is also a useful catague, *Bayerische Akademie der schönen Künste... Ausstellung zum 100. Todestag*, ed. Inge Feuchtmayer, Munich, 1957, 134 pp.

e **General studies.** Oskar Seidlin's essays in his *Versuche über E.*, Göttingen, Vandenhoeck & Ruprecht, 1965, 303 pp., contain the most perceptive writing about him. Egon Schwarz's general introd., *J. v. E.*, New York, Twayne, 1972, 184 pp., is acceptable, and there are essays by Helmut Koopmann, in *DDRW*, pp. 416–41 (good), and Gillian Rodger, in *German Men of Letters*, ed. Alex Natan, London, Wolff, 1961, pp. 59–78. Lawrence Radner, *E.: The Spiritual Geometer*, Lafayette, Purdue U. Studies, 1970, 372 pp., is opinionated and ill written, but stimulating on what he conceives to be the irrelevancy of nature for E.; contrast for scholarship and argument, though not for rebarbativeness, Alexander von Bormann, *Natura loquitur. Naturpoesie und emblematische Formel bei J. v. E.*, Tübingen, Niemeyer, 1969, 312 pp.

Gerhard Möbus, *Der andere E.*, Osnabrück, Fromm, 1960, 206 pp., remains important. There are two respectable studies of the function of the poet for E.: Volkmar Stein, *Morgenrot und falscher Glanz*, Winterthur, Keller, 1964, xvii, 160 pp., and, more speculatively interesting, Hans Jürg Lüthi, *Dichtung und Dichter bei J. v. E.*, Bern and Munich, Francke, 1966, 311 pp.

f **Individual topics.** The three classic essays on landscape in E. are in all the bibls: Alewyn (1957), Mayer (1957) and Spitzer (1958). A related work of considerable merit is Peter Paul Schwarz. *Aurora. Zur r.en Zeitstruktur bei E.*, Bad Homburg, Gehlen, 1970, 236 pp. See also Marshall Brown, 'E.'s Times of Day', *GQ*, l (1977), 485–503.

Günter Strenzke, *Die Problematik der Langeweile bei J. v. E.*, Hamburg, Lüdke, 1973, 415 pp., is of broader interest than the title suggests, as is Elisabeth Stopp,' The Metaphor of Death in E.', *OGS*, iv (1969), 67–89. Theresia Sauter Bailliet, *Die Frauen im Werk E.s: Verkörperungen heidnischen und christlichen Geistes*, Bonn, Bouvier, 1972, 240 pp. (=AKML, 118), documents the already known. Detlev W. Schumann has two illuminating arts, on E.'s relationship with Fr. Schlegel in *JFDH*, 1966, pp. 336–83, and with Goethe in *LJb*, ix (1968), 159–218. Siegfried Hajek, 'Der Wanderer, der Philister, der Scheiternde. Grundfiguren bei E.', *Jb. der Raabe-Gesellschaft*, 1975, pp. 42–65.

Kohlschmidt's essay 'Die symbolische Formelhaftigkeit', *OL*, viii (1950), 322–54, and Rehder's 'Ursprünge dichterischer Emblematik', *JEGP*, lvi (1957), 528–41, remain basic to any consideration of E.'s style, but one may now add several other works of importance: Hillmann, *Bildlichkeit* [V.f. Imagery], pp. 207–328; Richard Alewyn, 'E.s Symbolismus', in his *Probleme und Gestalten*, Frankfurt, Insel, 1974, pp. 232–44 (originally in *Neue Deutsche Hefte*, xliii (1958), 977–85); Martin Wettstein, *Die Prosasprache J. v. E.s*, Zürich and Munich, Artemis, 1975, 100 pp. (=ZBLG, 43), a lucid re-examination of crit. clichés; Klaus-Dieter Krabiel, *Tradition und Bewegung. Zum sprachlichen Verfahren E.s*, Stuttgart, Kohlhammer, 1973, 107 pp., with excellent analyses of some poems and passages; Ansgar Hillach, 'Dramatische Theologie und christliche R. Zur geschichtlichen Differenz von calderonischer Allegorie und E.scher Emblematik', *GRM*, lviii (1977), 144–68.

g **Poetry.** Paul Gerhard Klussmann, 'Über E.s lyrische Hieroglyphen', in *Lit. und Gesellschaft. F.st.* von Wiese, ed. Hans Joachim Schrimpf, Bonn, Bouvier, 1963, pp. 113–41.

For interpretations of single poems see the *E.-Kommentar* vols, but add William R. Gilby on 'Der stille Grund', *Seminar*, ix (1973), 127–33.

h **Prose.** Josef Kunz, *E. Höhepunkt und Krise der Spätr.*, Oberursel, Altkönig, 1951, 255 pp., was a pioneering work that still has value. Ursula Wendler,

E. und das musikalische Theater. Untersuchungen zum Erzählwerk, Bonn, Bouvier, 1969, 191 pp (=AMML, 75), is interesting in its comparisons with the Singspiel tradition. Albrecht Schau, *Märchenformen bei E.*, Freiburg, Becksmann, 1970, 214 pp., aims to trace their importance in his development, with partial success. Eric A. Blackall, 'Moonlight and Moonshine: A disquisition on E.'s novels', *Seminar*, vi (1970), 111–27.

For *Ahnung und Gegenwart* see bibl. in *E.-Kommentar* II, 218, particularly Killy (1962), Kafitz (1971) and Meixner, *Figuralismus* [III, 2b], but add Worthmann, *Zeitroman* [III. 2b], pp. 24–9.

For *Dichter und ihre Gesellen* see Ernst L. Offermanns in *Lit. wissenschaft und Geschichtsphilosophie*, Fest. Emrich, ed. Helmut Arntzen, Berlin, de Gruyter, 1975, pp. 383–87.

For the *Taugenichts* see bibl. in G. T. Hughes, *E.: Aus dem Leben eines Taugenichts*, London, Edward Arnold, 1961, 64 pp. (=Studies in German Lit., 5), and in *E.-Kommentar* II, 219, and add: Dierk Rodewald, *ZDP*, xcii (1973), 231–59, good; Gertrud Bauer Pickar, in *Studies in 19th and Early 20th c. German Lit.*, Fest. Whitaker, Lexington, APRAP Press, 1974, pp. 131–7; Wolfgang Paulsen, *E. und sein Taugenichts*, Bern and Munich, Francke, 1976, 129 pp., clear and intelligent but not very original; W. G. Hesse, in *Fest.* Farrell, ed. Anthony Stevens, Bern, Lang, 1977, pp. 81–95, discursive; Carel tar Haar, *J. v. E.: 'Aus dem Leben eines T.s'. Text, Materialen, Kommentar*, Munich, Hanser, 1977, 204 pp., also with a substantial bibl.

For other Novellen see *E.-Kommentar* II, 218–19 and 214, particularly Helmut Koopmann on *Das Schloß Dürande*, *ZDP*, lxxxix (1970), 180–207, and add: on *Eine Meerfahrt*, Anselm Maler, *GRM*, lvi (1975), 47–73; on *Das Schloß Dürande* and *Die Entführung*, Detlev W. Schumann, *JDSG*, xviii (1974), 466–81; on *Das Marmorbild*, Lothar Pikulik, *Euph*, lxxi (1977), 128–40, and Valentine C. Hubbs, *GR*, iii (1977), 243–59.

Fichte

a   There is a bibl. by Hans Michael Baumgartner and Wilhelm G. Jacobs, Stuttgart, Frommann, 1968, 346 pp.; just under 4,000 items, extremely well indexed.

b   **Texts.** The crit. ed. Stuttgart, Frommann Holzboog, ed. Reinhard Lauth et al., began to appear in 1962 and is to be completed in some 30 vols. For single works see, in Meiner's 'Philosophische Bibliothek' series (Hamburg), the separate and slightly revd reprints from the 6 vols of selected works ed. Fritz Medicus in 1908–12, notably *Grundlage der gesamten Wissenchaftslehre (1794)*, 1956, xxxi, 247 pp., and *Reden an die deutsche Nation*, 1955, xvii, 253, pp., both with a useful index.

There is a handy selection of letters with an introd. by Manfred Buhr, *Briefe*, Leipzig, Reclam, [ca 1962], 317 pp.

c   Studies. Views about F. have changed rather less than those about Schelling so that it is still reasonably safe to rely on older works, such as Léon (3 vols, 1922–7), Wundt (1927 and 1929, both repr. Frommann, 1975), or even, in English, Adamson (1881). Among later studies of value are: Wolfgang

Janke, *F. Sein und Reflexion*, Berlin, de Gruyter, 1970, xvi, 428 pp.; Günter Schulte, *Die Wissenschaftslehre des späten F.*, Frankfurt, Klostermann, 1971, 264 pp., with an ed. of the 1810 text by the same publishers, 1976; Peter Baumanns, *F.s Wissenschaftslehre*, Bonn, Bouvier, 1974; Bernard Willms, *Die totale Freiheit. F.s politische Philosophie*, Cologne and Opladen, Westdeutscher Verlag, 1967, x, 170 pp.

d **Influence.** See Géza von Molnár [VI. Novalis, d]; Stefan Summerer. *Wirkliche Sittlichkeit und ästhetische Illusion. Die F. rezeption in den Fragmenten und Aufzeichnungen Fr. Schlegels und Hardenbergs*, Bonn, Bouvier, 1974, 294 pp.; and Kürt Röttgers, 'F.s Wirkung auf die Frür.er, am Beispiel Fr. Schlegels. Ein Beitrag zur "Theoriepragmatik"', *DVLG*, li (1977), 55–77, portraying him as more than an equal partner.

Fouqué

a **Texts.** There is no satisfactory ed., though *R.e. Erzählungen*, ed. Gerhard Schulz, Munich, Winkler, 1977, 514 pp., is now the preferred text for the tales. Otherwise use the ed. by Walter Ziesemer, Berlin, Bong [1908], 3 parts in one vol.

Undine has been ed. by W. W. Chambers, London and Edinburgh, Nelson, 1956, xxx, 97 pp. It was first transl. into English in 1818 and there are very many later versions, inc. one by Edmund Gosse, 1896, which is in the Oxford World's Classics series. The most recent is by Paul Turner, London, Calder, 1960, 128 pp.

b **Studies.** Arno Schmidt, *F. und einige seiner Zeitgenossen*, 2nd, much enlarged ed., Darmstadt, Bläschke, [1960], 733 pp. (first ed., Karlsruhe, Stahlberg, 1958); a great deal of information and unpubl. material, though not arranged with conventional neatness.

For *Undine* see W. J. Lillyman, *SiR*, x (1971), 94–104, and Burton R. Pollin, '*Undine* in the Works of Poe', *SiR*, xiv (1975), 59–74, with some discussion of transls. Korff, *Geist der Goethezeit*, vol. IV, has an important section on *Undine*.

See also Edward Mornin, 'Some Patriotic Novels and Tales by La Motte F.' *Seminar*, xi (1975), 141–56; and Jean T. Wilde's study of his wife, *The R. Realist. Caroline de la Motte F.*, New York, Bookman Associates, 1955, 474 pp.

Görres

a **Texts.** *Gesammelte Schriften* [GS], ed. Wilhelm Schellberg et al., Cologne, Bachem, began to appear in 1926; 15 of the promised 28 vols have been publ. *Ausgewählte Werke und Briefe*, 2 vols, ed. Schellberg, Kempten and Munich, Kösel, 1911; a very long introd., good notes and indexes.

b **Studies.** There is no satisfactory modern biography, but for introductory essays largely directed towards the life see Heribert Raab in *DDRW*, pp. 341–70, and Golo Mann in *Die Großen Deutschen*, ed. Hermann Heimpel, Berlin, Propyläen, 1956, II, 518–31.

Two works of considerable quality throw light on G.'s connexions with R. and Naturphilosophie: Georg Bürke, *Vom Mythos zur Mystik. J. v. G.'*

mystische Lehre und die r.e. Naturphilosophie, Einsiedeln, Johannes Verlag, 1958, 256 pp., and Reinhardt Habel, *J. G., Studien über den Zasammenhang von Natur, Geschichte und Mythos in seinen Schriften*, Wiesbaden, Steiner, 1960, 196 pp.

Grimm, Jakob and Wilhelm

a **Texts.** Of the many eds of *Kinder- und Hausmärchen* the most generally useful is that in 2 vols ed. Gisela Spiekerkötter, Munich, Bong, [1964]. There are also convenient Winkler (1949, 1-vol.) and Insel (1974, 3-vol.) eds. The 1812 and 1815 versions are used in Munich, Fischer, 1962. The indispensable eds for comparison of versions are now *Die älteste Märchensammlung der Brüder G.*, ed. Heinz Rölleke, Cologny-Geneva, Foundation Martin Bodmer, 1975, 403 pp., and his *Märchen der Brüder G.: unbekannte Texte*, Bonn, Bouvier, 1977, 120 pp. See also his art in *Euph*, lxxii (1978), 102–5.

b **Translations.** The tales have been repeatedly transl., first by Edgar Taylor in 1823, with illustrations by George Cruikshank, now in Puffin Books. Good versions are those by James Stern, London, Routledge, 1975; Francis P. Magoun Jr and Alexander H. Krappe, Carbondale, Southern Illinois U.P., 1960; a selection by Lore Segal and Randall Jarrell, New York, Farrar, Straus & Giroux, 1973, and London, Bodley Head, 1974; and Ralph Mannheim, London, Gollancz, 1978.

c **General studies.** The best concentrated guide is Ludwig Denecke, *J. G. und sein Bruder W.*, Stuttgart, Metzler, 1971, xi, 228 pp. (=SM, 100), with a very extensive bibl.

Hermann Gerstner, *Brüder G. in Selbstzeugnissen und Bild-dokumenten*, Reinbek, Rowohlt, 1971, 154 pp., is reliable and has a goodish bibl. There are two sensible general introds in English: Ruth Michaelis-Jena, *The Brothers G.*, London, Routledge, 1970, xvi, 212 pp., and Murray B. Peppard, *Paths through the Forest: A Biography of the Brothers G.*, New York, Holt, Rinehart and Winston, 1971, xvi, 266 pp. *Brüder G. Gedenken 1963*, ed. Ludwig Denecke, Marburg, Elwert, 1963, ix, 610 pp., is particularly valuable for their influence abroad; vol. II, 1965, ix, 304 pp., has a varied selection of essays, incl. an important one by Heinz Rölleke, 'Die Beiträge der Brüder G. zu "Des Knaben Wunderhorn"', pp. 28–42.

d **The Märchen.** Wilhelm Schoof, *Zur Entsehungsgeschichte der G. schen Märchen*, Hamburg, Hauswedell, 1959, 247 pp., is to be read with the important corrections by Rölleke in *GRM*, lvi (1975), 74–86. Of recent works see also: Max Lüthi, *Märchen*, Stuttgart, Metzler, 4th ed. 1971, xi, 124 pp. (=SM, 16); Hugo Moser, 'Sage und Märchen in der deutschen R.', in *Die deutsche R.*, ed. Steffen [I.6a], pp. 253–76; and, for a full Freudian analysis, Bruno Bettelheim, *The Uses of Enchantment. The Meaning and Importance of Fairy Tales*, New York, Knopf, and London, Thames & Hudson, 1976, vii, 328, xi pp.

Hauff

a **Texts.** The most reliable ed. is *Sämtliche Werke*, Munich, Winkler, 1970, 3 vols, ed. Sibylle von Steinsdorff and Uwe Schweikert, with a postscript by Helmut Koopmann. Other acceptable eds are: in 2 vols, ed. Bernhard Zeller, Frankfurt, Insel, 1969 (1976 in paperback); in 2 vols, ed. H. Engelhard, Stuttgart, Cotta, 1961–2; and in 3 vols, ed. G. Speikerkötter on the basis of Max Drescher's ed., Munich, Bong, 1961.

b **Translations.** There were many English versions of the tales and of *Lichtenstein* in the 19th c.; most recently, *H.'s Fairy Tales*, London, Cape, 1971, 225 pp.

c **Studies.** Apart from the introds to the eds and the general works on Swabian R. there has only been one substantial work on H. in recent years: Sabine Beckmann, *W. H.: seine Märchenalmanache als zyklische Kompositionen*, Bonn, Bouvier, 1976, 368 pp. (=AKML, 201). But see also Fritz Martini in *DDRW*, pp. 442–72; and Egon Schwarz in *Fest*. Dieckmann [II. 3], pp. 1–17. 'There is also a monograph by E. Martinez, *Guglielmo H.*, Florence, 1966.

Hoffmann

a **Bibliography.** The best starting-point is Jürgen Voerster, *160 Jahre E. T. A. H.-Forschung 1805–1965*, Stuttgart, Eggert, 1967, 220 pp.; it has the special value of giving refs to themes, individual works, etc., within books as well as in separate publs. There is a good conventional bibl. by Helmut Riege in Gabrielle Wittkop-Ménardeau, *E. T. A. H. in Selbstzeugnissen und Bilddokumenten*, Reinbek, Rowohlt, 1966, 189 pp., updated in her *E. T. A. H.s Leben in Daten und Bildern*, Frankfurt, Insel, 1968, 442 pp. (We might here mention a similar work by Ulrich Helmke, *E. T. A. H. Lebensbericht mit Bildern und Dokumenten*, Kassel, Wenderroth, 1975, 180 pp.)

There are also surveys and listings by Klaus Kanzog in the annual *Mitteilungen der E. T. A. H.-Gesellschaft*. Individual arts from the *Mitteilungen* are only rarely listed below. Hartmut Steinecke, 'Zur E. T. A. H.-Forschung', *ZDP*, lxxxix (1970), 222–34, is chiefly a review of Voerster and of the Winkler eds of works and letters.

The musical works are listed in Gerhard Allroggen, *E. T. A. H.s Kompositionen*, Regensburg, Bose, 1970, 143 pp., also with a survey of lit. on his music.

b **Texts.** Maassen's crit. ed. was never completed, but there are many quite acceptable substitutes; see Voerster, pp. 22–6. The 5-vol. Winkler (Munich) ed. issued as separate vols, 1960–5, is perhaps the best; *Poetische Werke* [PW] in 6 vols, ed. Gerhard Seidel, *Berlin*, Aufbau, 1958–63, is useful though it lacks the musical writings, which will however be in the promising new Aufbau ed. in 10 vols, ed. R. Mingau, 1976 ff., with a selection of compositions and reproductions of all his drawings.

The best single eds are the new Reclam (Stuttgart) vols, with their excellent apparatus and careful text: *Die Elixiere des Teufels*, ed. Wolfgang Nehring, 1975, 376 pp. (=UB, 192 [4]): *Lebens-Ansichten des Katers Murr*, ed. Hartmut Steinecke, 1972, 512 pp. (=UB, 153–8); *Meister Floh*, ed. Wulf Segebrecht, 1970, 239 pp. (=UB, 365–7); *Prinzessin Brambilla*, ed. Nehring,

1971, 171 pp. (=UB, 7953-4). The latter also ed. M. M. Raraty, Oxford, Blackwell, 1972, li, 132 pp.

For Winkler, Munich, Friedrich Schnapp has ed. the letters, in 3 vols based on Hans von Müller's 1912 ed.: *E. T. A. H.s Briefwechsel*, 1967-9; the *Tagebücher*, 1971; and *E. T. A. H. in Aufzeichnungen seiner Freunde und Bekannten*, 1974, all now the standard eds. Schnapp has also ed. the admirable *Dichter über ihre Dichtungen: E. T. A. H.*, Munich, Heimeran, 1974, 435 pp. For biographical selections see also *E.T.A.H. Sein Leben und Werk in Briefen*, ed. K. Günzel, Berlin, Verlag der Nation, 1975, 500 pp.

c **Translations.** Chief among the many versions in English is *Selected Writings*, 2 vols, ed. and transl. Leonard J. Kent and Elizabeth C. Knight, Chicago and London, U. of Chicago P., 1969, 315 and 364 pp..; sensible introd., vol. II devoted to *Murr*, lists of trans in III, 354-5. *Selected Letters* have been transl. and ed. Johanna C. Sahlin, 1977, also Chicago, vii, 360 pp., with an introd. by Kent. One may also mention: *Three Märchen ... Zaches... Brambilla; Master Flea*, transl. and with an introd. by Charles E. Passage, Columbia, U. of South Carolina P., 1971, xxviii, 403 pp.; and *The Devil's Elixirs*, transl. Ronald Taylor, London, Calder, 1963, xi, 324 pp.

d **General studies.** Several of the earlier surveys are still valuable: Sakheim (1908), Harich (1920), Schenck (1939) particularly, Ricci (1948), Hewett-Thayer (1948). Ronald Taylor, *H.*, London, Bowes & Bowes, 1963, 112 pp., is a good clear guide. The best short introd. is, however, by Wulf Segebrecht in *DDRW*, pp. 391 414; supp. with his art. in *Neue Deutsche Biographie*, vol. IX (1972), 407-14. His *Autobiographie und Dichtung: Eine Studie zum Werk E. T. A. H.s*, Stuttgart, Metzler, 1967, x, 240 pp., is a profoundly important re-examination of the relationship between life and works. See also John Reddick in *German Men of Letters V* [VI. Brentano, c], pp. 77-105.

Three very different interpretations are offered by: Kenneth Negus, *E. T. A. H.'s Other World. The R. Author and his 'New Mythology'*:, Philadelphia, U. of Pennsylvania P., 1965, 183 pp., excellent on the Märchen; Peter von Matt, *Die Augen der Automaten: E. T. A. H.s Imaginationslehre als Prinzip seiner Erzählkunst*, Tübingen, Niemeyer, 1971, 192 pp., relating motifs to the creative fictional processes as deducted from the stories; and Horst S. Daemmrich, *The Shattered Self. E. T. A. H.'s Tragic Vision*, Detroit, Wayne State U.P., 1973, 141 pp.—the magic in the stories is a projection of crisis and despair. (See also his 'Fragwürdige Utopie: E. T. A. H's geschichtsphilosophische Position', *JEPG*, lxxv (1976), 503-14). Stress on the realistic aspect of H. comes from East Germany in Hans-Georg Werner, *E. T. A. H.: Darstellung und Deutung der Wirklichkeit*, 2nd revd ed., Berlin and Weimar, Aufbau 1971, 294 pp. (first ed., 1962); and Hans Mayer, 'Die Wirklichkeit E. T. A. H.'s', in his *Von Lessing bis Thomas Mann*, Pfullingen, Neske, 1959, pp. 198-246.

See also: Siegfried Schumm, *Einsicht und Darstellung. Untersuchung zum Kunstverständnis E. T. A. H.s*, Göppingen, Kümmerle, 1974, v. 186 pp.; Volkmar Sander, 'Realität und Bewußtsein bei E. T. A. H.', in *Studies in Germanic Languages and Lit. Fest.* Rose, ed. Robert A. Fowkes, Reutlingen,

Hutzler, 1967, pp. 115-26; Gisela Vitt-Maucher, 'Die wunderlich wunderbare Welt E. T. A. H.s', *JEGP*, lxxv (1976), 515-30; Peter Faesi, *Künstler und Gesellschaft bei E. T. A. H.*, Basel, aku-Fotodruck, 1975, 188 pp.—a Basel diss.; Robert Mollenauer, 'The Three Periods of E. T. A. H.'s R.' *SiR*, ii (1963), 213-43; Nora E. Haimberger, *Vom Musiker zum Dichter. Eine Studie zu E. T. A. H.s Akkordvorstellung*, Bonn, Bouvier, 1976, 140 pp.

There are several colls of essays: *E. T. A. H.*, ed. Helmut Prang, Darmstadt, Wiss BG, 1976, vi, 425 pp., with 18 previously publ. contributions; *ZDP*, xcv (1976) *Sonderheft E. T. A. H.*, with 8 new essays; *JEGP*, lxxv, 4 (Oct. 1976) also devoted to H.; Hans von Müller, *Gesammelte Aufsätze über E. T. A. H.*, ed. Schnapp, Hildesheim, Gerstenberg, 1974, 815 pp., with 35 essays dating from 1901 to 1936; Claudio Magris, *Tre studi su H.*, Milan, Cisalpino, 1969, 123 pp. Robert Mühlher has 10 essays on H. in his *Deutsche Dichter der Klassik und R.*, Vienna, Braumüller, 1976; significant forerunners of his announced 2-vol. study.

Comparative studies are: Marianne Frey, *Der Künstler und sein Werk bei W. H. Wackenroder und E. T. A. H.*, Bern, Lang, 1970, vi. 202 pp., with little new; Steven Paul Scher also on W. and H. in *JEGP*, lxxv (1976), 492-502; Günter Wöllner, *E. T. A. H. und Franz Kafka*, Bern, Haupt, 1971, 187 pp., with discussions of 'Das fremde Kind' and 'Der goldne Topf'.

Elizabeth Teichmann, *La Fortune d'H. en France*, Geneva, Droz and Paris, Minard, 1961, 288 pp.; Norman W. Ingham, *E. T. A. H.'s Reception in Russia*, Würzburg, Jal, 1974, 303 pp., is a Harvard diss. of great thoroughness.

e **Individual topics.** On motifs generally: Robert Mühlher, in *LJb*, iv (1963), 55-72. On the dream: Diana Stone Peters, *OGS*, viii (1973), 60-85, and Inge Stegmann, *ZDP*, xcv (1976), 64-93. On the eye: Helga Slessarev, *Monatshefte*, lxiii (1971), 358-71, and Yvonne Jill Kathleen Holbecke, *Optical Motifs in the works of E. T. A. H.*, Göppingen, Kümmerle, 1975, 248 pp. On music: Pauline Watts, *Music: The Medium of the Metaphysical in E. T. A. H.*, Amsterdam, Rodopi, 1972, 96 pp., inadequate; better, Norbert Miller, *Akzente*, xxiv (1977), 114-35; and, more generally, Ronald Taylor, *JEGP*, lxxv (1976), 477-91. On the supernatural: Lee B. Jennings, *JEGP*, lxxv (1976), 559-67. On nonsense: Francis J. Nock, *GQ*, xxxv (1962), 60-70. And Natalie Reber, *Studien zum Motiv des Doppelgängers bei Dostojevskij und E. T. A. H.*, Giessen, Wilhelm Schmitz, 1964, 240 pp.

On language and style: Helmut Müller, *Untersuchungen zum Problem der Formelhaftigkeit bei E. T. A. H.*, Bern, Haupt, 1964, 128 pp., discovering 'conflict-formulas'; an important counterpart to Kohlschmidt on Eichendorff. Also Francis J. Nock, *JEGP*, lv (1956), 588-603; Hillmann, *Bildlichkeit* [V.f. Imagery], pp. 131-266; Wolfgang Nehring, 'Die Gebärdensprache E. T. A. H.s', *ZDP*, lxxxix (1970), 207-21, incl. not only gestures, but dress, intonation, etc.; Erwin Rotermund, 'Musikalische und erzählerische "Arabesken" bei E. T. A. H.', *Poetica*, ii (1968), 48-69, with a good deal on *Murr*.

On structure: Lothar Köhn, *Vieldeutige Welt: Studien zur Struktur der Erzählungen E. T. A. H.s*, Tübingen, Niemeyer, 1966, vii, 252 pp.; structural

analyses contradict the traditional 'dualist' view of H.; Victor Terras, *GQ*, xxxix (1966), 549–69; Wolfgang Nehring, pp. 3–24, and Klaus Kanzog, pp. 42–63 of *ZDP*, xcv (1976); Wolfgang Preisendanz in *E. T. A. H.* ed. Prang, pp. 270–91, originally in *Fest.* Trier, ed. Wilhelm Foerste, Cologne and Graz, Böhlau, 1964, pp. 411–29; Jocelyne Kolb, *Monatshefte*, lxix (1977), 34–44.
Barbara Elling, *Leserintegration im Werk E. T. A. H.s*, Bern, Haupt, 1973, 88 pp., incls both real and fictive reader; she has a related note in *JEGP*, lxxv (1976), 546–58. Heide Eilert, *Theater in der Erzählkunst. Eine Studie zum Werk E. T. A. H.s*, Tübingen, Niemeyer, 1977, 200 pp.

f **Novels.** *Die Elixiere:* see the bibl. in the Reclam ed. and add: Meixner, *Figuralismus* [III. 2b], pp. 155–230; J. Milfull, *Ro*, iv (1962); Renate Moering, *JWGV*, lxxv (1971), 56–73; Charles E. Passage, *JEGP*, lxxv (1976), 531–45.
Kater Murr: to the bibl. in the Reclam ed. add: Peter J. Graves, *MLQ*, xxx (1969), 222–33; Charles Finlay, *GLL*, xxvii (1973), 22–34; Lawrence O. Frye, *DVLG*, xlix (1975), 520–45; Steven Paul Scher, comparison with *Tristram Shandy*, *ZDP*, xcv (1976), 24–42, and *CL*, xxviii (1976), 309–25; Michael T. Jones, *Monatshefte*, lxix (1977), 45–57.
For both novels add: Dietrich Raff, *Ich-Bewußtsein und Wirklichkeitsauffassung bei E. T. A. H.*, Rottweil, Emmanuel, 1971, 208 pp.

g **Märchen and tales.** See Voerster and Osborne, *R.*, adding or emphasizing the following:
Fritz Martini, 'Die Märchendichtungen E. T. A. H.s', *DU*, vii, 2 (1955), 56–78; Bonaventura Tecchi, *Le fiabe di E.T.A.H.*, Florence, Sansoni, 1962, 228 pp.; Christa-Maria Beardsley, *E. T. A. H.: Die Gestalt des Meisters in seinen Märchen*, Bonn, Bouvier, 1975, 200 pp. (=AKML, 182); Klaus Günther Just, 'Die Blickführung in den Märchennovellen E. T. A. H.s', *WW*, xiv (1964), 389–97, now in *E. T. A. H.*, ed. Prang, pp. 292–306.
Falun and *Das Majorat* both in Heinisch, *Deutsche R.* [I.6c], pp. 134–53 and 171–81.
Der goldne Topf: Lothar Pikulik, 'Anselmus in der Flasche', *Euph*, lxiii (1969), 341–70, important; Knud Willenberg, *ZDP*, xcv (1976), 93–113; Armand De Loecker, *Duitse Kroniek*, xxv (1973), 116–39.
Klein Zaches: Jürgen Walter, *Mitteilungen der E. T. A. H.-Gesellschaft*, xix (1973), 27–45, now in *E. T. A. H.*, ed. Prang, pp. 398–423; Lee B. Jennings, *DVLG*, xliv (1970), 687–703; Furio Jesi, *Studi Germanici*, xi (1973), 25–50.
Meister Floh: the Reclam ed. and Horst Rüdiger in *Deutsche Weltlit. Fest.* Pfeffer, ed. Klaus W. Jonas, Tübingen, Niemeyer, 1972, pp. 89–114.
Nußknacker und Mausekönig: Günter Heintz, *Lit. in Wissenschaft und Unterricht*, vii (1974), 1–15.
Brambilla: Claus F. Köpp, *WB*, xii (1966), 57–80; Helga Slessarev, *SiR*, ix (1970), 147–60; Hough-Lewis Dunn, *SiR*, xi (1972), 113–37, largely about the influence of Shakespeare's comedies; Jean Starobinski, *Critique*, xxii (1966), 438–57, on the influence of Gozzi. Reinhold Grimm, 'Die Formbezeichnung "Capriccio" in der deutschen Lit. des 19. Jhs, in *Studien zur*

Triviallit., ed. Heinz Otto Burger, Frankfurt, Klostermann, 1968, pp. 101–16. Schumm [d, above] and *MLN*, xciii (1978), 399–415, centres on *Brambilla*.

Rat Krespel: Giesela Vitt-Maucher, *Monatshefte*, lxiv (1972), 51–7; La Vern J. Rippley, *Papers on Language and Lit.*, vii (1971), 52–60; John M. Ellis, in his *Narration in the German Novelle*, London, Cambridge U.P., 1974.

Ritter Gluck: Vitt-Maucher, comparison with Poe, *GQ*, xliii (1970), 35–46; John Fetzer, *GQ*, xliv (1971), 317–30; Christa Karoli, *Mitteilungen der E. T. A. H.-Gesellschaft*, xiv (1968), 1–17, now in *E. T. A. H.*, ed. Prang, pp. 334–58.

Scuderi: Hellmuth Himmel, *Mitteilungen*, vii (1960), 1–15, and Klaus Kanzog, xi (1964), 1–11, both now in *E. T. A. H.*, ed. Prang, pp. 215–36 and 307–21; J. M. Ellis, *MLR*, lxiv (1969), 340.50; Edgar Marsch, in his *Die Kriminalerzählung*, Munich, Winkler, 1972, pp. 141–54; Klaus D. Post, *ZDP*, xcv (1976), 132–56; Hermann F. Weiss, *GR*, li (1976), 181–9.

Sandmann: Ursula D. Lawson, *Monatshefte*, lx (1968), 51–61; Raimund Belgardt, *GQ* xlii (1969), 686–700; Jean Giraud, *RG*, iii (1973), 102–24; Charles N. Hayes, in *Ideologiekritische Studien zur Lit. Essays I*, ed. Volkmar Sander, Frankfurt, Athenäum, 1972, pp. 169–214; Irving Massey, *Genre*, vi (1973), 114–20; Ursula Mahlendorf, *American Imago*, xxxii (1975), 217–39; Ingrid Aichinger, *ZDP*, xcv (1976), 113–32, on Freud's interpretation; Lienhard Wawrzyn, *Der Automaten-Mensch, E. T. A. H.s Erzählung vom Sandmann*, Berlin, Wagenbach, 1976, 160 pp.; Günter Hartung, *WB*, xxiii (1977), 45–65.

Kerner

There is no recent coll. ed., but *Die Reiseschatten*, ed. Walter P. H. Scheffler, Stuttgart, Steinkopf, 1964, 244 pp., has a good crit. apparatus. *Das Leben des J. K.*, ed. Karl Pörnbacher, Munich, Kösel, 1967, is abbreviated but has good notes.

Hartmut Fröschle, *J. K. und Ludwig Uhland*, Göppingen, Kümmerle, 1972, 159 pp., has an English summary. There are four crit. arts in *Antaios*, x (1968), 109–83. Gabriel Peterli, *Zerfall und Nahklang. Studien zur deutschen Spätr.*, Zürich, Atlantis, 1958 (=ZBLG, 14), devotes pp. 11–22 to K., but then moves outside R. Alan P. Cottrell interprets a sonnet in *GQ*, xxxix (1966), 173–86. The Mitteilungen of the J.-K.-Verein und Frauenverein Weinsberg reached issue 12 in 1975.

Müller, Adam

For a bibl. and a review of research see *Kritische, ästhetische und philosophische Schriften*, 2 vols, ed. Walter Schroeder and Werner Siebert, Neuwied, Luchterhand, 1967; a splendid ed. *Vermittelnde Kritik*, ed. Anton Kröttli, Zürich and Stuttgart, Artemis, 1968, 311 pp.; good introd. *Zwölf Reden über die Beredsamkeit*, ed. and with a hostile introd. by Walter Jens, Frankfurt, Insel, 1967, 211 pp.

There is a massive gathering of biographical material in *A. M.s Lebenszeugnisse*, ed. Jakob Baxa, Munich, Paderborn, Vienna, Schöningh, 1966, vol. I (1779–1816), 1208 pp., vol. II (1817–29), 1186 pp. *Katholizismus, konservative Kapitalismuskritik und Frühsozialismus bis 1850*, ed. Albrecht Langer,

Paderborn and Vienna, Schöningh, 1975, 250 pp., has essays on him by Ernst Klein and Ralph-Rainer Wuthenow ('R. als Restauration bei A. M.', pp. 79–97) and a note by the editor.

Müller, Wilhelm

Hatfield's 1906 ed. of the poems must still be used.

There have been four recent works of crit. value: Klaus Günther Just, 'W. M.s Liederzyklen', *ZDP*, lxxxiii (1964), 452–71, repr. in his *Übergänge*, Bern, Francke, 1966, pp. 133–52; Nigel Reeves, 'The Art of Simplicity: Heinrich Heine and W. M.', *OGS*, v (197), 48–66, substantially repeated in his *Heinrich Heine: Poetry and Politics*, Oxford U.P., 1974; the judicious Alan P. Cottrell, *W. M.'s Lyrical Song-Cycles: Interpretations and Texts*, Chapel Hill, U. of North Carolina P., 1970, ix, 170 pp. (=UNCSGLL, 66); and Günter Hartung, 'W. M. und das deutsche Volkslied', *WB*, xxiii (1977), 46–85.

Die Nachtwachen

As good an ed. as any is that of Wolfgang Paulsen, Stuttgart, Reclam, 1964, 180 pp. (=UB, 8926–7). Good introd. to the bilingual ed. by Gerald Gillespie, Edinburgh U.P., 1972, xv, 254 pp.

The latest discussion of the authorship, with the Klingemann hypothesis, in Jost Schillemeit, *Bonaventura — Der Verfasser der 'N.'*, Munich, Beck, 1973, 125 pp., but see note 7 to Chapter 2 above for later reservations. For a full earlier account, with important crit. material, see Jeffrey L. Sammons, *The N. v. B.: A Structural Interpretation*, The Hague, Mouton, 1965, 128 pp., and Max Rouché, 'B. ne serait-il pas Jean Paul Richter lui-même?', *EG*, xxiv (1969), 329–45, interesting if unconvincing.

General studies. See Dorothee Sölle-Nipperdey, *Untersuchungen zur Struktur der N. v. B*, Göttingen, Vandenhoeck & Ruprecht, 1959, 110 pp. (=Palaestra, 230); Richard Brinkmann, *N. v. B.: Kehrseite der Frühr.*, Pfullingen, Neske, 1966, 32 pp., also in *Die deutsche R.*, ed. Steffen [I.6a], pp. 134–58; Peter Küpper, 'Unfromme Vigilien. B. s. N.', in *Fest.* Alewyn [I.6b], pp. 309–27: Arendt [V.r. Nihilism].

For individual topics see: Gerald Gillespie, *Arcadia*, viii (1973), 284–95, on Hogarth; and again in *Herkommen und Erneuerung. Fest.* Seidlin, ed. Gillespie, Tübingen, Niemeyer, 1976, pp. 185–200, on *commedia dell'arte*; Klaus Kanzog, in *Großbritannien und Deutschland. Fest.* Bourke, ed. Ortwin Kuhn, Munich, Goldmann, 1974, pp. 347–71, on Shakespeare; Russell Neuswanger, *GLL*, xxx (1976), 15–23, on laughter.

Novalis

a **Texts.** The new crit. ed. publ. by Kohlhammer, Stuttgart, is the surest guide not only on textual matters, but also for biographical and bibl. detail. Nominally based on the 1929 ed. of Paul Kluckhohn (d. 1957) and Richard Samuel, it is really a new undertaking by Samuel and several collaborators. Vol. I, *Das dichterische Werk*, was first issued in 1960 just before the main bulk of N. manuscripts became available for study; the vol. has therefore been thoroughly revd and appeared as the 3rd ed. [*KS* I³] in 1977. Vols

II (1965) and III (1968) contain *Das philosophische Werk*, and vol. IV (1975) has *Lebensdokumente*, incl. diaries, letters to and from him, testimonies of friends, reading lists. Vol. V is to contain indexes, bibls and other material.

All other eds now become of historical interest, with the exception of that by Gerhard Schulz, Munich, Beck, 1969, which is valuable for its notes, bibl. and extensive indexes. A model of an intelligent single-vol. ed. Hanser announce a 3-vol. ed. by Mähl and Samuel.

The only separate text to be mentioned is the Reclam ed. of *Ofterdingen* by Wolfgang Frühwald, Stuttgart, 1965, 247 pp. (=UB, 8939–41), with a useful bibl. and postscript. See also *N.*, ed. Hans-Joachim Mähl, Munich, Heimeran, 1976, 263 pp. (=Dichter über ihre Dichtungen, 15).

b **Translations.** There are modern transls of *Hymns to the Night* by Mabel Cottrell, London, Phoenix, 1948, and, with *Klingsohr, Christendom* and some aphorisms, by Charles E. Passage, New York, Bobbs-Merrill, 1960; of *Henry of Ofterdingen* by Palmer Hilty, New York, Ungar, n.d.; of *The Novices of Sais* by Ralph Mannheim, New York, Valentin, 1949; and of some of the aphorisms by Michael Hamburger, *Quarterly Review of Lit.*, xviii (1972), 167–72.

c **General studies.** For a balanced general introd. see Hans-Joachim Mähl in *DDRW*, pp. 190–224, and, in English, the chapter in Michael Hamburger, *Reason and Energy*, London, Routledge, 1957, pp. 71–104. Friedrich Hiebel, *N.: deutscher Dichter, europäischer Denker, christlicher Seher*, Bern and Munich, Francke, 1972, 392 pp., is the much revd 2nd ed. of *N.: Der Dichter der blauen Blume*, 1951, which appeared in an English adaptation of 1954, revd 1959, in the series UNCSGLL, 10. The 1972 ed., though anthroposophically committed, is reliable and comprehensive. Gerhard Schulz, *N. in Selbstzeugnissen und Bilddokumenten*, Reinbek, Rowohlt, 1969, 189 pp., is one of the best of the series, with a good bibl. Schulz has also ed. *N.*, Darmstadt, Wiss BG, 1970, xx, 423 pp., with 12 essays written between 1839 and 1963, incl. the editor's own 'Die Berufslaufbahn F. v. H.s (N.)', pp. 283–356, originally publ. *JDSG*, vii (1963), 253–312, the most important contribution to the biography. Heinz Ritter, *Der unbekannte N.*, Göttingen, Sachse & Pohl, 1967, 365 pp., is speculative but knowledgeable.

d **Topics.** Works on N. are not easily categorized; one topic readily runs into another.

Theodor Haering, *N. als Philosoph*, Stuttgart, Kohlhammer, 1954, 648 pp., is not easy to consult and has in some respects been overtaken by later interpretations; but it remains the most comprehensive account. Géza von Molnár, *N.'s Fichte Studies*, The Hague, Mouton, 1970, 117 pp., notes his changes of emphasis from Fichte. Hannelore Link, *Abstraktion und Poesie im Werk des N.*, Stuttgart, Kohlhammer, 1971, 189 pp., explores modes of thought and linguistic structures; among the most important recent studies, with good comments on works. See also Winfried Weier, 'Die Verwandlung der idealistischen Abstraktion in die Emotion bei N.' *EG*, xxiii (1968), 548–73. Eckhard Heftrich, *N.: Vom Logos der Poesie*, Frankfurt, Klostermann, 1969, 184 pp., deals with poetry as religion; much incidental information. Ernst-Georg Gäde, *Eros und Identität. Zur Grundstruktur der Dichtungen F. v.*

H.s (N.), Marburg, Elwert, 1974, 294 pp. Rolf-Peter Janz, *Autonomie und soziale Funktion der Kunst: Studien zur Ästhetik von Schiller und N.*, Stuttgart, Metzler, 1973, vi, 157 pp., relates art, religion and the social order.

Ulrich Gaier, *Krumme Regel: N.s 'Konstruktionslehre des schaffenden Geistes' und ihre Tradition*, Tübingen, Niemeyer, 1970, 268 pp., finds the structures based on the magic number seven; there is a lengthy analysis of the *Lehrlinge*. Helmut Schanze, *R. und Aufklärung. Untersuchungen zu Fr. Schlegel und N.*, Nuremberg, Hans Carl, 1966, xiii, 172 pp., with a revd 2nd ed. 1976, xii, 186 pp., has been an influential work showing particularly the 'encyclopaedic' connexions. Now see also Hans Hegener, *Die Poetisierung der Wissenschaften bei N... Studien zum Problem enzyklopädischen Welterfahrens*, Bonn, Bouvier, 1975, 521 pp. (=AKML, 170).

On science, in addition to Kapitza [IV.a], see John Neubauer, *Bifocal Vision: N.'s Philosophy of Nature and Disease*, Chapel Hill, 1971, 194 pp. (= UNCSGLL, 68); Martin Dyck, *N. and Mathematics*, Chapel Hill, 1960, 109 pp. (=UNCSGLL, 27); Roger Cardinal, 'Werner, N. and the Signature of the Stones', in *Deutung und Bedeutung. Fest.* K.-W. Maurer, ed. Brigitte Schludermann, The Hague, Mouton, 1973, pp. 118–33.

A work of beautiful scholarship is Hans-Joachim Mähl's *Die Idee des goldenen Zeitalters im Werk des N.*, Heidelberg, Winter, 1965, viii, 496 pp. Karl Kaspar Groß, *Ursprung und Utopie. Aporien des Textes. Versuche zu Herder und N.*, Bonn, Bouvier, 1976, 179 pp.

For history generally see Kuhn (Chapter 4, note 6 above); Peter Küpper, *Die Zeit als Erlebnis des N.*, Cologne and Graz, Böhlau, 1959, viii, 139 pp.; Peter Berglar, 'Geschichte und Staat bei N.', *JFDH*, 1974, pp. 143–208; Gerda Heinrich, *Geschichts-philosophische Positionen der Frühr. (Fr. Schlegel und N.)*, Berlin, Akademie, 1976, 261 pp.

Klaus Ruder, *Zur Symboltheorie des N.*, Marburg, Elwert, 1974, 168 pp., is much the most full and sophisticated treatment; another vol. is planned. See also Steven C. Schaber, ''N.' Theory of the Work of Art as Hieroglyph', *GR*, xlviii (1973), 35–43. Bruce Haywood, *The Veil of Imagery. A study of the poetic works of F. v. H. (1772–1801)*, Cambridge (Mass.), Harvard U.P. and The Hague, Mouton, 1959, 159 pp., is still of interest; but supp. with William E. Yuill, '"Gehaltlos wie ein Sieb": Zu den elementaren Metaphern des N.', *Deutsche Beiträge zur geistigen Überlieferung*, vi (1970), 26–44.

Studies of limited themes are: on play, Viorica Niscov, *DVLG*, xlix (1975), 662–79; on death, Leonard P. Wessell Jr, *SiR*, xiv (1975), 425–52; on water, R. Leroy, *Revue des langues vivantes*, xxxiv (1968), 50–7; on the blue flower see Chapter 4, note 11 above.

e **Influences and relationships.** Three important arts by Mähl are, to a considerable extent, gutted in *KS*: on N. and Plotinus, *JFDH* 1963, pp. 139–250, repr. in *N.*, ed. Schulz, pp. 357–423; on his *Wilhelm Meister* studies, *Neophilologus*, xlvii (1963), 286–305; and on Goethe's view of N., *JFDH*, 1967, pp. 130–270. Carl Paschek's 1967 diss. has yielded his rich 'N. und Böhme', *JFDH*, 1976, pp. 138–67. See also: Paul E. Gottfried, 'Ideologische Ästhetik: Kunst und Politik bei Burke und N.', *Zeitschrift für Ästhetik*, xix

(1974), 240–51; Wolfgang Sommer, *Schleiermacher und N.*, Bern, Lang, 1973, 149 pp.; Marianne Kesting, 'Aspekte des absoluten Buches bei N. und Mallarmé', *Euph*, lxviii (1974), 420–36; Eudo C. Mason, 'Hölderlin und N.', *Hölderlin Jb. 1958–60*, pp. 72–119.

On *Meister* see also Géza von Molnár, in *Versuche zu Goethe. Fest.* Heller, ed. Volker Dürr, Heidelberg, Stiehm, 1976, pp. 235–47.

f **Genres.** On the novel one must read Gerhard Schulz, 'Die Poetik des Romans bei N.', *JFDH*, 1964, pp. 120–57, repr. in *Deutsche Romantheorien* [III.2b], pp. 81–110.

For *Ofterdingen* see bibls in *KS* I³, 623–4 and 637–8, adding J. Christopher Middleton, in *Literary Symbolism*, ed. Helmut Rehder, Austin, U. of Texas P., 1965, pp. 85–109; Lawrence O. Frye, *DVLG*, xlix (1975), 520–45; Elwin E. Rogers, *GQ*, 1 (1977), 130–7. Works of special value are: Oskar Serge Ehrensperger, *Die epische Struktur in N.s' H. v. O.*, Winterthur, Schellenberg, 1965, viii, 109 pp.; Johannes Mahr, *Der Übergang zum Endlichen. Der Weg des Dichters in N.s' 'H. v. O.'*, Munich, Fink, 1970, 272 pp.; Richard Samuel, in *Der deutsche Roman I*, ed. von Wiese, Düsseldorf, Bagel, 1963, pp. 252–300 and 433–7; Elisabeth Stopp, *DVLG*, xlviii (1974), 318–41; and, in a different way, Helmut Schanze's concordance *Index zu N. H. v. O.*, Frankfurt, Athenäum, 1968, ix, 193 pp., with references to *KS* I².

For the *Lehrlinge* see again bibl. in *KS* I³, 593, especially Ulrich Gaier [d, above].

For *Die Christenheit oder Europa* see Wilfried Malsch, *'Europa', Poetische Rede des N.: Deutung der französischen Revolution und Reflexion auf der Poesie in der Geschichte*, Stuttgart, Metzler, 1965, xiv, 207 pp., with much bibl. information in the excellent notes; and Barbara Steinhäuser-Carvill, *Seminar*, xii (1976), 73–88.

On the fragments see Manfred Dick, *Die Entwicklung des Gedankens der Poesie in den Fragmenten des N.*, Bonn, Bouvier, xii, 476 pp., one of the most illuminating of all recent studies; Hugo Kuhn, in his *Text und Theorie*, Stuttgart, Metzler, 1969, pp. 246–83 and 369–73; Gerhard Neumann, *Ideenparadiese. Untersuchungen zur Aphoristik von Lichtenberg, N., Fr. Schlegel und Goethe*, Munich, Fink, 1976, 863 pp.

For the *Hymnen* and the *Geistliche Lieder* see bibls in *KS* I³, 600–1 and 608, adding Winfried Kudszus, *Euph*, lxv (1971), 298–311. Notes 7 and 10 to Chapter 4 above refer to some of the works; the two arts by Lawrence Frye in *DVLG*, xli (1967), 568–91, and *Euph*, lxi (1967), 318–36, deserve special mention. Janet Gardner, 'N., Das Gedicht', *JFDH*, 1974, pp. 209–34, deals with the poem 'Himmlisches Ieben', *KS* I³, 409.

Ritter.
Walter D. Wetzels, *J. W. R.: Physik im Wirkungsfeld der deutschen R.*, Berlin, de Gruyter, 1973, 135 pp. is a first-rate study, throwing much light on other R. figures and with an extensive bibl.

Schelling
a **Bibliography.** There is a bibl. by Guido Schneeberger, Bern, Francke,

1954, 190 pp. Supp. with Hans Jörg Sandkühler, *F. W. J. S.*, Stuttgart, Metzler, 1970, viii, 108 pp. (=SM, 87), both for bibl. and general introd.; and Hermann Zeltner, *S.-Forschung seit 1954*, Darmstadt, Wiss BG, 1975, viii, 115 pp. Joseph A. Bracken, *Freiheit und Kausalität bei S.*, Freiburg and Munich, Alber, 1972, 128 pp., has a survey of lit. on S., pp. 11–16.

b **Texts.** Some measure of the change in S.'s status is the inauguration of a vast new crit. ed. in some 80 vols, of which I, 1, ed. W. G. Jacobs, appeared in 1976, Stuttgart, Frommann-Holzboog. For existing eds see the bibls, adding two selections: *Frühschriften. Eine Auswahl*, 2 vols, ed. Helmut Seidel and Lothar Kleine, Berlin, Akademie, 1971, 1251 pp., and *S. ou la quête du secret de l'être*, ed. Claude Bruaire, Paris, Seghers, 1970, 181 pp. *Briefe und Dokumente*, ed. Horst Fuhrmanns, to be completed in 4 vols, Bonn, Bouvier, I (1962), II (1973), III (1975), is an important coll. See also *S. und Cotta Briefwechsel 1803–1849*, ed. Horst Fuhrmanns and Liselotte Lohrer, Stuttgart, Klett, 1965, 359 pp.

c **Studies.** Karl Jaspers, *S. Größe und Verhängnis*, Munich, Piper, 1955, 346 pp.; Hermann Zeltner, *S.*, Stuttgart, Frommann, 1954, xii, 335 pp.; *S. Einführung in seine Philosophie*, ed. Hans Michael Baumgartner, Freiburg, Alber, 1975, 208 pp.; Xavier Tilliette, *S.: Une philosophie en devenir*, 2 vols, Paris, Vrin, 1970. Tilliette has also ed. *S. im Spiegel seiner Zeitgenossen*, Turin, Bottega d'Erasmo, 1974, 657 pp.

Materialen zu S.s philosophischen Anfängen, ed. Manfred Frank and Gerhard Kurz, Frankfurt, Suhrkamp, 1975, 476 pp., is an important coll. of essays; Dieter Jähnig, *S.: Die Kunst in der Philosophie*, 2 vols, Pfullingen, Neske, 1966–9, 264 and 366 pp.; Hinrich Knittermeyer, *S. und die r.e Schule*, Munich, Reinhardt, 1928, 482 pp., awkward to use but much useful material; Manfred Schröter, *Kritische Studien über S.*, Munich, Oldenbourg, 1971, 160 pp.; Peter Szondi, 'S.s Gattungspoetik', in his *Poetik und Geschichtsphilosophie*, II, Frankfurt, Suhrkamp, 1974, pp. 185–307; Karl-Heinz Volkmann-Schluck, *Mythos und Logos. Interpretationen zu S.s Philosophie der Mythologie*, Berlin, de Gruyter, 1969, 152 pp.; E. D. Hirsch Jr, *Wordsworth and S.: A Typological Study of R.*, New Haven, Yale U.P., 1960, xxiv, 214 pp.; Harald Holz, *Die Idee der Philosophie bei S.*, 144 pp., and Werner Marx, *S.: Geschichte, System, Freiheit*, 160 pp., both Freiburg, Alber, 1977.

There are special nos of *Les Etudes philosophiques* (1974, 2) and *Archives de philosophie*, xxxviii (1975) devoted to S.; *Die Philosophie des jungen S.*, ed. E. Lange, Weimar, Böhlau, 1977, 220 pp., contains studies presented at a Jena conference in 1975.

Schlegel, August Wilhelm
a There is no recent bibl.

b **Texts.** A sound ed. is now available in the 7 vols of *Kritische Schriften und Briefe*, ed. Edgar Lohner, Stuttgart, Kohlhammer, 1962–74; no claims as a crit. text, but each vol. has brief notes and vol. VII has invaluable indexes to the whole. The Bonn lectures of 1819–20 are being ed. by Frank Jolles in 5 vols of which vol. I, *Vorlesungen über das akademische Studium*, has appeared: Heidelberg, Stiehm, 1971, 111 pp., with a sound short introd. *Kritische Schriften*, ed. Emil Staiger, Zürich and Stuttgart, Artemis, 1962, 367 pp.; good selection and introd. with popular notes. *Observations sur la langue et la litt. provençales*, Tübingen, 1971, xiv, 122 pp. (=Tübinger Beiträge zur Linguistik, 7), is a repr. of the 1818 ed. with a preface by Gunter Narr.

c **General studies.** Straightforward introd. by Edgar Lohner in *DDRW*, pp. 135–62. *A. W. S.*, Bad Godesberg, Inter Nationes, 1967, 60 pp., has a mainly biographical essay by Marianne Thalmann and some notes on the Shakespeare transls. Three lectures given in London in 1938 by Walter Schirmer are still of value and are in his *Kleine Schriften*, Tübingen, Niemeyer, 1950, pp. 153–200. See also note 1 to Chapter 3 above. Stiehm, Heidelberg, announces that a study by Frank Jolles is in preparation.

d **Individual studies.** Ralph W. Ewton, *The Literary Theories of A. W. S.*, The Hague, Mouton, 1972, 120 pp.; informative. Wellek's chapter in his *History of Modern Crit.* [III.2g] is indispensable. See also note 6 to Chapter 3 above, and Hans-Dietrich Dahnke, 'A. W. S.s Berliner und Wiener Vorlesungen und die r.e Lit.', *WB*, xiv (1968), 782–96. Silke Reavis, *A. W. S.s Auffassung der Tragödie*, Bern, Lang, 1977, 190 pp.

For the Shakespeare transls see note 5 to Chapter 3 above.

Schlegel-Schelling, Caroline

Briefe aus der Frühr., first ed. Georg Waitz, Leipzig, 1871, but use the enlarged ed. by Erich Schmidt, also in 2 vols, Leipzig, Insel, 1913 (repr. Bern, Lang, 1968); a great quarry for R. history.

There are several recent studies, the best being Eckart Kleßmann, Munich, List, 1975, 316 pp. Gisela F. Richter, Bonn, Bouvier, 1968, 335 pp. (=AKML, 50), comparing her biography with its presentation in mainly obscure novels is of questionable utility; Elisabeth Mangold, Kassel, Wenderoth, 1973, 228 pp., has much quotation; Rudolf Murtfeld, Bonn, Bouvier, 1973, 104 pp. (=AKML, 141), adds little; Carmen Kahn-Wallerstein, Bern, Francke, 1959, 286 pp. (also on Pauline Schelling), is lightweight but evocative; Eckart von Naso, Stuttgart, Krüger, 1969, 156 pp., is semi-fictional; Irma Brandes, Berlin, Blanvalet, 1970, is a novel.

Schlegel, Dorothea

Florentin is ed. Paul Kluckhohn, *DL*, VII, 1933, pp. 89–244, 305–7; see also Hans Eichner, '"Camilla". Eine unbekannte Fortsetzung von D. S.s Florentin', *JFDH*, 1965, pp. 314–68.

The only recent crit. assessment is by Karin Steuben, *GQ*, xxxix (1966), 162–72.

Schlegel, Friedrich

a **Bibliography.** There is a full review of recent research by Volker Deubel, 'Die F. S.-Forschung 1945–72', *DVLG*, xlvii (1973), Sonderheft, 48*–181*. Earlier surveys by Ernst Behler, *JDSG*, i (1957), 253–89, and *GRM*, xxxix (1958), 350–65, are also still worth consulting.

b **Texts.** The *Kritische F.-S.-Ausgabe* [KA], publ. by Schöningh, Paderborn, began to appear in 1958; of the 35 projected vols, 15 had appeared by the end of 1976. The editorial principles have been questioned, but there can be no doubt of the great value of the ed., particularly of the newly publ. material from the notebooks. Lengthy introds, notably by the general editor Ernst Behler and by Hans Eichner, are often extended essays of the first importance, and the comprehensive indexes are excellent for tracing concepts. Behler has also ed. *Schriften und Fragmente*, Stuttgart, Kröner, 1956, xlviii, 396 pp., and, with Roman Struc, has transl., introd. and ann. the *Dialogue on Poetry and Literary Aphorisms*, University Park, Pennsylvania State U.P., 1968, vi, 167 pp.

Kritische Schriften, ed. Wolfdietrich Rasch, Munich, Hanser, 3rd ed., 1971, 734 pp., is abbreviated as *Schriften zur Lit.*, Munich, dtv, 1972, 391 pp.; handy selections. Hans Eichner's ed. of the *Literary Notebooks 1797–1801* [LN], London, Athlone Press, 1957, 342 pp., is both textually and critically of major importance.

The periodicals *Athenaeum*, 1960, *Europa*, 1963, *Deutsches Museum*, 1975, and *Concordia*, 1967, have been repr., with postscripts by Behler, by the Wiss BG, Darmstadt. Selections from the *Athenaeum*, ed. Curt Grützmacher, Reinbek, Rowohlt, 2 vols, 1969.

The best separate ed. of *Lucinde* is that by Jean-Jacques Anstett, Paris, Augier-Flammarion, 1971, 248 pp. There is an excellent English version, *F. S.'s Lucinde and the Fragments*, transl. with an introd. by Peter Firchow, Minneapolis, U. of Minnesota P., 1971, xi, 277 pp.

Ten vols of letters from and to F. and Dorothea are promised for *KA*. See older bibls for existing colls but add *F. S. und Novalis ... in ihren Briefen*, ed. Max Preitz, Darmstadt, Gentner, 1957, 271 pp.; Raymond Immerwahr, 'Bisher unbekannte Briefe...', *JFDH*, 1967, pp. 386–405; and *Ludwig Tieck und die Brüder S.: Briefe*, ed. Edgar Lohner, on the basis of Henry Lüdeke's ed., Munich, Winkler, 1972, 275 pp.; important.

c **General studies.** There is an excellent introd. in English: Hans Eichner, *F. S.*, New York, Twayne, 1970, 176 pp.; good ann. bibl. Ernst Behler's *F. S. in Selbstzeugnissen und Bilddokumenten*, Reinbek, Rowohlt, 1966, 185 pp., and his essay in *DDRW*, pp. 163–89, are both reliable.

ZDP, lxxxviii (1969), has a special F. S. no., with 9 essays, some of which are referred to below. One, 'Die Grundzüge des Athenaeums', pp. 19–41, by Alfred Schlagdenhauffen, recapitulates the argument of his *Frédéric S. et son Groupe. La doctrine de l'Athenaeum*, Paris, Les Belles Lettres, 1934, xxii, 430 pp.

d **Literary theory.** For a general discussion of F. S.'s theory of crit. one might start with 2 essays: Victor Lange, *CL*, vii (1955), 289–305, and Hans Eichner, in the *ZDP* special no., pp. 2–19.

Stimulating surveys of his literary and aesthetic views may then be found in a number of recent works: Jost Schillemeit, 'Systematische Prinzipien in F. S.s Lit. theorie', *JFDH*, 1972, pp. 137–62, excellent on the definition of terms; Heinz-Dieter Weber, *F. S.s 'Transzendentalpoesie'*, Munich, Fink, 1973, 247 pp., is a highly intelligent, though opaquely written, account of S.'s theory as a confrontation with 18th-c. crit. positions: see also his 1971 work [IV.a]; Franz Norbert Mennemeier, *F. S.s Poesiebegriff*, Munich, Fink, 1971, 414 pp., examines his search for 'objective' poetry and excels in close analysis: see also his 'Fragment und Ironie beim jungen F. S.', *Poetica*, ii (1968), 348–70; compare Klaus Peter, 'Objektivität und Interesse. Zu zwei Begriffen F. S.s', in *Ideologiekritische Studien* [VI. Hoffmann, g], pp. 9–34; Karl Konrad Polheim, *Die Arabeske. Ansichten und Ideen aus F. S.s Poetik*, Paderborn, Schöningh, 1966, 406 pp., is a significant work ranging much further than the title suggests and incl. an excellent index of topics; Peter Szondi, 'F. S.s Theorie der Dichtarten', *Euph*, lxiv (1970), 181–99; see also his *Poetik* ... II [VI. Schelling, c], pp. 94–151.

Three important slightly older works are: Richard Brinkmann, 'R.e Dichtungstheorie in F. S.s Frühschriften und Schillers Begriff des Naiven und Sentimentalischen', *DVLG*, xxxii (1958), 344–71; Hans Eichner, 'F. S.'s Theory of R. Poetry', *PMLA*, lxxi (1956), 1018–41; and Klaus Briegleb, *Ästhetische Sittlichkeit. Versuch über F. S.s Systementwurf zur Begründung der Dichtungskritik*, Tübingen, Niemeyer, 1962, viii, 262 pp. (= Hermaea, n.ser. 12), under crit. attack but a pioneering effort at systematization and still of considerable use for concepts.

Somewhat more run-of-the-mill but still valuable are: Raimund Belgardt, *R.e Poesie. Begriff und Bedeutung bei F. S.*, The Hague, Mouton, 1970, 257 pp., and an essay in *GQ*, xl (1967), 165–85; Eberhard Huge, *Poesie und Reflexion in der Ästhetik des frühen F. S.*, Stuttgart, Metzler, 1971, 184 pp.; Helmut Schanze, 'Shakespeare-Kritik bei F. S.', *GRM*, xlvi (1965), 40–50; Bausch [II.2a], mainly on F. S.; Raymond Immerwahr, 'Die symbolische Form des "Briefes über den Roman"', in the *ZDP* special no., pp. 41–60; Larry H. Peer, 'F. S.'s Theory of the Novel revisited', *CG*, x (1976–7), 25–40, is a partly successful attempt to clear the ground; Hans Robert Jauß, 'F. S.s und Fr. Schillers Replik auf die "Querelle des Anciens et des Modernes"', in *Europäische Aufklärung. Fest.* H. Dieckmann, ed. H. Friedrich, Munich, Fink, 1967, pp. 117–40, and in his *Lit.geschichte als Provokation*, 2nd ed., Frankfurt, Suhrkamp, 1970, pp. 67–106; E. Keller, *Kritische Intelligenz: Lessing-S.-Börne. Studien zu ihren lit.kritischen Werken*, Bern, Lang, 1975, 230 pp. Of two works by Eugeniusz Klin the first, *Die frühr.e Lit.theorie F. S.s*, Wrocław, 1964, 134 pp. (= Acta Universitatis Wratislaviensis, 26), is outdated; the other, *Die hermeneutische und kritische Leistung F. S.s in den r.en Krisenjahren*, Wrocław, 1971, 159 pp. (= Travaux de la Société des Sciences et des Lettres de Wrocław, A 143), is worthy but adds little. The same is true of Ursula Klein, 'Der Beitrag F. S.s zur Entwicklung der frühr.en Kunstanschauung', *WB*, xx (1974), 80–101.

e **Philosophy and politics.** Klaus Peter, *Idealismus als Kritik. F. S.s Philosophie der unvollendeten Welt*, Stuttgart, Kohlhammer, 1973, 140 pp., and Werner Weiland, *Der junge F. S. oder die Revolution in der Frühr.*, Stuttgart, Kohlhammer, 1968, 58 pp., are both subtle examinations of his youthful

ideals and their outcome. Balance them with the sensible lecture by Clemens Menze, *Der Bildungsbegriff des jungen F. S.*, Ratingen, Henn, 1964, 37 pp. Gerd Peter Hendrix, *Das politische Weltbild F. S.s*, Bonn, Bouvier, 1962, 198 pp.; Bernd Bräutigam, 'Eine schöne Republik. F. S.s Republikanismus im Spiegel des Studium-Aufsatzes', *Euph*, lxx (1976), 315–39.
Hans-Joachim Heiner, *Das Ganzheitsdenken F. S.s. Wissenssoziologische Deutung einer Denkform*, Stuttgart, Metzler, 1971, vi, 132 pp., explains the intellectual development in terms of his distancing himself as a writer from social problems; the clear analyses are more significant than the conclusion. Leonard P. Wessell, *SiR*, xii (1973), 648–69, is interesting on the relationship to Kant and Fichte.
Achim Heiner, 'Der Topos "goldenes Zeitalter" beim jungen F. S.', in *Toposforschung*, ed. Peter Jehn, Frankfurt, Athenäum, 1972, pp. 293–314. Jean-Jacques Anstett, 'Mystisches und Okkultisches in F. S.s spätem Denken und Glauben', in the *ZDP* special no., pp. 132–50.

f **Individual genres.** On the novel in general see Helmut Schanze's excellent chapter in *Deutsche Romantheorien* [III.2b], pp. 61–80.
For *Lucinde* see the introds to their transls by Anstett and Firchow; K. K. Polheim in the *ZDP* special no., pp. 61–90; Wolfgang Paulsen, *GR*, xxi (1946), 173–90; M. Kay Flavell, *MLR*, lxx (1975), 550–66; Baerbel Becker-Cantarino, *CG*, x (1976–7), 128–39; and Richard Littlejohns, *MLR*, lxxii (1977), 605–14, demonstrating that S. is less emancipatory than is often claimed. John Hibberd, 'The Idylls in F. S.'s *Lucinde*', *DVLG*, li (1977), 222–46.
One art. on a poem deserves mention: Jean-Jacques Anstett, 'F. S.s "Hieroglyphenlied"', in *Stoffe—Formen—Strukturen. Fest.* Borcherdt, ed. Albert Fuchs, Munich, Hueber, 1962, pp. 303–14.
Periodicals: one may here mention Margaret Stoljar's *Athenaeum: a Crit. Comm.*, Bern, Lang, 1973, 152 pp., a straightforward and fairly reliable introd. See also Raymond Immerwahr, 'F. S.: Der Dichter als Journalist und Essayist', *JiG*, viii (1976), 145–68.

Schleiermacher

a There is an ann. bibl. by Terrence N. Tice, Princeton Theological Seminary, 1966, with 1,928 items. Of the general surveys, Friedrich Wilhelm Kantzenbach, *F. D. E. S. in Selbstzeugnissen und Bilddokumenten*, Reinbek, Rowohlt, 1967, 181 pp., also has an extensive bibl., and a useful little booklet, *F. S.* by Stephen Sykes, London, Lutterworth, 1971, viii, 52 pp., has a list of the principal works available in English. See also Martin Redeker, *F. S.: Leben und Werk*, Berlin, de Gruyter, 1968, 320 pp. (=Sammlung Göschen, 1177/77a).

b **Texts.** The two most useful eds of individual texts are: *Monologen ... Kritische Ausgabe*, by Friedrich Michael Schiele, 2nd ed. revd Hermann Mulert, Leipzig, Meiner, 1914, xlviii, 199 pp., and *Über die Religion*, ed. Hans-Joachim Rothert, Hamburg, Meiner, 1958, xiv, 176 pp., both in the series 'Philosophische Bibliothek', 84 and 225.

c **Studies.** Of the many special studies the following may be mentioned: Jerry F. Dawson, *F. S. The evolution of a nationalist*, Austin and London, U. of Texas P., 1966, x, 173 pp.; Richard R. Niebuhr, *S. on Christ and Religion*, London, SCM, 1965, xiv, 267 pp.; Paul Seifert, *Die Theologie des jungen S.*, Gütersloh, Gerd Mohn, 1960, 208 pp.; Erwin E. U. Quapp, *Christus im Leben S.s. Vom Herrnhuter zum Spinozisten*, Göttingen, Vandenhoeck & Ruprecht, 1973, 439 pp.; Gerhard Spiegler, *The Eternal Conflict. S.'s Experiment in Cultural Theology*, New York, Evanston and London, Harper & Row, 1967, xvii, 205 pp.; Hermann Patsch, 'Fr. Schlegels "Philosophie der Philologie" und S.s frühe Entwürfe zur Hermeneutik', *Zeitschrift für Theologie und Kirche*, lxiii (1966), 434–72; Marianna Simon, *La philosophie de la religion dans l'œuvre de S.*, Paris, Vrin, 1974, 349 pp.

Vol. x, 3 (1968), of the *Neue Zeitschrift für systematische Theologie* was a special S. number.

Schubert, Gotthilf Heinrich von

There have been reprs of the 1808 ed. of the *Ansichten von der Nachtseite*, Darmstadt, Wiss BG, 1967, 464 pp.; of the 1814 ed. of *Die Symbolik des Traumes*, Heidelberg, Schneider, 1968, 206, xxxi pp., with a good postscript and bibl. by Gerhard Sauder; and of the 5th, 1877–8 ed. of *Die Geschichte der Seele*, Hildesheim, Olms, 1961, 926 pp.

Adalbert Elschenbroich, *R.e Sehnsucht und Kosmogonie. Eine Studie zu G. H. S.s 'Geschichte der Seele' und deren Stellung in der deutschen Spätr.*, Tübingen, Niemeyer, 1971, 107 pp., is the necessary introd., with copious bibl. material.

(Catherine Crowe, *The Night Side of Nature*, London, 1848, is not a transl. but her own credulous coll. of tales. She does, however, owe a good deal to S. and to Kerner, and, in turn, considerably influenced Baudelaire.)

Steffens

For bibl., in addition to Goedeke VI and XV, see Poggendorf, *Biographisch-literarisches Handwörterbuch der exakten Naturwissenschaften*, VIIa supp., Berlin, Akademie, 1971; and Aage Jørgensen, 'Litteraturen om Henrik Steffens: En bibliografi', *Nordisk tidsskrift för bok- och biblioteksväsen*, lii (1965), 19–29, and lvii (1970), 8–15.

There are no recent eds but there is now a good general study up to 1804: Fritz Paul, *H. S. Naturphilosophie und Universalr.*, Munich, Fink, 1973, 252 pp. One still relevant art. is that by René Guignard, 'H. S. et la litt. allemande', *Revue Germanique*, xxvii (1936), 337–52.

Werner Abelein, *H. S.' politische Schriften. Zum politischen Denken in Deutschland in den Jahren um die Befreiungskriege*, is announced as a substantial study by Niemeyer, Tübingen.

Tieck

a **Bibliography.** A bibl. by Uwe Schweikert and Giuliano Merz is announced by Lothar Stiehm, Heidelberg. Meanwhile use, for earlier works, the excellent crit. bibl. in Minder, 1936 [d, below], pp. 455–95.

There are several surveys of scholarship: E. C. Stopp, *DVLG*, xvii (1939), 252–76; Marianne Thalmann, *Monatshefte*, xlv (1953), 113–23, repr. in her

R. in kritischer Perspektive. Zehn Studien, ed. Jack D. Zipes, Heidelberg, Stiehm, 1976, pp. 63–75; Robert Minder, in *Fest.* Ziegler, ed. Eckehard Catholy, Tübingen, Niemeyer, 1968, pp. 181–204: see also his 'Redécouverte de T.', *EG*, xxiii (1968), 537–47; Roger Paulin, 'Der alte T.', in *Zur Lit. der Restaurationsepoche, Fest.* Sengle, ed. Jost Hermand, Stuttgart, Metzler, 1970, pp. 247–62, good; and Wulf Segebrecht in his introd., pp. vii–xxix, to the 1976 vol. of essays [d, below]. On a slightly different tack see José Lambert, *L. T. dans les lettres françaises*, Paris, Didier, 1977, 490 pp.

b **Texts.** The most accessible ed. is now the 4-vol. *Werke* [*WTh*], ed. Marianne Thalmann, Munich, Winkler, 1963–6, though this still leaves a good deal to be desired and omits letters and crit. works. It is therefore still necessary to refer to the *Schriften* in 28 vols, Berlin, 1828–54, and to the *Kritische Schriften*, 4 vols, Leipzig, 1848–52, repr. Berlin, de Gruyter, in 1966 and 1974 respectively. Two recent publs have, however, gone a considerable way towards filling the gaps: *L. T.*, 3 vols, ed. Uwe Schweikert, Munich, Heimeran, 1971, 361, 361 and 399 pp. (=Dichter über ihre Dichtungen, 9); and *Ausgewählte kritische Schriften*, ed. Ernst Ribbat, Tübingen, Niemeyer, 1975, xxi, 224 pp.

A modest 2-vol. ed. by Hermann Kasack and Alfred Mohrhenn, Berlin, Suhrkamp, 1943 (=Die Gefährten I/II), has a useful selection from the crit. works and the letters. For an indication of the scattered sources of the letters see Minder and note 17 to the Segebrecht introd., where the main colls are listed.

Individual works. There are four eds of high quality in the Reclam, Stuttgart, series: *Franz Sternbalds Wanderungen*, ed. Alfred Anger, 1966, 584 pp. (=UB, 8715–21); *Vittoria Accorombona*, ed. W. J. Lillyman, 1973, 416 pp. (=UB, 9458–63); *Der gestiefelte Kater*, ed. Helmut Kreuzer, 1964, 80 pp. (=UB, 8916); and *Merkwürdige Lebensgeschichte Sr. Majestät Abraham Tonelli*, 1974, 87 pp. (=UB, 9748). See also *Trois contes fantastiques de Louis T.*, ed. Jean Boyer, Paris, P.U.F., 1954, 208 pp., with *Eckbert, Eckart* and *Runenberg*; *T. 'Der Blonde Eckbert' and Brentano '... Kasperl und... Annerl'*, ed. Margaret E. Atkinson, Oxford, Blackwell, 1952, xliii, 72 pp.; *Der gestiefelte Kater, Puss-in-boots*, ed. and transl. Gerald Gillespie, Edinburgh U.P., 1974, xi, 137 pp.; *Die Verkehrte Welt*, ed. Karl Pestalozzi, Berlin, de Gruyter, 1964, 148 pp. (=Komedia, 7), with a very extensive comm.

c **Translations.** There were many versions of the tales in the 19th c., notably by Carlyle. *The Rebellion in the Cevennes* was transl. in 1845 by Madame Burette, and there is a version of *Vittoria Accorombona*, as *The Roman Matron*, in the same year. *Sternbald* appears not to have been transl.

d **Biography and general studies.** It is still necessary to refer to Rudolf Köpke's 1855 reminiscences, repr. Darmstadt, Wiss BG, 1970; to Robert Minder's profound psychological study. *Un poète r. allemand: L.T.*, Paris, Les Belles Lettres, 1936, viii, 516 pp., with its full crit. apparatus;

and to Edwin H. Zeydel's informative if unsubtle *L. T.*, *the German R.ist*, Princeton U.P., 1935, xvi, 406 pp., repr. with a short new introd. by Zeydel, Hildesheim, Olms, 1971.

The most prolific recent interpreter of T. has been Marianne Thalmann: in the postscripts to her ed.; in *L. T.*, *der r.e Weltmann aus Berlin*, Bern, Francke, 1955, 144 pp.; in her study of the later Novellen writer, *L. T.*, *'Der Heilige von Dresden'*, Berlin, de Gruyter, 1960, vii, 194 pp.; and in sections of her more general works listed earlier in this guide.

Christian Gneuss, *Der späte T. als Zeitkritiker*, Düseldorf, Bertelsmann, 1971, 164 pp., is an unchanged version of a 1948 Würzburg diss., but the dogged analysis of political and social attitudes is still of value. For the earlier period see James Trainer's well argued *L. T.: from Gothic to R.*, The Hague, Mouton, 1964, 113 pp.; his short essay in *German Men of Letters* [VI. Eichendorff, e], pp. 41–57, is a more satisfactory introd. than Heinz Hillmann's sociologically tendentious chapter in *DDRW*, pp. 111–34. The contribution by Paul Gerhard Klussmann to the parallel *Deutsche Dichter des 19. Jhs*, 1969, pp. 15–52, is more judicious; but the most penetrating short interpretation is still Emil Staiger, 'L. T. und der Urpsrung der deutschen R.', *NRu*, lxxx (1960), 596–622, also in his *Stilwandel*, Freiburg and Zürich, Atlantis, 1963, pp. 175–204.

There is an important new study in the Thalmann tradition by Johannes Kern, *L. T.: Dichter einer Krise*, Heidelberg, Stiehm, 1977, 243 pp., emphasizing the unity of his outlook. *L. T.*, ed. Wulf Segebrecht, Darmstadt, Wiss BG, 1976, xxx, 471 pp., is a coll. of 12 essays, dating from 1838 to 1969. Ernst Ribbat, *L. T.: Studien zur Konzeption und Praxis r.er Poesie*, Kronberg, Athenäum, 1978, 290 pp.; wide-ranging and significant.

e **Topics.** On general poetic problems see Gerhard Kluge, 'Idealisieren — Poetisieren', *JDSG*, xiii (1969), 308–60, shortened in *L.T.*, ed. Segebrecht, pp. 386–443; and Raimund Belgardt, 'Poetic Imagination and External Reality in T.', in *Essays in German Lit. Fest.* Hallamore, ed. Michael S. Batts, U. of British Columbia and U. of Toronto Ps, 1968, pp. 41–61. Hillmann has a chapter on T. and Wackenroder in his *Bildlichkeit* [V.f. Imagery], pp. 53–130. See also Rosemarie Hellge, *Motive und Motivstrukturen bei L. T.*, Göppingen, Kümmerle, 1974, 287 pp.; and Friedrich Carl Scheibe, 'Aspekte des Zeitproblems in T.s früh.er Dichtung', *GRM*, xlvi (1965), 50–63; also Frank [V.y. Time].

Two very good arts by Roger Paulin are: '"Ohne Vaterland kein Dichter"', *LJb*, xiii (1972), 125–50, on the late T.; and 'The Early L. T. and the Idyllic Tradition', *MLR*, lxx (1975), 110–24.

Gisela Brinker-Gabler, *T.s Bearbeitung altdeutscher Lit.*, Cologne, Diss.-Druck, 1973, 287 pp.; her 'T und die Wissenschaft', *JFDH*, 1976, pp. 168–77. is a short survey of his scholarly activities. See, for T.'s ideas on art, Lippuner [VI. Wackenroder, c], and Christa Franke [II.1].

Michel-François Demet, 'L'expérience de la folie et le fantasme dans la femme-de-pierre chez L.T.', *Ro*, xv (1977), 57–70. Margaret C. Ives, 'Pope's "Windsor Forest" as a Possible Source of R. "Waldeinsamkeit"', *Comparison*

(U. of Warwick), no. 3 (1976), 65–87, is perhaps more intriguing than convincing.

f **Märchen and Novellen.** One of the most illuminating arts on T. is that by Paul Gerhard Klussmann, 'Die Zweideutgkeit des Wirklichen in T.s Märchennovellen', *ZDP*, lxxxiii (1964), 426–52, repr. in *L. T.*, ed. Segebrecht, pp. 352–85. See also Gonthier-Louis Fink, 'Le conte fantastique de *T.*', *RG*, iv (1974), 71–94. Rolf Stamm, *L. T.s späte Novellen*, Stuttgart, Kohlhammer, 1973, 156 pp., is a work of importance arguing that T. consciously used the literary associations of the marvellous to enhance the prestige of the Novelle form; good analyses of individual works.

For *Der blonde Eckbert* see the bibl. in J. M. Ellis, *Narration in the German Novelle* [VI. Hoffmann, g], pp. 77 and 215–16 (with a proper singling out of W. J. Lillyman in *Seminar*, vii (1971)), 144–55), and add: Heinz Schlaffer, in *Gestaltungsgeschichte und Gesellschaftsgeschichte*, ed. Helmut Kreuzer, Stuttgart, Metzler, 1969, pp. 224–41, repr. in *L. T.*, ed. Segebrecht, pp. 444–64; Diether Haenicke, in *Vergleichen und Verändern, Fest. Motekat*, ed. Albrecht Goetze, Munich, Hueber, 1970, pp. 170–87; Richard W. Kimpel, *SiR*, ix (1970), 176–92 (also on *Der Runenberg*); Otto K. Liedke, *GQ*, xliv (1971), 311–16; Ralph W. Ewton, *GQ*, xlvi (1973), 410–27; Thomas Fries, *MLN*, lxxxviii (1973), 1180–1211; Martin Swales, *GLL*, xxix (1975), 165–75; Christa Bürger, in *Lit. soziologie II*, ed. Joachim Bark, Stuttgart, Kohlhammer, 1974, pp. 139–58; and her *Der blonde Eckbert/Die Elfen. Materialen zur r.en Gesellschaftskritik*, Frankfurt, Diesterweg, 1976, 106 pp.

For *Der Runenberg* see primarily W. J. Lillyman, *Monatshefte*, lxii (1970), 231–44; also Wolfdietrich Rasch, in *The Discontinuous Tradition. Fest. Stahl*, ed. P. F. Ganz, Oxford, Clarendon Press, 1971, pp. 113–28; Harry Vredeveld, *GR*, xlix (1974), 200–14; Ralph W. Ewton, *GR*, I (1975), 19–33; Gonthier-Louis Fink, *RG*, viii (1978), 20–49.

For *Abraham Tonelli* see Gonthier-Louis Fink, *Euph*, lxvii (1973), 287–305; for *Des Lebens Überfluß*, W. J. Lillyman, *GQ*, xlvi (1973), 393–409, and Rolf N. Linn, *WB*, xviii (1972), 164–70.

g **Novels.** *William Lovell:* See James Trainer, *EG*, xxiii (1968), 191–201; François Jost, in *Irrationalism in the 18th c.*, ed. Harold E. Pagliaro, Cleveland, Case Western Reserve U., 1972, pp. 181–93, and *EG*, xxviii (1973), 29–48, with interesting French parallels also pointing up the individual character of the novel; Karlheinz Weigang, *JWGV*, lxxv (1971), 41–56, perceptive—and see now his Frankfurt diss., *T.s 'William Lovel': Studie zur fruhr.en Antithetik*, Heidelberg, Winter, 1975, 196 pp.; Françoise Knopper, *RG*, iv (1974), 3–15, and viii (1978), 3–19; and Walter Münz's Regensburg diss., *Individuum und Symbol in T.s 'William Lovell'*, Bern and Frankfurt, Lang, 1975, 338 pp., wide-ranging and effective on the themes.
Sternbald: See the bibl. in the Reclam ed., adding Roland Hoermann, *Monatshefte*, xlvii (1955), 209–20; Jeffrey L. Sammons, *SiR*, v (1965), 30–43; Hans Geulen, *GRM*, xlix (1968), 281–98; Robert L. Kahn, *SiR*, vii (1967), 40–64; Eberhard Wilhelm Schulz, in his *Wort und Zeit*, Neumünster,

Wachholtz, 1968, pp. 35–48; W. J. Lillyman, *GRM*, lii (1971), 378–95; Gonthier-Louis Fink, *RG*, iv (1974), 16–70.
Vittoria Accorombona: See the bibl. in the Reclam ed., adding Lillyman himself in *JEGP*, lxx (1971), 468–87; and Christiane E. Keck, *Renaissance and R.: T.'s Conception of Cultural Decline as portrayed in his 'V.A.'*, Bern, Lang, 1976, 120 pp.

h **Drama.** See Marianne Thalmann, *Provokation* [II.2f]; Raymond M. Immerwahr, *The Esthetic Intent of T.'s Fantastic Comedy*, Saint Louis, Washington U. Studies, 1953, x, 150 pp.; Ernst Nef, 'Das Aus-der-Rolle-Falllen als Mittel der Illusionszerstörung bei T. und Brecht', *ZDP*, lxxxiii (1964), 191–215.

For *Der gestiefelte Kater* see under b above, and add: Helmut Kreuzer, *DU*, xv, 6 (1963), 33–44, and Karl Pestalozzi, in *Die deutsche Komödie*, ed. Walter Hinck, Düsseldorf, Bagel, 1977, pp. 110–126, bibl. p. 377.

For *Kaiser Octavianus* see Ernst Halter, *K.O.: Eine Studie über T.s Subjecktivität*, Zürich, Juris, 1967, 204 pp.

For *Leben und Tod des kleinen Rotkäppchens* see Hans-Wolf Jäger's interpretation of the political content in *Lit.soziologie II* [f, above], pp. 159–80.

Uhland

There have been no recent eds of importance, though Wiss BG have (1977) repr. Fischer's 1892 ed. Useful selections are: *Dichtungen, Briefe, Reden*, ed. Walter P. H. Scheffler, Stuttgart, Steinkopf, 1963, 502 pp., textually and critically good; *Frühlingsglaube. Gedichte-Betrachtungen-Reden-Briefe*, ed. Uwe Berger, Berlin, Rütten & Loening, 1974, 302 pp., with a good postscript; *Gedichte*, ed. Peter von Matt, Stuttgart, Reclam, 1974, 80 pp. See Scheffler on a new letter in *JDSG*, xx (1976), 3–37.

Hugo Moser's introd. in *DDRW*, pp. 473–98, is unexceptionable. The only other works that need to be mentioned are: Hartmut Froeschle, *L.U. und die R.*, Cologne and Vienna, Böhlau, 1973, x, 358 pp., the most satisfactory modern study (see also VI, Kerner); Hellmut Thomke, *Zeitbewußtsein und Geschichtsauffassung im Werke U.s*, Bern, Haupt, 1962, 207 pp.; Marguerite Wieser, *La fortune d'U. en France*, Paris, Nizet, 1972, 288 pp.

The poems as a whole were first transl. into English in 1848 by Alexander Platt: other versions followed in 1864 and 69.

Varnhagen, Rahel Four vols of selections from Rahel's correspondence have been publ. under the editorship of Friedhelm Kemp by Kösel, Munich, in the series *Lebensläufe*, nos 8, 9, 10, 14, 1966–8; good notes, postscripts and indexes.

There are significant biographies by Herbert Scurla, *Begegnungen mit R.*, Berlin, Verlag der Nation, 1962, 631 pp., and Hannah Arendt, *R.V.: Lebensgeschichte einer deutschen Jüdin aus der R.*, Munich, Piper, 1959, 298 pp. (now also Ullstein pocketbook, 3091), written in the main before 1933 and first publ. in an English transl., London, East and West Library, 1958, xiv, 222 pp.; a distinguished sociological interpretation. See also Alan Bird, 'R.V. von Ense and Some English Assessments of her Character', *GLL*, xxvi

(1973), 183–92; and Doris Starr Guilloton in *Monatshifte*, lxix [1977], 391–403.

Wackenroder

a **Texts.** There are two acceptable eds, both in 2 vols: ed. Friedrich von der Leyen, Jena, Diederichs, 1910, and ed. Lambert Schneider, Berlin, Schneider, 1938, repr. Heidelberg, Schneider, 1967. A handy text is *Schriften*, ed. Curt Grützmacher, Reinbek, Rowohlt, 1968, 218 pp., with a good bibl.

The *Herzensergießungen* have been ed. by many, incl.: Oskar Walzel, Leipzig, Insel, 1921; A. Gillies, Oxford, Blackwell, 1948, 2nd ed. 1966, with a useful factual introd.; and August Langen, Kempen, Thomas, 1948, the best interpretative comm. The *Phantasien* have been ed. Wolfgang Nehring, Stuttgart, Reclam, 1973, 160 pp. (=UB, 9494–5), with a good postscript. The *Reisebriefe* were ed. Heinrich Höhn, Berlin, Schneider, 1938, 218 pp. For clarifications and corrections see Oscar Fambach, 'Zum Briefwechsel W. H. W.s mit L. Tieck', *JFDH*, 1968, pp. 257–82; and Alfred Anger, 'Zwei ungedruckte Briefe von W. H. W.', *JFDH*, 1972, pp. 108–36.

b **Translations.** *Confessions and Fantasies*, transl. and ann. and with a long crit. introd. by Mary Hurst Schubert, University Park and London, Pennsylvania State U.P., 1971, 219 pp., is a work of quality. She, Kahnt and Heftrich (both in c. below) also review the lit. *Outpourings of an Art-Loving Friar*, transl. E. Mornin, New York, Ungar, 1975, xxxii, 124 pp., has a reasonable introd.; *Fantaisies sur l'Art*, transl. and with a long introd. by Jean Boyer, Paris, Aubier, 1945, 400 pp., should not be overlooked.

c **Studies.** Bonaventura Tecchi's *W.*, Florence, 1927 (in Italian), was transl. into German with little revision in 1962, Bad Homburg, Gentner, 85, xxiii pp. There is a satisfactory general introd. by Siegfried Sudhof in *DDRW*, pp. 86–110.

Of the older works, Paul Koldewey, *W. und sein Einfluß auf Tieck*, Altona, 1903, and Leipzig, 1904, 212 pp., is still useful. The main modern studies are: Heinz Lippuner, *W. Tieck und die bildende Kunst*, Zürich, Juris, 1965, viii, 225 pp., a detailed and careful restatement of the known; Elmar Hertrich, *Joseph Berglinger. Eine Studie zu W.s Musiker-Dichtung*, Berlin, de Gruyter, 1969, xi, 238 pp., attempting to argue beyond the autobiographical commonplaces; Rose Kahnt, *Die Bedeutung der bildenden Kunst und der Musik bei W. H. W.*, Marburg, Elwert, 1969, 128 pp., convincingly differentiating between his attitude to the two arts. For Frey and Scher see VI. Hoffmann, d; for Christa Franke, II.1.

Other studies on the arts in W. are: Gerhard Fricke, 'Bemerkungen zu W. H. W.s Religion der Kunst', in *Fest.* Kluckhohn and Schneider, Tübingen, Mohr, 1948, pp. 345–71, repr. in his *Studien und Interpretationen*, Frankfurt, Menck, 1956, pp. 186–213; Jürg Kielholz, *W. H. W.: Schriften über die Musik*, Bern, Lang, 1970, 135 pp., with some relatively new if ill organized thoughts on the affective intent of his musical language; Ruthann Richards, 'Joseph Berglinger: A Radical Composer', *GR*, I (1975), 124–39; Rolf Wiecker, 'Kunstkritik bei W. Zu Polemik und Methode des Klosterbruders in den *Herzensergießungen*', *Text und Kontext*, iv (1976), 41–94; Gustav Lohmann's art. 'W.' in *Die Musik in Geschichte und Gegenwart*, vol. XIV, Kassel, Bärenreiter, 1968, is interesting generally as well as on music.

Other arts of interest are: Richard Alewyn, 'W.s Anteil', *GR*, xix (1944), 48–58; Werner Kohlschmidt, 'Der junge Tieck und W.', in *Die deutsche R.*, ed Steffen [I.6a], pp. 30–44—a foretaste of his History of Lit.—and 'W. und die Klassik', in *Unterscheidung und Bewahrung, Fest.* Kunisch, ed. K. Lazarowicz, Berlin, de Gruyter, 1961, pp. 175–84, also in his *Dichter, Tradition und Zeitgeist*, Bern, Francke, 1965, pp. 83–92; Hans Joachim Schrimpf, 'W.H.W. and K.Ph. Moritz', *ZDP*, lxxxiii (1964), 385–409; Karin Thornton, 'W.'s objective R.', *GR*, xxxvii (1962), 161–73; Jack D. Zipes, 'W. H. W.: in defense of his r.', *GR*, xliv (1969), 247–58; and David B. Sanford, 'Dürer's Role in the *Herzensergießungen*', *JAAC*, xxx (1972), 441–8, an interesting if shakily buttressed thinkpiece. Linda Siegel, also *JAAC*, xxx, 350–8, is a modest piece on the musical essays.

Werner

a **Texts.** *Ausgewählte Schriften*, 15 vols, Grimma, 1840–1, have been repr. Haupt, Bern, 1970, but one also needs to use *DL.*, vol. XX, *Dramen*, 1937 (for *Das Kreuz an der Ostsee* and *Wanda*); and *Der vierundzwanzigste Februar*, ed. Johannes Krogoll, Stuttgart, Reclam, 1967, 96 pp. (=UB, 107). *JFDH*, 1962, pp. 69–96, has a fragment of the drama *Der Ostermorgen* presented by Birgot Heinemann, who also publs 10 new letters in *JFDH*, 1963, pp. 251–95.

b **Translations.** *The Twenty-Fourth of February* was transl. by E. Riley in 1844, and there are versions by Elisabeth E. M. Lewis of *The Brethren of the Cross* (1892) and *The Templars in Cyprus* (1886).

c **Studies.** Recent works, however much they disagree with Paul Hankamer's attempt to connect W.'s peculiar personality and the history of ideas, still find they need to take account of his *Z. W.*, Bonn, Cohen, 1920, 346 pp. Four extensive studies, all with substantial bibls, are informative on the life and ideas (Guinet) and moderately convincing on the works (Koziełek): Louis Guinet, *Z. W. et l'ésotérisme maçonnique*, Paris and The Hague, Mouton, 1962, 426 pp., and *De la franc-maçonnerie mystique au sacerdoce, ou La vie r. de F.-L.-Z.-W.*, Caen, 1964, 246 pp. (=Publs de la Faculté des Lettres et Sciences Humaines de l'Université de Caen); Gerard Koziełek, *F. L. Z. W. Sein Wegzur R.*, Wrocław, 1963, 172 pp. (=Trauvaux de la Société des Sciences et des Lettres de Wrocław, A 88), and *Das dramatische Werk Z. W.s*, Wrocław, 1967, 362 pp. (Travaux . . ., A 120).

Elisabeth Stopp examines the relationship of Goethe and W. in *PEGS*, xl (1970), 123–50, and *LJb*, xi (1970), 67–86. Colin Walker, 'Z. W. and the "Martyrdom of Abraham"', *MLR*, lxx (1975), 333–46, looks at the various forms of unhealthy readiness to sacrifice the life of others.

For *Der vierundzwanzigste Februar* see the bibl. in the Reclam ed., adding: Heinz Moenkemeyer, 'The Son's Fatal Homecoming in W. and Camus', *MLQ* xxvii (1966), 51–67; Lee B. Jennings, *Symposium*, xx (1966), 24–42; and Herbert Kraft, *Das Schicksalsdrama*, Tübingen, Niemeyer, 1974, 127 pp.

Index

This index does not include every minor reference to the principal figures mentioned. Subjects are indexed very selectively. Titles of works, given in full in the text, are generally abbreviated but fully translated. The author section of the Bibliographical Guide is on the whole not included, but some references not under their own obvious headings have been picked out.

alchemy, 6, 18, 65, 68, 77, 120
allegory, 34, 35, 74, 77, 84, 86, 101, 106, 108, 119, 120, 130, 139
Altdorfer, Albrecht, 93
Anacreontics, 46
analogy, 14, 15, 18, 65, 67
Antiquity, 2, 4, 28, 50, 51, 72, 107
anti-semitism, 4, 90
arabesque, 29, 56n, 83, 86, 107, 158, 168
architecture, 5n, 16, 59, 94
Ariosto, Lodovico, 2n, 52, 142
Arndt, Ernst Moritz, 8
Arnim, Achim von, 2, 4, 7n, 24, 79, 80, 82, 89–97, 130
  Aloys und Rose, 90
  Die Ehenschmiede (The Marriage Smiths), 90
  Gräfin Dolores (The Poverty, Riches, Guilt and Atonement of the Countess Dolores), 90–92, 121
  Halle und Jerusalem, 96–7
  Hollins Liebeleben (Hollin's Love-Life), 89
  Isabella von Ägypten (Isabella of Egypt, the first youthful love of the Emperor Charles the Fifth), 94–5, 115
  Kriegslieder (War Songs), 90
  Die Kronenwächter (The Guardians of the Crown), 90, 92–4
  Das Loch (The Hole, or Paradise Regained), 96
  Die Majoratsherren (The Heirs in Tail), 95–6
  Owen Tudor, 90
  Schaubühne (The Stage), 96
  Der tolle Invalide (The Mad Veteran of Fort Ratonneau), 89, 96
  Versuch einer Theorie der elektrischen Erscheinungen (An Attempted Theory of Electrical Phenomena), 89
Arnim, Bettina von, 82, 89, 92
  Frühlingskranz (A Springtime Garland woven for him from the Letters of Youth), 82
Athenäum, 7, 18, 29, 47, 51, 52, 62, 71
autobiography, 99, 113, 123, 140, 157

Baader, Franz Xaver von, 6, 17–18, 20, 59, 66n
Baggesen, Jens, 2, 28n, 128

Balzac, Honoré de, 120
Basile, Giambattista
  Pentamerone, 85
Baudelaire, Charles, 120, 170
Bellori, Giovanni Pietro, 23
Béranger, Pierre-Jean de, 115
Bernhardi, August Ferdinand, 141
Bernhardi, Sophie, 48
Bible, the, 141–2; a new, 54, 57
Biedermeier, 27, 40, 127, 128, 136, 140
Blake, William, 6
Blechen, Karl, 108
blue, 68, 75, 122
Boccaccio, Giovanni, 32
Böhme, Jacob, 4, 5, 6, 18, 24, 29, 33, 74, 75, 77, 103, 106, 126, 163
Boisserée, Sulpiz and Melchior, 49, 59
'Bonaventura'
  Nachtwachen (The Night Watches), 28–9, 161
Böttiger, Karl August, 35
Bouterwek, Friedrich, 2
Brahms, Johannes, 111
Brentano, Bettina. *See* Arnim, Bettina von
Brentano, Clemens, 2, 14, 28, 79, 80, 81–9, 90, 91, 95, 102, 129
  Das bittere Leiden (The Bitter Sufferings of Our Lord Jesus Christ), 82
  Blätter aus dem Tagebuch der Ahnfrau (Leaves from the Journal of the Ancestress), 85
  Chronika eines fahrenden Schülers (From the Chronicles of a Wandering Scholar), 88
  Geschichte vom braven Kasperl (The Story of Honest Kasperl and Pretty Annerl), 86–7
  Gockel, Hinkel und Gackeleia, 85
  Godwi (Godwi, or the Stone Image of the Mother. A Novel run wild), 56, 83–4
  Die Gründung Prags (The Founding of Prague), 84
  Gustav Wasa, 84
  'Hörst du wie die Brunnen rauschen?' (Do you hear how the fountains rustle?), 88
  Leben der Heiligen Jungfrau Maria (The Life of the Blessed Virgin Mary), 82
  'Lureley', 84, 88

Brentano, Clemens—contd.
　Ponce de Leon, 84
　Die Romanzen vom Rosenkranz (The Rosary Romances), 86, 122
　'Säusle liebe Mirte' (Murmur Sweet Myrtle), 88
　'Der Spinnerin Nachtlied' (The Spinner as she sings at Night), 88
　'Sprich aus der Ferne' (Speak from Afar), 84, 88
Breton, André, 96
Brown, John, 13n, 65, 66
Bruno, Giordano, 12, 77
Büchner, Georg, 84
Bürger, Gottfried August, 5, 41
Buffon, Georges-Louis Leclerc, Comte de, 58
Burdach, Karl Friedrich, 14

cabbalism, 6, 18, 86, 116
Calderón de la Barca, Pedro, 36, 37, 44, 45, 57, 86, 97, 103n, 108, 109, 142, 152
Callot, Jacques, 113, 114
Carlyle, Thomas, 126
Carus, Carl Gustav, 16–17
Catholicism, 2n, 17, 18n, 24, 49, 59, 69, 70, 82, 86, 101, 108, 123, 126, 160
Cervantes, Miguel de, 29, 30, 45, 54, 56, 142
Chamisso, Adelbert von, 12, 110, 114–15
chaos, 27, 28, 39, 45, 54, 57, 78, 83
Charpentier, Julie, von, 62
chemistry, 13, 141
childhood, 71, 85, 99, 101, 107, 110, 111, 148
chiliasm, 7, 68, 69
Christian-German Dining Club, 90
clairvoyance, 16, 17, 95
Classicism, 4, 9, 43, 47, 53, 72, 107
Claudius, Matthias, 3n
Cleve, Joos van, 23
Coleridge, Samuel Taylor, 42, 44, 61
comedy, 35–6, 140
Concordia, 59
conservatism, 3, 38n, 59, 90, 108
Constant, Benjamin, 42n
Contessa, Karl Wilhelm, 114
contradictions, 19, 53, 54, 56
Cornelius, Peter, 25
Cramer, Carl Gottlob, 35
Cranach, Lukas, 93
Creuzer, Friedrich, 3n, 54n
Czech literature, 49

daemonic, the, 82, 87, 96, 106, 107, 108, 115, 124
Danish literature, 142
Dante Alighieri, 44, 45, 52, 75
death, 62, 68, 71, 72, 87, 115, 128, 152, 163
Diderot, Denis, 56
distance, 5, 75, 105, 122
Doppelgänger, 121, 122
Dostoevsky, Fedor Mikhailovich, 120
drama, 34–37, 44, 86, 140
dreams, 16, 33, 34, 72, 74–7, 93, 95, 100, 101, 107, 110, 111, 116, 119, 122, 123, 142, 158
Droste-Hülshoff, Annette von, 38, 110
dualism, 50, 87, 116, 121
Dürer, Albrecht, 22, 24, 93, 176

Echtermeyer, Theodor, 3n
Eckartshausen, Franz Karl von, 71

Eckhart, Meister, 18
ego, the Fichtean, 10–11, 26, 55, 63, 65–6, 68. *See also* self *and* subjectivism
Eichendorff, Joseph Freiherr von, 28, 79, 98, 99, 100–111, 129
　Der Adel und die Revolution (The Nobility and the Revolution), 108
　Ahnung und Gegenwart (Presentiment and Present), 101–102, 104n, 105
　Auch ich war in Arkadien (And I too was in Arcadia), 108
　Aus dem Leben eines Taugenichts (Memoirs of a Good-for-Nothing), 103, 107–108, 110, 115
　Dichter und ihre Gesellen (Poets and their Companions), 102–103, 105, 106n
　Die Entführung (The Abduction), 109
　Die Freier (The Suitors), 109
　Gedichte (Poems), 110
　Geschichte der poetischen Literatur Deutschlands (History of the Poetic Literature of Germany), 110
　Die Glücksritter (The Knights of Fortune), 109
　Halle und Heidelberg, 79n, 99, 103n
　Libertas und ihre Freier (Liberty and her Suitors), 108
　Das Marmorbild (The Marble Statue), 105, 107, 110
　Eine Meerfahrt (Ocean Voyage), 109
　Das Schloß Dürande (The Castle of Durande), 108
　Viel Lärmen um Nichts (Much Ado about Nothing), 104n
　Die Zauberei im Herbste (Enchantment in the Autumn), 107
'Zur Geschichte der neuern romantischen Poesie' (On the History of the New Romantic Poetry in Germany), 2
Emmerick, Anna Katharina, 82
Empfindsamkeit (sensibility), 5, 26, 46
encyclopaedia, 4, 48, 52, 53, 67
Enlightenment, the, 4, 5, 19, 43, 44, 69, 70, 126
Ennemoser, Joseph, 13
Enzensberger, Hans Magnus, 88
Erhard, Johann Benjamin, 28n
Eschenburg, Johann Joachim, 46
Euripides, 43
Europa, 59
evening, 32, 100, 106

fate, 87, 93, 123, 126
feudalism, 3, 91, 108
Fichte, Johann Gottlieb, 2, 6, 9, 10–11, 12, 27, 27, 29, 53, 54, 63, 90
　Reden an die deutsche Nation (Addresses to the German Nation), 8
　Wissenschaftslehre (Theory of Knowledge), 7
Fischer, Johann Karl Christian, 28
Flögel, Carl Friedrich
　Geschichte der komischen Literatur (History of Comic Literature), 120
flowers, 68, 75, 94, 122, 129
folk elements, 3, 8, 79, 129
folksong, 80, 85, 88, 92, 110
folktales, 26, 32, 79, 85, 91
forest, 32, 33, 98, 99, 105, 106n, 110. *See also* Waldeinsamkeit
formulas, 32, 104, 110, 152, 158

Index 179

Forster, Johann Georg Adam, 5n, 8, 33, 48, 51
Fouqué, Friedrich Baron de la Motte, 81, 101, 110, 114, 118n
fragment, 4, 28, 64–5, 78, 164
freedom, 10, 11, 72, 165; artistic, 55, 83
Freiberg Mining Academy, 65, 67, 127
French Revolution, 3, 7, 18, 91, 92, 115, 127, 137
Freud, Sigmund, 12n, 17, 121
Friedrich, Caspar David, 16n, 105n, 114, 136–7, 143
Friedrich Wilhelm III, 69

galvanism, 13, 14, 77
garden, 83, 90, 104, 105, 108, 111
genres, 10, 52, 57, 78, 168
Gerhardt, Paul, 80
Geßner, Salomon, 63
Gleim, Johann Wilhelm Ludwig, 63
Gluck, Christoph Willibald Ritter von, 116
Görres, Johann Joseph von, 2, 8, 79, 99–100, 101, 103, 106, 107
  Mythengeschichte der asiatischen Welt (History of the Myths of the Asiatic World), 99
  Die teutschen Volksbücher (German Chapbooks), 79
  Wachstum der Historie (The Growth of History), 99
Goethe, Johann Wolfgang von, 2, 4, 9, 22, 29, 30, 36, 43, 50, 53, 57, 59, 75, 76, 88, 90, 125, 129, 137
  Faust, 77, 86, 146
  Die Wahlverwandtschaften (Elective Affinities), 91, 139
  Werther (The Sorrows of Young Werther), 19, 26, 27, 89
  Wilhelm Meister, 7, 30, 52, 73, 76, 83, 124, 130n, 139, 163
Gogol, Nikolai Vasilievich, 120
golden age, 7, 15, 24, 54, 58, 63, 68, 69, 71, 72, 73, 76, 106, 119, 145, 163, 169
Gorki, Maksim, 120
Gothic novel, the, 26, 93, 122, 123
Gotter, Friedrich Wilhelm, 63
Gozzi, Carlo, 26, 35, 118, 142, 159
Grimm, Jacob and Wilhelm, 79, 80–1, 85
  Deutsche Sagen (German Legends), 79
  Kinder- und Hausmärchen (Nursery and Household Tales), 79, 80, 81, 85
Grimm, Jacob, 95
Grimm, Wilhelm, 93, 97
Grimmelshausen, Hans Jakob Christoffel von, 95, 108
Grosse, Karl, 122
grotesque, the, 93, 95, 96, 113, 118, 122
Gutzkow, Karl Ferdinand, 57, 102, 129

Hamann, Johann Georg, 3n, 5, 9
Hardenberg, Friedrich von. *See* Novalis
harmony, 14, 15, 50, 68, 72, 73, 74, 76, 91, 106, 111, 116, 119, 123, 124
Hartmann, Eduard von, 17
Hauff, Wilhelm, 129–30
Hawthorne, Nathaniel, 121
Haym, Rudolf, 3
Hazlitt, William, 42
Hebel, Johann Peter, 121
Hegel, Georg Wilhelm Friedrich, 6, 9, 13, 55, 138

Heidelberg Circle, the, 2, 79
Heine, Heinrich, 2n, 121, 128
  Buch der Lieder (Book of Songs), 128
  Die romantische Schule (The Romantic School), 2, 42, 59, 95, 110, 135
Heinse, Wilhelm, 3n, 27, 30, 57, 83
Hemsterhuis, Frans, 63, 65, 67
Hensel, Luise, 86
Herder, Johann Gottfried, 2, 5, 9, 22, 43, 51, 52, 71, 103, 106
hermeneutics, 20n
Herz, Henriette, 19
Herzen, Aleksandr Ivanovich, 120
Hesse, Hermann, 53
Heyne, Christian Gottlob, 41
hieroglyph, 6, 14, 18, 32, 54, 56, 58, 68, 73, 75, 86, 89, 100, 103, 104, 106, 107, 108, 110, 111, 117, 152, 163
historical novel, 39, 92–4, 130
history, 4, 58, 59, 69, 70, 73, 90, 92, 99, 100, 103, 105, 106, 111, 130, 137, 138
Hitzig, Julius Eduard, 114
Hölderlin, Friedrich, 54, 72, 88, 164
Hoffmann, Ernst Theodor Amadeus, 2, 7n, 26, 28, 56, 95, 112–14, 116–25, 130
  Die Automate (The Automata), 121
  Die Bergwerke zu Falun (The Mines at Falun), 117, 121
  Cornaro, 112
  Die Elixiere des Teufels (The Devil's Elixirs), 122–3
  Fantasiestücke in Callots Manier (Fantasias after Callot), 113
  Das Fräulein von Scuderi (Mademoiselle de Scudéry), 121–2
  Der Geheimnisvolle (The Mysterious Man), 112
  Der goldne Topf (The Golden Pot. A Märchen of Modern Times), 117–18, 119
  Kater Murr (Murr the Tom-Cat's Views on Life; together with the fragmentary Biography of Musical Director Johannes Kreisler on random waste sheets), 112, 123–5
  Klein Zaches (Little Zaches, called Zinnober), 118, 119
  Kreisleriana, 124
  Meister Floh (Master Flea. A Märchen in Seven Adventures of Two Friends), 117, 119–20
  Prinzessin Brambilla, 118–19
  Ritter Gluck (Chevalier Gluck), 112, 116
  Der Sandmann (The Sandman), 121
  Die Serapionsbrüder (The Serapion Brethren. Collected Tales and Märchen), 113, 114
  Des Vetters Eckfenster (My Cousin's Corner-Window), 113
Hofmannsthal, Hugo von, 121
Hogarth, William, 113, 161
Homer, 44
Huch, Ricarda, 3
Hugo, Victor Marie, 42
Humboldt, Alexander von, 15n
Huysmans, Joris-Karl, 120

Iffland, August Wilhelm, 35, 43
illusion, aesthetic, 34, 83; dramatic, 35, 36
imagery, 70, 71, 72, 85, 88, 99, 100, 101, 142, 163

imagination, 5, 10, 17, 31, 53, 54, 74, 89, 99, 102, 111, 116, 119, 122, 126
Immermann, Karl Leberecht, 121
India, 42, 50, 58, 59, 72, 75, 144
infinite, the, 2, 3, 10, 19, 26, 31, 44, 48, 53, 55, 56, 58, 59, 73, 78, 129
irony, 34, 35, 38, 96, 107, 118, 119, 125, 142–3
Irving, Washington, 120
Italy, 31, 39, 107

Jacobi, Friedrich Heinrich, 27, 59
Jacobinism, 3, 5n, 8, 137
Jahn, Friedrich Ludwig, 8
Jean Paul, 2n, 28, 38, 56, 71, 83, 113, 123, 135, 161
Jena, 8, 9, 29, 47, 79, 82
Joyce, James, 6, 76, 125
Jung, Carl Gustav, 17

Kafka, Franz, 76, 118n, 121
Kamptz, Karl Albert von, 119
Kanne, Johann Arnold, 143
Kant, Immanuel, 9, 29, 50, 95
Kerner, Justinus, 3n, 110, 128, 170
  Die Seherin von Prevorst (The Seeress of Prevorst), 128
Kielmeyer, Carl Friedrich, 12n
Kieser, Dietrich Georg, 14
Kleist, Heinrich von, 30, 90, 96, 108–09, 123n
Klingemann, August Friedrich, 28
Koreff, David Ferdinand, 114
Korff, Hermann August, 3
Kotzebue, August von, 35, 43
  Der hyperboreische Esel (The Hyperborean Ass), 43
Kühn, Sophie von, 61, 62, 63, 64, 65, 69, 71

Lafontaine, August Heinrich Julius, 43
landscape, 5, 22, 31, 32, 68, 74, 90, 93, 94, 98, 103, 104, 105, 110, 143, 152
language, 4, 5, 44, 59, 63, 87, 88, 110, 111, 130
Laube, Heinrich, 102
Lavoisier, Antoine, 58
Lenz, Jakob Michael Reinhold, 30
Lessing, Gotthold Ephraim, 2, 43, 51, 52, 86
Lewis, Matthew Gregory, 122
light, 65, 72, 115
Linden, Walther, 3
Linder, Emilie, 82
Loeben, Otto Heinrich Graf von, 77, 102, 105
love, 57, 58, 63, 64, 68, 69, 71, 75, 102, 106, 120, 121, 125, 126
Lukács, Georg, 50
Lukasbruderschaft. *See* Nazarenes
Luther, Martin, 93
Lyceum, 51, 52
lyric, 87, 88, 89, 109–111, 138

Märchen, 32, 33, 34, 37, 73, 76, 81, 85, 114, 115, 117–20, 130, 139, 140, 141, 153, 155
magic, 73, 78, 86, 93, 105, 107, 117, 119, 121
'magic idealism', 10, 66
magnetism, 13, 16, 18, 116
Mann, Thomas, 56, 115, 121
Mannerism, 143
Manzoni, Alessandro, 42
Mark, Julia, 112, 113, 118

marriage, 57, 90, 91
marvellous, the, 37, 39, 143
Matthisson, Friedrich von, 43
medievalism, 1, 2, 5, 17, 24, 50, 54, 59, 69, 70, 75, 76, 93, 114, 126, 129, 143
medicine, 13n, 65, 66, 143, 163
Mendelssohn, Felix, 111
mesmerism, 13, 16, 95, 119, 122
Metternich, Klemens Wenzel Lothar Prince von, 60, 82
Mickiewicz, Adam, 42
mining, 61, 65, 74, 94, 97, 121
Moravians, 20, 61, 62, 69, 70
Mörike, Eduard, 110
Moritz, Karl Philipp, 22, 135
morning, 32, 106, 107, 108
motifs, 31, 32, 85, 87, 94, 96, 98, 104, 106, 107, 110, 117, 130, 142
Mozart, Wolfgang Amadeus, 113, 117
Müller, Adam, 18, 20, 35, 56, 59, 70, 90
Müller, Friedrich (Maler Müller), 30
Müller, Hans von, 112n, 124
Müller, Wilhelm, 110, 127–28
  'Die schöne Müllerin' (The Fair Maid of the Mill), 128
  'Winterreise' (Winter Journey), 128
music, 25–6, 88, 92, 112, 116, 124, 135, 137, 143, 148, 158
Musset, Alfred de, 120
mysticism, 5, 6, 17, 18, 49, 60, 72, 73, 75, 123, 126, 129, 135, 175–6
myth, mythology, 4, 15, 54, 56, 58, 69, 72, 73, 76, 80, 82, 84, 86, 87, 92, 93, 94, 100, 107, 116, 118, 119, 121, 143

Nachtwachen. *See* Bonaventura
Nadler, Josef, 3
Napoleon Bonaparte, 8, 20, 42, 70, 95, 97, 101, 127
narrative, 57, 113, 119, 122, 123, 125, 138
nature, 5, 10, 11, 12, 15, 32, 33, 54, 67, 68, 72, 73, 78, 95, 100, 102, 105, 106, 107, 110, 121, 123, 129
Naturphilosophie, 11, 13–17, 18, 29, 36n, 54, 64, 76, 99, 114, 120, 128, 138, 154–5
Nazarenes, the, 24–5, 49n, 67, 108
Nees von Esenbeck, Christian Gottfried, 14
Nicolai, Friedrich, 9n, 27
  Vertraute Briefe (Confidential Letters of Adelheid B* to her friend Julie S*), 43
night, 72, 100, 105, 106, 107, 115, 144
nihilism, 27, 28, 29, 144
noon, 106, 108
Novalis, 2, 5n, 6, 8, 13n, 14, 32, 47, 51, 53, 58, 61–78, 106, 116, 118
  'Allgemeine Brouillon' (The General Rough-Book), 65n, 67
  Blütenstaub (Pollen), 62, 64–5
  Die Christenheit oder Europa (Christendom or Europe), 69–70
  Geistliche Lieder (Spiritual Songs), 61, 67, 70–71
  Glauben und Liebe (Faith and Love), 69
  Heinrich von Ofterdingen, 54, 61, 67, 74–7, 93
  Hymnen an die Nacht (Hymns to the Night), 67, 71–3
  Die Lehrlinge zu Sais (The Disciples at Sais), 67 9

Index

novel, the, 1, 30, 52, 56, 57, 58, 73, 78, 83, 91, 94, 124–5, 139, 168
Novelle, the, 37–8, 87, 95, 96, 140, 173
numerology, 6, 14, 163
Nuremberg, 24, 31

occultism, 13, 60
Oken, Lorenz, 14
Opitz, Martin, 80
opium, 72
organicism, 3, 12, 14, 18, 20, 33, 44, 59, 99, 107, 120
Orient, the, 2n, 5n, 54, 77, 144
Overbeck, Friedrich, 25

pantheism, 19, 103
Paracelsus (Theophrastus von Hohenheim), 114
parody, 28, 29, 43
patriotism, 8, 80, 90
Percy, Thomas
  Reliques of Ancient English Poetry, 89
Perrault, Charles, 34
Pestalozzi, Johann Heinrich, 29
Petrarch (Francesco Petrarca), 45
Pfitzner, Hans, 111n
Pforr, Franz, 25
philosophy, 8–12, 137
physics, 14, 54, 67, 78, 138, 164
Pietism, 5, 6, 7, 65, 103
play, 84, 85, 96, 163
Poe, Edgar Allan, 121
poetics, 43, 51, 78, 120, 134, 141
poetry, 58, 73, 74, 75, 76, 77, 80, 92, 102, 107, 117, 119
polarity, 11, 12, 13, 14, 16, 123
politics, 18, 69, 90, 144
Preromanticism, 4, 5n, 135
progressive poetry, 52–3, 56, 58, 129
Proust, Marcel, 99
psychology, 15–17
puppet plays, 96, 109
Pushkin, Aleksandr, 42, 120

Raabe, Wilhelm, 121
Raphael (Raffaello Sanzio), 23, 24, 25
rationalism, 4, 34, 72, 108
Reichardt, Johann Friedrich, 22, 51, 80n
Reil, Johann Christian, 123
Reinhold, Karl Leonhard, 63
religion, 5, 17–20, 23, 39, 59, 67, 70, 85, 87, 94, 96, 100, 102, 126, 138, 144
Renaissance, 6, 24, 31, 39, 93
Restoration, 3, 82, 90, 127
Rétif de la Bretonne, 27
revolution, 29, 38, 58, 59, 91, 108. *See also* French Revolution
Richter, Johann Paul Friedrich. *See* Jean Paul
Ritter, Johann Wilhelm, 14, 16, 65
  Fragmente (Posthumous Fragments of a Young Physicist), 14
Robespierre, Maximilien de, 58
rococo, 63, 82, 104
Romantic, as a term, 1, 2, 3, 51–2, 134
Romantic Irony, 34, 55–6
Romanticism
  critical approaches to, 3–4, 44, 129, 133, 134–5
  decline of, 127
  origins of, 4–6, 135

Romantikertreffen (the 1799 gathering), 29n
Rosicrucians, 5n, 6, 68
Rothe, Richard, 62n
Rousseau, Jean-Jacques, 5, 50, 54, 58
Ruge, Arnold, 3n
Runge, Philipp Otto, 24, 32, 81, 85, 86, 100, 106, 137

Saint-Martin, Louis Claude de, 6, 126
Sandrart, Joachim von, 23
Sanscrit, 42, 49, 58
satire, 34, 43, 97, 101, 104, 108, 118, 119, 120, 124
Schelling, Caroline von. *See* Schlegel, Caroline
Schelling, Friedrich Wilhelm Joseph von, 6, 9, 11–12, 13, 14, 17, 28, 29, 33, 44, 53, 65, 68, 92, 116, 123
Scherer, Wilhelm, 94
Schillemeit, Jost, 28
Schiller, Friedrich von, 4, 9, 43, 50, 57, 63, 68, 129, 163
  'Über naive und sentimentalische Dichtung' (On Naive and Sentimental Poetry), 50, 168
Schlegel, August Wilhelm von, 2, 5n, 9, 18, 34, 41–7, 48, 52, 59, 62, 63, 71, 126
  Ehrenpforte und Triumphbogen (Gate of Honour and Triumphal Arch for Kotzebue), 43
  Ion, 43
  Über dramatische Kunst und Literatur (On Dramatic Art and Literature), 41–2
Schlegel, Caroline, 28, 30, 41, 46, 48
Schlegel, Dorothea, 9, 29, 48, 57, 100, 101, 104n
Schlegel, Friedrich von, 1, 2, 4, 5n, 7, 9, 10, 13n, 14, 18, 19, 29, 30, 34, 36, 41, 43, 47–60, 63, 64, 66, 67, 70, 83, 100, 101, 126
  Alarcos, 56–7
  Geschichte der alten und neuen Literatur (History of Ancient and Modern Literature), 49, 51
  Gespräch über die Poesie (Dialogue on Poetry), 51, 58
  Die Griechen und Römer (The Greeks and Romans), 50
  Lucinde, 43, 57–8, 73, 83, 89
  Rede über die Mythologie (Address on Mythology), 54
  'Die Signatur des Zeitalters' (The Character of the Age), 59
  Über die Sprache und Weisheit der Indier (On the Language and Wisdom of India), 58
Schlegel, Johann Adolf, 48
Schlegel, Johann Elias, 48
Schleiermacher, Friedrich Daniel Ernst, 9, 17, 18–20, 29, 41, 47, 53, 54, 70, 99, 164
  Monologen (Soliloquies), 19
  Über die Religion (On Religion. Addresses to the Cultured among its Despisers), 19
Schmidt, Arno, 114
Schmidt, Friedrich Wilhelm August (Pfarrer Schmidt of Werneuchen), 43
Schnorr von Carolsfeld, Julius, 25
Schubert, Franz, 128
Schubert, Gotthilf Heinrich von, 6, 15–16, 17, 119
  Ansichten von der Nachtseite (Remarks on the Night-Side of the Natural Sciences), 15, 126
  Geschichte der Seele (History of the Soul), 15
  Symbolik des Traumes (Symbolism of the Dream), 15
Schumann, Robert, 111

182 Index

science, 6, 12–15, 115, 120
Scott, Sir Walter, 38, 90, 130, 146
Sehnsucht (yearning), 55, 74, 75, 105
self, 4, 9, 10, 11, 19, 27, 30, 63, 64, 103, 104, 115, 118, 121. *See also* ego, the Fichtean *and* subjectivism
sensibility. *See* Empfindsamkeit
sentimentality, 1, 5, 34, 103, 126, 128
Serapion Brethren, the, 114, 120n
Shaftesbury, Anthony Ashley Cooper, third Earl of, 23
Shakespeare, William, 2n, 29, 33, 36, 45–7, 48, 50, 52, 54, 97, 103n, 159, 161, 168
Shelley, Percy Bysshe, 57
signatures, doctrine of, 6, 92
society, 4, 7–8, 18, 144
Solger, Karl Wilhelm Ferdinand, 29, 37, 56, 126
somnambulism, 16, 95, 100, 122, 123, 128
Sonntagsblatt für gebildete Stände (Sunday Paper for the Educated Classes), 128n
sound, 104, 106
Southey, Robert, 7
South Seas, 5
space, 65, 104–105, 106
Spee, Friedrich von, 80, 88
Spinoza, Baruch, 4, 12, 19
Staël, Anne-Louise-Germaine, Mme de, 2, 9, 41, 42
state, 18, 59, 69, 70, 76, 100
Steffens, Henrik, 3n, 14–15, 17, 29, 32, 33, 99
  Anthropologie, 15
  Beiträge zur inneren Naturgeschichte der Erde (Contributions towards an Inner Natural History of the Earth), 14
  Was ich erlebte (What I experienced), 14
Stein Hardenberg reforms, 8
Stephanie, Gottlieb (the Younger), 35
Sterne, Laurence, 26, 27, 35, 36, 56, 123, 125, 159
stones, 74, 75, 77, 117, 163
Storm and Stress (Sturm und Drang), 3n, 4, 23, 45, 46, 55, 86
Stransky, Christine von, 60
Strauss, Richard, 111
Strich, Fritz, 3
subjectivism, 32, 55, 103, 104. *See also* ego, the Fichtean *and* self
supernatural, the, 33, 39, 87, 93, 97, 111, 117, 123, 158
Swabian school, the, 128–30
symbol, symbolism, 4, 6, 33, 38, 54, 66–9, 73–5, 77, 84, 93–5, 97, 100, 102, 104, 106–108, 110, 126, 129, 144, 163
Symbolists, French, 78
Symphilosophieren, 47, 63
synaesthesia, 34n, 37, 85, 111
synthesis, 55, 64, 66, 67, 75, 83, 88

Tasso, Torquato, 52
Thalmann, Marianne, 33, 36
theatre, 30, 34, 35, 36, 40, 96, 112, 126
theosophy, 6, 13, 18
Tieck, Dorothea, 46
Tieck, Friedrich, 27
Tieck, Ludwig, 1, 2, 6, 7, 8, 13n, 21, 22, 26–8, 29–40, 47, 56, 67, 74, 76, 82, 83, 84, 91, 130, 167
  Der Aufruhr in den Cevennen (The Uprising in the Cevennes), 39
  Der blonde Eckbert (Fair-Haired Eckbert), 32–4
  Die Elfen (The Elves), 32
  Fortunat, 36–7
  Franz Sternbalds Wanderungen (Franz Sternbald's Travels), 24, 26, 30–32, 93
  Genoveva (The Life and Death of St Genevieve), 36
  Der gestiefelte Kater (Puss in Boots), 34–5, 36
  Der getreue Eckart (Faithful Eckart), 32
  Der junge Tischlermeister (The Young Master-Joiner), 40
  Kaiser Octavianus, 30, 36–7
  Des Lebens Überfluß (Life's Profusion), 38–9
  Peter Leberecht, 27
  Prinz Zerbino (Prince Zerbino, or the Journey to Good Taste), 34–5
  Ritter Blaubart (Sir Bluebeard), 27
  Der Runenberg (The Runic Mountain), 32
  Die verkehrte Welt (The World Upside Down), 35
  Vittoria Accorombona, 39
  William Lovell, 27–8
Tieck, Sophie, 27
time, 65, 144
towns, 22, 24, 35, 142
Trakl, Georg, 121
translations, 29, 45–7, 109, 145
Treviranus, Gottfried Reinhold, 14
trivial literature, 27, 93, 122, 144
Trösteinsamkeit (Consolation in Solitude), 79
Troxler, Ignaz Paul Vital, 14
Tübinger Romantik, 128
Turgenev, Ivan, 120
turning-point. *See* Wendepunkt

Uhland, Ludwig, 3n, 110, 129
'Über das Romantische' (On the Romantic), 129
unconscious, the, 12, 16–17, 26, 33, 95, 100, 121
Unger, Friederike, 43
unity, 12, 19, 64, 74, 92, 93, 100, 106, 120
universality, 52–3, 100, 104, 129, 141
Uz, Johann Peter, 63

Varnhagen, Rahel, 48
Vasari, Giorgio, 23
vegetative, the, 100, 103, 106
Veit, Dorothea. *See* Schlegel, Dorothea
Veit, Philipp and Johannes, 25
Venus, 102, 106, 107, 108
visions, 62, 63, 70, 92, 97, 99, 111, 122
visual arts, 16, 22–5, 83, 88, 113, 114, 135, 175
Volta, Alessandro, 13
Voß, Johann Heinrich, 2, 43, 46, 128

Wackenroder, Wilhelm Heinrich, 7, 19, 21–5, 76
  Herzensergießungen (Confessions from the Heart of an Art-Loving Friar), 22, 31
  Phantasien über die Kunst (Fantasies on Art for Friends of Art), 22
Wagner, Johann Jakob, 14
Waldeinsamkeit, 34, 110, 172. *See also* forest
wanderlust, 31, 101, 104, 110
Webster, John, 39
Weishaupt, Adam, 7

Wendepunkt (turning-point), 37–8
Werner, Abraham Gottlob, 65, 68
Werner, Zacharias, 59, 125–26
  Der vierundzwanzigste Februar (The Twenty-Fourth of February), 126
Wetzel, Friedrich Gottlob, 28
Wiegleb, Johann Christian
  Die natürliche Magie (Natural Magic), 121
Wieland, Christoph Martin, 46, 63
Willkur, defined, 55, 66n
Winckelmann, Johann Joachim, 22, 50
window, 105, 113
Witz (wit), 53–4, 56, 67
Wölfflin, Heinrich, 3

Wolf, Hugo, 111
woman, 57, 84
word-play, 84–5
Wordsworth, William, 98, 111, 165
world-soul, 11, 15, 16, 17, 32, 68
Wunderhorn, Des Knaben (The Youth's Magic Horn), 79–80, 89, 98, 110, 128, 129, 147

Young, Edward
  Night Thoughts, 71
Young Germany, 3n, 102

Zeitung für Einsiedler (Hermits' Journal), 79, 95
Zinzendorf, Nikolaus Ludwig Count von, 70, 71n

LIBRARY OF DAVIDSON COLLEGE